MW01612312

...ed into the batting order. No multiple substitutions may be made
...after the batting rotation. A designated hitter may be used in
...the two scenarios:

...e designated hitter may be a 10th starter hitting for any one of
...starting defensive players. If the designated hitter (DH) is used
...manner, the role of the DH is terminated for the remainder of
...e when the defensive player, or any previous defensive player
...m the designated hitter batted, subsequently bats, pinch-hits
...-runs for the designated hitter, or the designated hitter or any
...s designated hitter assumes a defensive position

...e starting designated hitter may be any one of the starting
...e players. In this manner, the starting defensive player has two
...s: the defensive player and the designated hitter. The role of the
...aerensive player may be substituted for by any legal substitute. If the
...defensive player has been substituted for, the original player/DH may
...re-enter one time. The role of the DH is terminated for the remainder of
...the game when a substitute or former substitute for the defensive role
...subsequently participates in an offensive role; or the starting defensive
...player/DH is substituted for either as a hitter or a runner (3-1-4).

Fundamental #3

The designated hitter, no matter how utilized, is locked into that spot in the
batting order.

3.1.4 SITUATION C: F4, for whom the DH is
pinch runs for the DH. **RULING:** The DH po...
remainder of the game. However, the startin...
player but not in the role of DH. If he does r...
the same position in the batting order, replac...

3.1.4 SITUATION D: The starting DH, who...
defense for F4 at the end of the second innin...
the DH position for the remainder of the gam...

*3.1.4 SITUATION E: Prior to the start of the...
conference meeting, the (a) home team's coa...
a lineup card with Holaday the DH for Feldt...
visiting team's coach presents a lineup card...
RF/DH. **RULING:** Legal in both (a) and (b)...
either DH option or no DH for a particular g...
their intentions prior to the start of the game

*3.1.4 SITUATION F: Sanders is listed as the...
position in the batting order. (a) In the fifth i...
game as pitcher with Sanders reaching his p...
continues as DH for McNeely; (b) in the sixt...
enters to pitch replacing McNeely, Sanders r...
and (c) in the seventh inning, Sanders return...
and is still listed as the DH: **RULING:** Legal

n and fielding position (1-1-3). Each
mum of nine players to start the game.
en in effect (4-1-3).
he official lineup card prior to the
hall pitch until the first opposing
oned to first base. In any other case,
f his team when the ball is dead and

regame conference, head coaches of
ineup cards to the umpire-in-chief.
all eligible substitutes are listed on
R's lineup card lists only starting
m B wishes to pinch hit with a
n the lineup card. **RULING:** The
eligible substitute shall be listed.
lineup card but encourages the head
Later, if Team B wishes to substitute
ineup card, it may do so without

am has returned to join the varsity
varsity game. A member of Team

3.1.1 SITUATION K: (a) Before the pregame conference, or (b) after the pregame conference, Team A's coach decides not to start F1. Lineups become official after they have been exchanged, verified and then accepted by the umpire-in-chief during the pre-game conference. In (a), lineup changes may be made without penalty. In (b) unless F1 is injured, ill or ejected, or removed by his coach for disciplinary reasons, F1 shall pitch to one batter. If F1 does not pitch to one batter, F1 shall not pitch for the remainder of the game, but he may play another position (1-1-1, 3-1-2).

Topic:
Designated Hitter

A hitter may be (not mandatory) designated for any one starting play-er (not just pitchers) and all subsequent substitutes for that player in the game. A designated hitter for said player shall be selected prior to the start of the game, and his name shall be included on the lineup cards presented to the umpire-in-chief and to the official scorer. A team forfeits the use of a designated hitter if it fails to declare a designated hitter prior to the game. If a pinch hitter or pinch runner for the designated hitter is used, that player becomes the new designated hitter. The player who was the designated hitter may re-enter as the designated hitter under the re-entry rule. A designated hitter and the player for whom he is batting

HIGH SCHOOL BASEBALL
RULES BY
TOPIC
2020

DR. KARISSA L. NIEHOFF, Publisher
B. Elliot Hopkins, Editor
NFHS Publications

To maintain the sound traditions of this sport, encourage sportsmanship and minimize the inherent risk of injury, the National Federation of State High School Associations (NFHS) writes playing rules for varsity competition among student-athletes of high school age. High school coaches, game officials and administrators who have knowledge and experience regarding this particular sport and age group volunteer their time to serve on the rules committee. Member associations of the NFHS independently make decisions regarding compliance with or modification of these playing rules for the student-athletes in their respective states.

NFHS rules are used by education-based and non-education-based organizations serving children of varying skill levels who are of high school age and younger. In order to make NFHS rules skill-level and age-level appropriate, the rules may be modified by any organization that chooses to use them. Except as may be specifically noted in this NFHS basketball rules book, the NFHS makes no recommendation about the nature or extent of the modifications that may be appropriate for children who are younger or less skilled than high school varsity athletes.

Every individual using the NFHS baseball rules is responsible for prudent judgment with respect to each contest, athlete and facility, and each athlete is responsible for exercising caution and good sportsmanship. The NFHS baseball rules should be interpreted and applied so as to make reasonable accommodations for athletes, coaches and officials with disabilities.

2020 High School Baseball Rules By Topic

Copyright © 2020 by the National Federation of State High School Associations with the United States Copyright Office.

Produced by Referee Enterprises Inc., publishers of *Referee* magazine.

Published by the
NATIONAL FEDERATION OF STATE HIGH SCHOOL ASSOCIATIONS
PO Box 690
Indianapolis, IN 46206
Phone: 317-972-6900, Fax: 317-822-5700
www.nfhs.org

ISBN-13: 978-158208-448-0
Printed in the United States of America

Table of Contents

2020 NFHS Baseball Rules Changes

Rule Changed

Points of Emphasis

1. Game-Ending Procedures

2. Player/Designated Hitter Role

3. Proper Pitching Positions

4. Force Play Slide Rule

5. Enforcement of NFHS Jewelry Rule

6. Compliance of Player's Equipment

New Caseplays for 2020

Introduction

Rules by Topic is a collection of information like no other.

Combining numerous NFHS educational elements into one collective resource will improve rules understanding and retention.

Included in the book:

Rules — Official NFHS rules book language and references are linked, combining related items by topic. That way, all related items are found in one location, from definitions to penalties.

Caseplays — Taken right from the NFHS case book, related caseplays are imbedded within the topic for easy reference.

Rationales — The reasons behind the rules are included, used from previous years' Comments on the Rules and rule change summaries. You not only see the rule, you learn the reason behind it.

Fundamentals — Related rules book fundamentals are connected to the specific topic.

In Simple Terms — Summary statements that take complex rules and make them easier to understand are found throughout the book.

Did You Know? — Historical tidbits provide basis for the rules as written today.

Rules by Topic is designed to complement the official NFHS publications. While not replacing the rules book and case book, *Rules by Topic* offers a different way to learn the rules. Some rules and case plays are repeated because they apply to more than one topic.

Rules by Topic will change the way you look at rules and will greatly enhance your rules knowledge.

Note: New baseball rules language is indicated with gray shading. New baseball case book plays, or those with new language, are preceded by an asterisk (*).

Topic 1
Pregame

Topic:
Umpires

Game officials include the umpire-in-chief and one, two, three or more field umpires. Whenever possible, at least two umpires are recommended. Any umpire has the authority to order a player, coach or team attendant to do or refrain from doing anything that affects the administration of these rules and to enforce prescribed penalties (10-1-1).

Umpires shall wear gray slacks and navy pullover shirt or state association-adopted shirt (10-1-9).

If there are two or more umpires, the umpire-in-chief shall stand behind the catcher. The umpire-in-chief, when behind the plate, shall wear proper safety equipment including but not limited to: chest protector, face mask, throat guard, plate shoes, shin guards and protective cup (if male). He shall call and count balls and strikes, signal fair and foul balls and make all decisions on the batter. When calling a foul ball, the umpire-in-chief should always signal a foul ball, but should only call out "Foul Ball," when the ball is not a caught foul fly ball. He shall make all decisions except those commonly reserved for the field umpire (10-2-1).

In Simple Terms

While crews may designate a senior umpire, the umpire-in-chief for a particular game is the plate umpire.

The umpire-in-chief has sole authority to forfeit a game and has jurisdiction over any rules matters not mentioned in 10-2-1 and not assigned to the field umpire (10-2-2).

Any umpire's decision which involves judgment, such as whether a hit is fair or foul, whether a pitch is a strike or a ball, or whether a runner is safe or out, is final. But if there is reasonable doubt about some decision being in conflict with the rules, the coach or captain may ask that the correct ruling be made. The umpire making the decision may ask another umpire for information before making a final decision. No umpire shall criticize or interfere with another umpire's decision unless asked by the one making it (10-1-4). The use of videotape or equipment by game officials for the purpose of making calls or rendering decisions is prohibited (10-1-5).

A field umpire shall aid the umpire-in-chief in administering the rules. He shall make all decisions on the bases except those reserved for the umpire-in-chief. He shall have concurrent jurisdiction with the umpire-in-chief in calling time, balks, infield fly, defacement or discoloration of the ball by the pitcher, illegal pitches, when a fly ball is caught, or in ejecting any coach or player for flagrant, unsportsmanlike conduct or infraction as prescribed by the rules. In some instances, he will rule on the ball being fair or foul (10-3-1).

No umpire may be replaced during a game unless he becomes ill or is injured. His right to disqualify players or to remove nonplayers for objecting to decisions or for unsportsmanlike conduct is absolute. Ejections will be made at the end of playing action (10-1-6).

When there is only one field umpire, he shall make all calls primarily at first, second and third unless the calls are more conveniently made by the umpire-in-chief (10-3-2). If additional field umpires are used, they are referred to as base umpires and their normal positions are behind third and second bases. They have concurrent jurisdiction with the first field umpire (10-3-3).

✍ Rationale

In 2009, the rules committee updated the uniform requirement for umpires. Umpires are no longer required to wear "heather" gray slacks. Because umpire pants fade over time and not all "heather" grays look the same, the word "heather" was deleted from the requirement. The only requirement is that umpires wear gray slacks.

Umpires: Caseplays

10.1.4 SITUATION: The coach of Team A informs the umpire that five runs scored in an inning by Team A, rather than the four credited, and that this fact can be verified on a parent's or team's videotape of the game. **RULING:** The umpire may not allow the use of video to assist in rendering any decision.

10.1.9 SITUATION A: Umpires arrive at the field wearing light gray slacks. Are these slacks legal? **RULING:** Yes. Umpires are no longer required to wear "heather" gray slacks.

10.1.9 SITUATION B: Umpires arrive at the field wearing (a) navy pullover shirts, or (b) red pullover shirts, or (c) one umpire is wearing a black shirt while the other umpire is wearing a gray shirt. **RULING:** (a) Legal (b) Umpires may wear an alternate shirt if approved by the state association; (c) Illegal. Both umpires shall be wearing identical, approved uniforms.

10.2.2 SITUATION A: With the home team behind by one run in the bottom of the seventh and two outs, B4 singles. R2 scores, but then maliciously runs over the catcher. The umpire ejects R2 and nullifies his run. As both teams begin to go to their respective dugouts, R2's coach informs an umpire that the run should score, since he touched the plate before the malicious contact. The umpire summons the other umpires and asks them to wait. The umpire disagrees, at which time the coach lodges a protest with the umpire-in-chief. **RULING:** The coach's protest is on record since he lodged the protest with an umpire before the umpires left the field. If the umpire-in-chief realizes an error has been made, the game would resume, as long as an umpire has remained on the field.

Jurisdiction

Umpire jurisdiction begins upon the umpires arriving at the field (within the confines of the field) and ends when the umpires leave the playing field at the conclusion of the game. The game officials retain clerical authority over the contest through the completion of any reports, including those imposing disqualification, that are responsive to actions occurring while the umpires had jurisdiction. State associations may intercede in the event of unusual incidents after the umpires' jurisdiction has ended or in the event that a game is terminated prior to the conclusion of regulation play (10-1-2). If there is only one umpire, he has complete jurisdiction in administering the rules and he may take any position he desires, preferably behind the catcher (10-1-3). The umpire-in-chief shall make the final decision on points not covered by the rules (10-2-3g).

Rationale

Since the umpires have pregame duties to perform (check field and backstop, etc.), the committee felt that official jurisdiction should begin upon arrival on the playing field. This change was made in 1995. Previously, the committee had ruled that jurisdiction began at the pre-game conference.

Jurisdiction: Caseplays

10.1.2 SITUATION A: Upon arriving on the playing field, the umpire(s) observe F1 warming up with F2 outside the confines of the field. The umpire informs F2 that he must wear a mask with a throat protector and a head protector to continue. F2 puts his mask and head protector on immediately and continues warming up F1. **RULING:** Legal. Umpire jurisdiction begins when the umpire arrives within the confines of the field.

10.1.2 SITUATION B: As an umpire is walking to the field, a player from one of the teams swears at the umpire. **RULING:** Unless the umpire is within the confines of the field, he cannot impose any penalties.

COMMENT: The umpire should inform the player's coach immediately, and if circumstances warrant, submit a written account to the state association.

10.2.2 SITUATION B: With the score tied in the bottom of the seventh and R3 on third and R1 on first, R1 is obstructed trying to steal second. The umpire awards R1 third base, which forces R3 home to win the game. Both teams leave the field and are entering their respective dugouts as the umpires leave. The coach of the defensive team, after talking to his assistant coach, realizes the obstruction award was misapplied. He finds the umpire-in-chief behind the backstop. Is the coach allowed to lodge a protest? **RULING:** No. A protest would have to have been lodged with an umpire before the umpires left the field. Once the umpires have left the field, even if nearby, it is too late.

Topic:
Equipment, Field Check

Ball
The ball shall meet the current NOCSAE standard for baseballs at the time of manufacture and is required on balls that will be used in high school competition (effective Jan. 1, 2020.) The SEI/NOCSAE mark is required on all balls that meet the NOCSAE standard that will be used in high school competition. Please see the mark below. A minimum of three  umpire-approved baseballs shall be provided to start the game. Unless otherwise mutually agreed upon, the home team has this responsibility. No less than two baseballs shall be used to complete a game. The NFHS Authenticating Mark is required on all balls that will be used in high school competition. A current list of NFHS authenticated products can be found on the Web site: www.nfhs.org (1-3-1).

Ball: Caseplay
1.3.1 SITUATION: (a) The home team provides the umpire-in-chief with three new baseballs or (b) game management at a tournament or a playoff site provides the umpire-in-chief with three new baseballs. **RULING:** Legal in both (a) and (b). In fact, some leagues may have a rule that the visiting team will supply one new baseball and the home team will supply two. That would be legal, too, since the intent of the rule is to have enough baseballs to keep the game from being delayed when a ball is hit out of play.

Bases

First, second and third bases shall be white bags, 15 inches square and 2 to 5 inches in thickness, and made of canvas filled with a soft material, or molded rubber or synthetic material, and must be securely attached to the ground. Bases may have tapered edges and/or be designed to disengage from their anchor systems. By state association adoption, a double first base is permitted. The double first base shall be a white base and a colored base. The colored base shall be located in foul territory (1-2-9).

When a double first base is used, the runner should use colored base on initial play at first base, unless the fielder is drawn to the side of the colored base, in which case the runner would go to the white base and the fielder to the colored. On a dropped third strike, the fielder and runner may touch white or colored base. A runner is never out for touching the white base rather than the colored base and once the runner reaches first base, the runner shall then use the white base (Suggested Double First Base Rules).

Home plate shall be a five-sided slab of whitened rubber or other suitable similar material. One edge is 17 inches long, two are 8 1/2 inches and two are 12 inches. It shall be set in the ground so that the two 12-inch edges coincide with the diamond lines extending from home plate to first base and to third base, with the 17-inch edge facing the pitcher's plate (1-2-10).

Bases: Caseplays

1.2.9 SITUATION A: With R1 on first base, B2 hits a fair ball to F8. B2, in rounding a double first base, (a) touches the colored part and continues to second, (b) touches the white part of the base and continues to second, (c) cannot make it to second safely and returns to first touching the colored part of the base. **RULING:** Legal in (a) and (b). In (c), the batter is out if tagged by defense before gaining the white part of the bag. The colored base should be used on the initial contact with the base.

 COMMENT: In (b), B2 is allowed to touch the white side of the base as long as the runner does not interfere with the fielder at first base.

1.2.9 SITUATION B: During the pregame conference the coach of the home team informs the umpire that a double first base is going to be used. The coach of the opposing team objects. **RULING:** A double first base is legal only by state association adoption. If the state association has adopted the double first base, it may be used.

Bats

The bat shall have the following characteristics and components. Each legal wood, aluminum or composite bat shall be one piece, multi-pieces and permanently assembled, or two pieces with interchangeable barrel construction (1-3-2a-1); shall not have exposed rivets, pins, rough or sharp edges or any form of exterior fastener that would present a hazard (1-3-2a-2); shall be free of rattles, dents, burrs, cracks and sharp edges. Bats that are broken, altered or that deface the ball are illegal. Materials inside the bat or treatments/devices used to alter the bat specifications and/or enhance performance are prohibited and render the bat illegal (1-3-2a-3).

Each legal wood, aluminum or composite bat shall have the following components. The bat knob shall protrude from the handle. The knob may be molded, lathed, welded or permanently fastened. Devices, attachments or wrappings are permitted except those that cause the knob to become flush with the handle. A one-piece rubber knob and bat grip combination is illegal (1-3-2b-1).

In Simple Terms

All BBCOR certification marks must be silk screened or other permanent mark.

The bat handle is the area of the bat that begins at, but does not include, the knob and ends where the taper begins (1-3-2b-2).

The barrel is the area intended for contact with a pitched ball. The barrel shall be round, cylindrically symmetric and smooth. The barrel may be aluminum, wood or composite (made of two or more materials). The type of bat (wood, aluminum or composite) shall be determined by the composition of the barrel (1-3-2b-3).

The taper is an optional transition area which connects the narrower handle to the wider barrel portion of the bat. Its length and material may vary but may not extend more than 18 inches from the base of the knob (1-3-2b-4).

The end cap is made of rubber, vinyl, plastic or other approved material. It shall be firmly secured and permanently affixed to the end of the bat so that it cannot be removed by anyone other than the manufacturer, without damaging or destroying it. By definition, a one-piece construction bat does not have an end cap (1-3-2b-5).

Each bat not made of a single piece of wood shall have a safety grip made of cork, tape (no smooth, plastic tape) or commercially manufactured composition material. The grip must extend a minimum of 10 inches, but not more than 18 inches, from the base of the knob. Slippery tape or similar material shall be prohibited. Resin, pine tar or any drying agent to enhance the hold are permitted only on the grip. Molded grips are illegal (1-3-2c-1); must be 2-5/8 inches or less in diameter at thickest part and 36 inches or less in length (1-3-2c-2); not weigh, numerically, more than three ounces less than the length of the bat (e.g., a 33-inch-long bat cannot be less than 30 ounces) (1-3-2c-3).

Did You Know? Aluminum bats were first allowed in 1974. Prior to that, only wood bats were allowed.

Bats that are not made of a single piece of wood shall meet the Batted Ball Coefficient of Restitution (BBCOR) performance standard, and such bats shall be labeled with a silkscreen or other permanent certification mark. No BBCOR label, sticker or decal will be accepted on any non-wood bat. The certification mark shall be rectangular, a minimum of one inch on each side and located on the barrel of the bat in any contrasting color to read: "BBCOR .50" (1-3-2d). The NFHS has been advised that certain manufacturers consider alteration, modification and "doctoring" of their bats to be unlawful and subject to civil and, under certain circumstances, criminal action (1-3-2d Note).

A bat made of a single piece of wood may be roughened or wound with tape not more than 18 inches from the handle end of the bat. No foreign substance may be added to the surface of the bat beyond 18 inches from the end of the handle. Each bat made of a single piece of wood shall be 2-3/4 inches or less in diameter at the thickest part and 36 inches or less in length (1-3-3a-b).

Did You Know? Grips on metal bats were required starting in 1981. Metal bats without grips were slipping out of batters' hands and causing an unnecessary injury risk.

Only bats may be used in warming up (including weighted bats used for this purpose) at any location. Only bats and items designed to remain part of the bat, such as weighted bats, batting donuts, and wind-resistant devices are legal at any location (1-3-4).

Bats that are altered from the manufacturer's original design and production, or that do not meet the rule specifications, are illegal (1-3-5, 7-4-1a). No artificial or intentional means shall be used to control the temperature of the bat. No foreign substance may be inserted into the bat. Bats that are broken, cracked or dented or that deface the ball, i.e., tear the ball, shall be removed without penalty. A bat that continually discolors the ball may be removed from the game with no penalty at the discretion of the umpire (1-3-5).

◢ Rationale

The NFHS is aware that the incidence of bat altering is on the rise. In addition, the bat manufacturers are also aware and extremely concerned about their products being misrepresented and altered. Modifying a bat from its original manufactured form is viewed as unlawful and, under specific circumstances, civil and criminal action could be taken.

Bats: Caseplays

1.3.2 SITUATION A: In the third inning, the batter comes to the plate with (a) a wood bat that has no certification mark; or (b) a non-wood bat with a visible certification mark. **RULING:** The wood bat, provided it is no thicker in diameter than 2-3/4 inches or longer than 36 inches in length, is legal and is not required to be BBCOR-certified. All non-wood bats shall meet the BBCOR standard and shall be labeled with a completely visible silkscreen or permanent certification mark. Accordingly, the bat in (b) is legal if the BBCOR certification is completely visible.

1.3.2 SITUATION B: B1 appears at bat with a bat that is (a) wood, (b) aluminum, (c) bamboo, (d) composite, (e) fiberglass or (f) titanium. All have the BBCOR certification mark. **RULING:** Not needed in (a). Legal in (b) – (f).

1.3.2 SITUATION C: In the top half of the fifth inning, a player enters the batter's box with a bat that has manufactured holes or ridges in the taper of the bat. **RULING:** Provided the bat meets all other bat requirements, it is a legal bat. Only the barrel is required to be round, cylindrically symmetric and smooth.

1.3.2 SITUATION D: During the game, B1 enters the batter's box with a wood composite bat without the BBCOR certification mark, or a bat made of a grass, such as bamboo. The umpire-in-chief questions the coach. It is the coach's opinion that since the bats are partially made of wood, the bats are not subject to the BBCOR standard and do not require the BBCOR certification mark. **RULING:** The coach is incorrect. A bat is either solid wood or non-wood. Any bat that is not solid wood is considered a non-wood bat and is subject to the BBCOR requirements. The bat is illegal, BI is out and the penalties of 4-1-3b are applied to the head coach.

1.3.2 SITUATION E: The batter enters the box with a non-wood bat (a) that has the BESR certification mark and appeared on the 2011 approved bat list, but does not have a BBCOR certification mark, or (b) that has a BBCOR certification mark. **RULING:** In (a), the bat is illegal and the penalty for an illegal bat shall apply, including the provisions of 4-1-3b applied to the head coach; in (b) the bat is legal for play.

1.3.2 SITUATION F: A batter enters the box with a non-wood bat that has a post-production sticker labeling it as BBCOR certified. **RULING:** The bat is illegal since BBCOR post-production labels, stickers or decals are not allowed. The batter is out and the penalties of 4-1-3b are applied to the head coach.

1.3.2 SITUATION G: A batter enters batting box with an illegal bat in the first inning. The umpire detects the illegal bat. In the third inning, another player for the same team enters the box with an illegal bat and it is detected. In the fifth inning, a third player from the same team enters the box with an illegal bat and it is detected. **RULING:** For the offense in the first inning, the batter is out (7-4-1a) and the head coach is restricted to the dugout. For the offense in the third inning, the batter is out (7-4-1a) and the head coach is ejected. For the offense in the fifth inning, the batter is out (7-4-1a) and the person who is now acting as head coach is ejected.

1.3.5 SITUATION D: The first baseman hits a home run with the bases empty using a bat that, while otherwise legal, has a small crack in the barrel. The plate umpire notices the crack: (a) as the batter enters the box; or (b) when the defense complains before the next pitch that it is an illegal bat. RULING: In (a), the bat is illegal upon detection as the head coach had verified that all equipment was legal. The first baseman is declared out and the penalties of 4-1-3b are applied to the head coach. In (b), the home run stands. The bat will be removed from the game. If the same bat were subsequently to be used later in the game, it would be subject to the illegal bat rule. **NOTE:** In (a), if the plate umpire feels that the damage to the bat was done during the course of play during that game, the bat may be removed from the game, and replaced with no penalty to the offense. If the same bat were subsequently used later in the game, it would be subject to the illegal bat rule.

1.3.5 SITUATION F: In between innings, the plate umpire notices that the home team is using an electric heater in its dugout to warm bats. **RULING:** Using any artificial means to control the temperature of a bat is illegal (4-1-3b, 7-4-1a).

Casts, Splints, Braces

Hard and unyielding items (guards, casts, braces, splints, etc.) must be padded with a closed-cell, slow-recovery foam padding no less than 1/2-inch thick. Knee and ankle braces which are unaltered from the manufacturer's original design/production do not require any additional padding. Each state association may, in keeping with applicable laws, authorize exceptions to NFHS playing rules to provide reasonable accommodations to individual participants with disabilities and/or special needs, as well as those individuals with unique and extenuating circumstances. The accommodations should not fundamentally alter the sport, allow an otherwise illegal piece of equipment, create risk to the athlete/others or place opponents at a disadvantage (1-5-8).

Umpires may wear casts, splints and braces, if padded. Umpires may wear prostheses and use mobility devices (10-1-7).

◪ Rationale

In 1991, umpires were specifically prohibited from working when mobility was restricted by equipment such as crutches, canes, and wheelchairs. The committee was concerned about jeopardizing the safety of the participants. To conform with ADA requirements, the rule was revised to its current form in 2002.

Casts, Splints, Braces: Caseplays

1.5.8 SITUATION A: F4, having broken his wrist the previous week, has a hard cast on his catching hand. The cast is not covered. **RULING:** The second baseman will not be allowed to participate until the cast is padded with at least one-half inch of closed-cell, slow-recovery rubber or other material of the same minimum thickness with similar properties.

1.5.8 SITUATION B: The shortstop's arm cast is covered with one-half inch of closed-cell, slow recovery rubber. **RULING:** With inspection and approval by the umpire-in-chief, the shortstop may play.

1.5.8 SITUATION C: The catcher comes to bat with a knee brace that, while padded, still has an exposed hinge. **RULING:** This is legal. Knee and ankle braces which are unaltered from the manufacturer's original design/production do not require any additional padding.

1.5.8 SITUATION D: The visiting team's head coach, while in the third-base coaching box, has an elbow brace with a pointed hinge at the end of the brace. **RULING:** This is legal. Braces which are unaltered from the manufacturer's original design/production do not require any additional padding.

Fundamental #1

Once the game begins, umpires have sole discretion over field conditions.

1.5.8 SITUATION E: The umpire notices R1 wearing (a) an elbow brace with an exposed metal hinge; or (b) a metal splint on his finger; or (c) a religious medallion around his neck. **RULING:** The brace in (a), if unaltered from the original manufactuerer's design and production does not require any additional padding. In (b), each item must be properly padded with at least 1/2 inch of closed-cell, slow-recovery rubber or other material of the same minimum thickness with similar properties. In (c), the umpire will ask the player to tape the medallion to his body and wear under the uniform.

1.5.8 SITUATION F: During the pregame meeting between both head coaches and the umpire, Team A's coach shows a letter from the local state association allowing one of its players with a forefinger prosthesis to play. **RULING:** Both the umpire and Team B's coach accept the letter from the state association because in the association's opinion it is no more dangerous than the corresponding human body part and does not place an opponent at a disadvantage.

1.5.8. SITUATION G: The umpire notices that F3's glove appears unusual. Upon further inspection, the glove is really a basket-shaped glove-like prosthesis designed for F3 while he is playing defense. **RULING:** The coach has a letter from the player's physician that the prosthesis was legally prescribed. The umpire advises that the prosthesis can not be used because the local state association did not approve it and must be replaced if possible. If the ball is touched with the illegal glove, the offensive team has the choice of taking the result of the play or having the award for use of an illegal glove or mitt (8-3-3a, b, c).

1.5.8 SITUATION H: Team A's coach inserts a substitute, who is in a wheelchair, to pinch hit. **RULING:** Because this accommodation may heighten the risk to the substitute — and other players — he should not be allowed to enter the game.

 COMMENT: These situations should be reviewed and approved by each state association.

10.1.7 SITUATION A: The base umpire takes the field in a wheelchair. **RULING:** This is allowed.

10.1.7 SITUATION B: The plate umpire must use a cane to assist his walking. **RULING:** This is allowed; however, the cane should be padded.

10.1.7 SITUATION C: During the pregame conference, the opposing coaches realize that one of the umpires: (a) needs a cane to walk; (b) has one arm; (c) is wearing a prosthesis that incorporates a metal hook for a hand; or (d) has an ankle cast. **RULING:** Legal in (a) and (b) because his physical challenge does not preclude him from officiating the contest. However, the cane should be padded. In (c) and (d), both pose a risk to players. In both scenarios they must be padded with a recommended 1/2 inch of closed-cell, slow-recovery rubber or other material of the same minimum thickness and having similar physical properties.

10.2.3 SITUATION D: In (a), F4 takes the field wearing a cast on his left wrist or (b) F1 appears wearing a cast on his non-pitching arm. **RULING:** Legal in (a) and (b). A player may participate in the game wearing a cast, provided the cast is padded with a recommended 1/2-inch closed-cell, slow-recovery rubber or other material of the same minimum thickness and having similar physical properties and free of attachments that could cut, scrape or puncture. The umpire has the final decision as to whether or not a cast is safe and should be allowed. A pitcher may compete with a cast on his nonpitching arm, provided the cast is padded with a recommended 1/2-inch closed-cell, slow-recovery rubber or other material of the same minimum thickness and having similar physical properties and not white or gray.

Condition of Field Before the Game

The home coach shall decide whether the grounds and other conditions are suitable for starting the game. After the game starts, the umpires are sole judges as to whether conditions are fit for play and as to whether or not conditions are suitable for starting the second game of a scheduled doubleheader (two games between the same teams during the same day) (4-1-1).

Any game started on a nonregulation facility by mutual agreement of the opposing coaches shall not be protested for this reason (1-2-12).

Condition of Field Before the Game: Caseplay

1.2.12 SITUATION: Prior to the game, coach of Team B notices that (a) the pitching mound is not regulation; or (b) there is an obstruction on fair ground 250 feet from home plate; or (c) all base bags and/or home plate are non-regulation. At the end of the second inning with Team A leading 4-0, he informs the umpire that he is protesting the game because of those deficiencies. **RULING:** The umpire informs the coach that a protest for such reasons will not be considered once the game has started.

COMMENT: Protests are allowed only when those state associations or allied groups have adopted that provision. Protests may no longer be honored because the game was played on a nonregulation facility. When a game is started on a nonregulation facility, the coaches have either by inference or by mutual agreement consented to play the game even though the field does not meet all rule specifications. There are many high school fields that are deficient in some part of the field requirements, but when coaches agree to play on such a field or the game is started, the nonregulation facility cannot be protested.

Equipment

Any player equipment judged by the umpire to be unreasonably dangerous is illegal (1-5-9). Non-traditional playing equipment must be reviewed by the NFHS Baseball Rules Committee before it will be permitted to be used (1-5-11).

Field Markings

The playing field includes both fair and foul territory. Any other areas beyond the playing field are defined as being outside the playing field (dead ball area). Any wall, fence, barricade, rope, wire, marked or imaginary line is considered a part of the playing field. Any areas beyond those boundaries are outside the playing field (2-42-1). A diamond (or infield) shall be 90-foot square. When measuring the distance to first base and third base, measure from the apex of home plate to the back edge of the base. The outfield is the area between two foul lines formed by extending two sides of the diamond. The infield and outfield, including the boundary marks from home plate to first and third and their extended foul lines, are fair ground. All other area is foul ground (1-2-1). All lines of the playing field shall be marked with a material which is not injurious to the eyes or skin. All non-permanent lines should be white. Lime or caustic material of any kind is prohibited (1-2-2).

The umpire-in-chief's duties include inspecting the condition of the field (10-2-3a).

When the dugout area is temporarily extended, for any reason, it shall be extended toward the outfield on a line parallel to the foul line. The extension of the dugout area shall be equally applied for both teams (1-2-4).

When constructing a new field for high school play, the distance from home plate to the nearest obstruction on fair ground should be at least 300 feet down the foul lines and at least 350 feet to center field. It is recommended that the line from home plate through the pitcher's plate to second base run east-northeast. This line, using a steel tape or a strong tape or a cord, must measure 127 feet, 3 3/8 inches from the rear tip of home plate to the middle of second base. The recommended width of a foul line is 2 1/2 inches (1-2-5).

Media shall be prohibited from being in live-ball area. If a designated media area is to be used, it shall be established before the game begins. The home team or game management shall designate a lined area for the media, which shall be considered dead-ball area (1-2-8).

The ball becomes dead immediately when a batted, thrown or pitched ball touches a designated media area or anyone or anything that is entirely or partially in the designated media area. The umpire has the authority to remove any member of the media for not staying in or keeping their equipment in the designated dead ball area (5-1-1l).

◪ Rationale

A 2010 rule change clarifies that temporary extensions of the dugout must be in a direction away from the plate. Previously, that was a recommendation. Now, dugouts may not be extended temporarily toward the plate or foul lines.

Field Markings: Caseplays

1.2.2 SITUATION A: Team A has constructed a new baseball field that has sports/field turf for the playing surface. The lines of the new field are "marked" in the school's official colors, black and red. **RULING:** This is legal since these lines are permanent.

1.2.2 SITUATION B: Team A has marked its foul lines with (a) maroon colored chalk, (b) a fire hose painted maroon, or (c) wood 2 X 4's painted maroon. **RULING:** Illegal in (a). Legal in (b) and (c) because these markings would be considered permanent in nature.

 COMMENT: Even though illegal in (a), the game will be played as scheduled. However, Team A should be informed that it is not a legal manner in which the lines shall be marked and the state association needs to be notified of this violation.

1.2.4 SITUATION A: Team A's has small dugouts at its baseball field. In an effort to accommodate the teams, Team A uses chalk to draw temporary lines which extend parallel with the foul line and toward the outfield. **RULING:** This is legal.

1.2.4 SITUATION B: Team A increases the size of the dugouts at their field by installing permanent railings or walls in front of each dugout. The new structures are closer to the foul lines and home plate. **RULING:** This is legal. The rule does not pertain to permanent structures.

1.2.4 SITUATION C: Team A extends their dugout parallel to the foul line and toward the outfield but does not do the same for the visitor's dugout. **RULING:** This is illegal. The expansion of the dugout must be equally applied. If Team A is unable to extend the visitor's dugout, it cannot extend their own.

1.2.4 SITUATION D: In constructing new dugouts, the home team extends both facilities equal distance down both foul lines toward the outfield. **RULING:** This is appropriate.

1.2.8 SITUATION A: During the game, a photographer positions himself in foul territory beyond first base to take pictures. The umpire tells him he must return to dead-ball territory. The photographer says that he would prefer that the umpire designate an area in live-ball territory for him to shoot. **RULING:** If an area has not been established for the media prior to the game, then the media shall not be permitted on the field in live-ball area. A dead-ball area shall not be established once the game begins. The responsibility for a media dead-ball area is the home team's or game management.

 COMMENT: If, in the judgment of the umpire, the designated media area is not safely located or could be involved in play too much, the umpire has the authority to prohibit the use of the designated media area.

1.2.8 SITUATION B: Designated media areas are determined and properly chalked before the game. During the game (a) a thrown or batted ball touches or lands in an occupied designated media area, (b) a thrown ball passes through the designated media area in flight, (c) a fielder outside the designated media area reaches over the plane of the designated media area to catch an overthrow or foul fly ball. **RULING:** In (a) the ball is dead immediately. A designated media area is a dead-ball area, even though it may not be occupied. Therefore, it is recommended that designated media areas be located in an area least likely to affect play. In (b), the ball remains live. In (c), a fielder may reach into the designated media area or "break the plane" of the designated media area to field a ball, provided the ball has not touched the designated media area or anything inside the designated media area.

Helmets

It is mandatory for on-deck batters, batters, runners, retired runners, players/students in the coaches boxes as well as non-adult bat/ball shaggers to wear a batting helmet that has a non-glare (not mirror-like)

surface and meets the NOCSAE standard at the time of manufacture. The batting helmet shall have extended ear flaps that cover both ears and temples and also display the NOCSAE stamp and the exterior warning statement. The warning statement may be affixed to the helmet in sticker form, or it may be embossed at the time of manufacture (1-5-1). A violation by a non-adult bat/ball shagger shall result in a warning to the coach of the team and the individual. A subsequent violation may result in the individual not being allowed on the field (1-5-1 exception).

In Simple Terms

Any non-adult member of the offensive team must wear a NOCSAE helmet while outside the dugout. In some states, a bullpen protector who is facing play may not be required to wear a helmet.

A face mask/guard may be attached to batting helmets at the time of manufacture. All face mask/guards shall meet the NOCSAE standard. A face mask/guard specifically designed for a particular helmet model may be attached after manufacture, provided that procedure is approved by the manufacturer and meets the NOCSAE standard (1-5-2).

Did You Know? In 1955, a head protector for batters was only recommended. They became required one year later. Baserunners were required to wear head protection starting in 1964.

Defensive players are permitted to wear face/head protection in the field. If a pitcher or any defensive player wears face/head protection, its outer covering shall have a non-glare surface (1-5-5).

The umpire shall call "Time" and play is suspended when a player is ordered to secure protective equipment (5-2-1c).

Helmets: Caseplays

1.5.1 SITUATION A: The bat boy, without a helmet, leaves the dugout to retrieve a ball between home plate and the backstop. **RULING:** Bat boys and shaggers shall wear helmets when in live-ball area, even if the ball is dead. After being warned, any subsequent violation could result in that individual not being allowed on the field.

1.5.1 SITUATION C: Between innings the umpire notices that a player in the coach's box is not wearing a batting helmet. **RULING:** The umpire shall have the player wear a batting helmet immediately. There is no penalty, since the ball was dead. If the ball had been live, the umpire would have issued a team warning to the coach of the involved team member. Subsequent players who may violate the rule while the ball is live shall be ejected.

1.5.1 SITUATION E: Non-adult bat/ball shaggers appear in live-ball area not wearing a helmet while (a) the ball is live or (b) the ball is dead. **RULING:** In both (a) and (b), the bat/ball shaggers have committed a violation. Batters, runners, on-deck batters, players/students who occupy coaches' boxes and retired runners are required to keep their helmets on in live-ball area while the ball is live. Non-adult bat/ball shaggers are required to wear a batting helmet whenever in live-ball area, even if the ball is dead.

1.5.1 SITUATION F: The visiting team wants to use non-adult bat/ball shaggers, but does not have any helmets for them. The coach secures a couple of helmets from his team's equipment. The helmets are noticeably incorrect in size, but the coach claims some protection is better than none, and that he is meeting the intent of the rule. **RULING:** The coach is incorrect. All helmets should fit reasonably well. A helmet that does not fit properly may not protect the wearer. Unless the coach can secure helmets that fit, the helmets shall not be worn and the bat/ball shaggers are prohibited from being in the live-ball area.

Jewelry, Bandanas

Jewelry shall not be worn except for religious or medical medals. A religious medal must be taped and worn under the uniform. A medical alert must be taped and may be visible (1-5-12). Players participating in the game shall not wear jewelry. No coach or player may wear a bandana (3-3-1d).

▨ Rationale

Prior to 1986, all exposed jewelry, including medical alert bracelets, were prohibited. The committee realized the need for these to be allowed, but still requires them to be taped to the body to minimize the risk for all participants.

Jewelry, Bandanas: Caseplays

1.5.12 SITUATION A: The umpire observes F2 wearing a loose-fitting bracelet. Examination shows that the bracelet describes F2's diabetic condition. **RULING:** The umpire will instruct F2 to have the bracelet securely taped to his wrist in such a way that it is visible but does not pose a potential risk to other players. Medical-alert bracelets are not considered jewelry.

1.5.12 SITUATION B: B1 is wearing a class ring. B1 tapes the ring so that it is no longer visible. **RULING:** Illegal. Jewelry, even though taped, may not be worn. The umpire will instruct B1 that he must remove the ring or he will not be permitted to play.

> **Did You Know ?** Warnings for violations (such as jewelry) may not be given until a violation has occurred. Blanket warnings for this type of violation cannot be issued at the pregame meeting.

3.3.1 SITUATION NN: In the first inning, the umpire issues a team warning to the coach of Team B because one of his players was discovered wearing jewelry. Later in the game, another player on that team is observed wearing (a) an earring or (b) a class ring. **RULING:** The first warning for a violation of the rule served as a warning to the entire team. A subsequent offense of that nature by a player from the same team shall result in ejection. Therefore, in (a) and (b), any player wearing jewelry shall be ejected.

3.3.1 SITUATION UU: A player from Team A is discovered wearing a bandana while (a) on the field, (b) on the bench or (c) behind the dugout. **RULING:** In (a) and (b), the umpire shall issue a team warning to the coach of the involved player. In (c), there is no violation because the rule is to be enforced within the confines of the field.

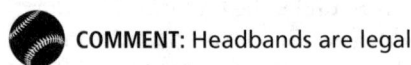 **COMMENT:** Headbands are legal.

Pitcher's Mound

On a sodded field, an unsodded area, commonly referred to as the "pitcher's mound," should have a radius of about nine feet centered 1 1/2 feet in front of the midpoint of the front edge of the pitcher's plate.

The top of the pitcher's plate must be 10 inches above the top surface of home plate. Inside the circle, a pitcher's mound should be constructed according to the specifications shown in the rules book diagram.

The degree of slope from a point 6 inches in front of the pitcher's plate to a point 6 feet toward home plate shall be one inch to one foot, and such degree of slope shall be uniform.

The pitching mound is an 18-foot diameter circle, the center of which is 59 feet from the back point of home plate.

Locate the front edge of the rubber 18 inches behind the center of the mound. The front edge of the rubber to the back point of home plate is 60 feet, 6 inches.

The slope starts 6 inches from the front edge of the rubber. The slope shall be 6 inches from the starting point, 6 inches in front of the rubber to a point 6 feet in front of the rubber.

The level area surrounding the rubber should be 6 inches in front of the rubber, 18 inches to each side and 22 inches to the rear of the rubber. The total level area is 5 feet x 34 inches (1-2-6).

The pitcher's mound may consist in part of synthetic material that is commercially manufactured for that purpose. If a mound pad is composed of natural soil and synthetic material, the synthetic material must be securely attached to the ground and be installed at least flush or slightly below the surface of the ground (1-2-7).

The pitcher's plate shall be a rectangular slab of whitened rubber or suitable material, 24 inches by 6 inches. It shall be set in the ground so that the distance between the nearer edge of the pitcher's plate and the rear tip of home plate shall be 60 feet, 6 inches (1-2-11).

Pitcher's Mound: Caseplay

1.2.7 SITUATION: The home team's coach purchases a commercially manufactured pitcher's mound pad for his field. The visiting team's coach protests the game because his pitchers are not accustomed to pitching on the artificial surface. RULING: The mound is legal if it meets the specifications under Rule 1-2-7. The protest would be invalid.

Uniforms

Uniforms of all team members should be of the same color and style. Caps and shoes are required equipment (no track spikes allowed). When a player is required to wear a head protector, it replaces the cap as mandatory equipment (1-4-1).

For individual players, uniform sleeve lengths may vary. However, sleeves of each individual player shall be approximately the same length and shall not be ragged, frayed or slit. If the pitcher's undershirt sleeves are exposed, they shall not be white or gray. A pitcher shall not wear any item on his hands, wrists or arms which may be distracting to the batter. A pitcher shall not wear white or gray exposed undershirt sleeves or any white or gray sleeve that extends below the elbow. If a pitcher is wearing a compression sleeve, it may only be a solid black or solid dark color. A vest and coordinating shirt that is worn underneath is viewed as a type of uniform top (1-4-2).

A uniform shall not have any dangerous or reflective buttons or ornaments. Each player shall be numbered on the back of his shirt with a plain number of solid color contrasting with the color of the shirt. This number shall be a plain Arabic style and shall be at least eight inches high, and no players on the same team shall wear identical numbers. A number may have a border of not more than one-quarter inch in width (1-4-3).

The school's official uniform (including uniform pants, jersey, visible undergarments, socks, stockings, caps and headwear) may bear only a visible single manufacturer's logo (partial or whole) or trademark. A manufacturer's logo/trademark shall not exceed 2 1/4 square inches with no dimension exceeding 2 1/4 inches. No more than one manufacturer's logo/trademark or reference shall be permitted on the outside of each item. (The same restriction shall apply to either the manufacturer's logo/trademark or reference.) One American flag 2 inches x 3 inches may be worn on each item of uniform apparel.

By state association adoption, to allow for special occasions, commemorative or memorial patches, that will be uniformly placed, not to exceed 4 square inches, to be worn on jerseys in an appropriate and dignified manner without compromising the integrity of the uniform (1-4-4).

Uniforms: Caseplays

1.4.4 SITUATION A: In (a), the coach and/or the player-coach wears a jacket while in the coach's box; or (b) players other than the pitcher request to wear jacket over their uniforms while on base. **RULING:** Legal in (a), illegal in (b). If players other than the pitcher request a jacket while running the bases, the request shall be denied. Jackets are also prohibited on defense.

1.4.4 SITUATION B: A team's uniforms have commercial advertising on them. **RULING:** There is no NFHS rule prohibiting advertising on uniforms. State associations may have rules that do prohibit advertising on uniforms.

1.4.4 SITUATION C: Five team members are wearing a commemorative patch on their arms. Four other players are wearing the same patch on their chests. Is this legal? **RULING:** No, patches must be placed and worn uniformly.

1.4.4 SITUATION D: For the upcoming season, team captains vote to dedicate the season in memory of two previous players. Two different patches are designed that meet NFHS specifications. Are these legal to be worn on uniforms? **RULING:** Yes, if approved by the state association.

1.4.4 SITUATION E: Team A arrives at the field and the American Flag has been sublimated on the entire uniform jersey. **RULING:** The uniform is illegal.

COMMENT: The American flag is limited to no larger than 2 inches x 3 inches and may be worn on each uniform item. The game shall be played and a report from the officials should be filed at the state association office.

1.4.4 SITUATION F: Team B has an American Flag located above the number on the back of the jersey. The dimensions of the patch are 2 inches x 3 inches. **RULING:** The uniform is legal. All uniforms must be compliant with Rule 1-4.

8.1.1 SITUATION Q: A 1-1 pitch, which is just off the plate, strikes an armband-type placard device used for play situations, which is loosely attached to the batter's waist. **RULING:** The umpire shall call the pitch and declare a dead ball. The batter shall not be awarded first base.

 COMMENT: The armband placard is not designed to be worn on the waistband of the uniform pants. It was intended to be properly worn on the wrist/forearm of the player.

Topic:
__Pregame Conference__

The pregame conference is a meeting involving the umpires, both head coaches and team captains (if available) near home plate. The meeting should begin approximately five minutes prior to the game.

The purpose of the pregame conference is to exchange and check each team's lineup cards and to discuss ground rules. Umpires also shall ask the head coaches of the two opposing teams if their players are legally and properly equipped. In addition, the expectation of good sporting behavior is shared with both teams and representatives. Both teams shall remain in their dugout (bench) or bullpen area until this meeting has concluded (2-10-2).

The head coach must attend the pregame conference, if available (3-2-4).

⬦ Rationale

The 2008 rule change that requires the head coach to attend the pregame conference, if available, was made because the head coach is the one ultimately responsible for his team. He should be the one certifying his team is legally equipped and needs to be aware of all ground rules.

Pregame Conference: Penalty

The head coach will be restricted to the dugout for the remainder of the game, except to attend to a sick or injured player, if he refuses to attend the pregame conference (3-2-4 penalty).

Pregame Conference: Caseplays

1.1.2 SITUATION C: Team A's head coach in the third inning wants to substitute a player who is not on the original lineup card. **RULING:** There is no penalty if a coach wants to substitute a player whose name was not listed as a substitute on the lineup card. However, to help improve the pace of the game, all known substitutes, with their name and shirt number, shall be listed on the lineup card submitted at the pregame conference.

2.10.2 SITUATION: Five minutes prior to the start of the game the home plate umpire calls both team representatives together for the pre-game conference (a) The home team sends out the assistant coach. (b) The home team sends out the team captain. (c) The visiting team sends out the head Coach and team captain. **RULING:** (a) Illegal, unless the head coach is not onsite or incapacitated and the assistant coach has assumed the responsibilities of the head coach (b) Illegal. While team captains are permitted to attend the pre-game conference, they do not replace the head coach. Head coaches must attend the pre-game conference (c) Legal.

3.2.4 SITUATION A: The head coach of Team A is caught in traffic and (a) has notified his assistant he will be 30 minutes late or (b) does not notify anyone at the game site. **RULING:** In both (a) and (b), the assistant coach may represent the team at the pregame conference and must certify that his team is legally and properly equipped. The head coach is not restricted and may assume normal duties upon his arrival.

3.2.4 SITUATION B: The head coach of Team A dislikes the umpire-in-chief and refuses to leave the dugout to attend the pregame conference. In his stead, he sends the assistant coach and team captain to the pregame conference. **RULING:** The head coach is restricted to the dugout for the duration of the game. The assistant coach must represent the team at the pregame conference and must certify that his team is legally and properly equipped.

3.2.4 SITUATION C: The head coach of Team A is (a) on the bus, tending to an injured player or (b) in the bullpen, supervising his pitcher's warmup or (c) finishing field preparations. In both (b) and

(c) he refuses the request of the umpire-in-chief to attend the pregame conference. In all cases, he sends the assistant coach and team captain to the pregame conference. **RULING:** In (a), the head coach is legal, is not restricted and may assume normal duties upon his return. In (b) and (c), the head coach is restricted to the dugout for the duration of the game. The assistant coach must represent the team at the pregame conference and must certify that his team is legally and properly equipped.

Ground Rules

If there are unusual conditions, such as spectators or obstacles too near the playing field, the home coach shall propose special ground rules. If sanctioned by the visiting team, these shall be in force. If the teams cannot agree, the umpires shall formulate ground rules. Ground rules do not supersede a rules book rule. All special rules shall be announced (4-1-2).

The field should be clearly marked. Markings should include poles along the foul lines at least 210 feet past first and third and vertical foul line markings on any wall that limits the outfield (4-1-2a).

When a fair or foul fly comes down near a stand or fence, 7-4-1d applies. If there is a screen behind the catcher or other permanent obstruction in front of the stand, a batted ball that goes behind these becomes dead and cannot be caught. It is recommended that no such obstruction be less than 60 feet from the diamond (4-1-2b).

Fundamental #2

Ground rules can not conflict with official playing rules.

Wild pitches, overthrows and batted balls that go over, through or wedges in a fence are governed by Rule 8-3-3. If the field has unusual obstructions, ground rules should, as nearly as possible, be similar to this rule (4-1-2c).

For a special field condition, such as a drain pipe that makes a spot where it is impossible or very difficult for a fielder to retrieve the ball, the ball should become dead if it goes to that spot and each runner's advance should be limited to two bases (4-1-2d).

In an unfenced field where cars are parked along the foul lines, umpires should consider these the same as bleachers and ball becomes dead if it bounces into the line of cars. They should anticipate such a situation and announce the ground rule in advance (4-1-2e).

Ground Rules: Caseplays

4.1.2 SITUATION A: During the pregame conference, the home team's coach, in covering the ground rules, explains that the fence does not go completely to the ground in right field and that a batted ball could go underneath it. Since the distance to the fence is more than 500 feet, should the ball go underneath the fence, the batter would automatically be awarded a home run. **RULING:** Ground rules shall be established if there are unusual conditions. However, ground rules do not supersede the NFHS Baseball Rules Book. Therefore, in this play the batter shall be awarded a ground-rule double.

4.1.2 SITUATION B: An outfield fence has a distance of 350 feet down the lines, but it is 270 feet to straightaway center field. During the pregame conference, the home team's coach informs the umpire that any batted ball that goes over the center-field fence shall be considered a ground-rule double. **RULING:** Ground rules shall not supersede the NFHS Baseball Rules Book. Therefore, the award shall be four bases, not two (8-3-3a).

Lineup Cards, Batting Order

The lineup card, presented by either the head coach or captain at the pregame meeting, shall include the name, shirt number, position and batting order of each starting player. The name and shirt number of each eligible substitute should also be listed. The umpire shall not accept the lineup card until all substitutes are listed. There is no penalty assessed (1-1-2).

For brevity in the play rulings, the home team is H and the visiting team V (2-1-1). Players of the team at bat are B1, B2, etc. The player who bats first in his half of an inning is designated B1. The second player to bat is B2, etc. Substitutes are S1, S2, etc. Runners are R1, R2 or R3. R1 occupies first base, R2 occupies second base, and R2 occupied third base (2-1-2). Fielding players are F1, F2, etc. (2-1-3, 2-13-5).

Each player of the team at bat shall become the batter and shall take his position within a batter's box, on either side of home plate, in the order in which his name appears on the lineup card as delivered to the umpire prior to the game. This order shall be followed during the entire game except that an entering substitute shall take the replaced player's place in the batting order (7-1-1).

◪ Rationale

In 2011, the rules committee required that subs be listed on the lineup card, although there is no penalty for non-compliance. That reverses a 2008 rule change.

Lineup Cards, Batting Order: Caseplays

1.1.2 SITUATION A: During the pregame conference, head coaches of Team A and Team B hand in their lineup cards to the umpire-in-chief.

Team A's starting players as well as all eligible substitutes are listed on the lineup card properly, but Team B's lineup card lists only starting players. During the first inning, Team B wishes to pinch hit with a substitute player who is not listed on the lineup card. **RULING:** The name and the shirt number of each eligible substitute shall be listed. The plate umpire accepts Team B's lineup card but encourages the head coach to list the eligible substitutes. Later, if Team B wishes to substitute a player who was not listed on the lineup card, it may do so without penalty.

1.1.2 SITUATION B: Team A's JV team has returned to join the varsity team during the sixth inning of the varsity game. A member of Team A's JV team attempts to enter the game as a pinch runner, but Team B's coach notices that Team A's JV player was not listed on the starting lineup card and argues he should not be allowed to enter the game. **RULING:** There is no penalty if the names are not listed on the lineup card. However, it is suggested that all players who might possibly enter the game be listed with their proper names and shirt numbers.

Confirm Players are Properly Equipped

Prior to the start of the game, the head coach shall be responsible for verifying to the umpire-in-chief that all his players are equipped in compliance with the above rules. Any questions regarding legality of a player's equipment shall be resolved by the umpire-in-chief (1-5-10).

The umpire in chief shall emphasize to both head coaches and captains that all participants are expected to exhibit good sporting behavior throughout the game(s) (4-1-3a).

The umpire-in-chief shall receive verification from each head coach that his participants are properly equipped in accordance with NFHS rules. In addition, each coach shall verify that his participants are using only legal equipment, including bats that are unaltered from the manufacturer's original design and production and that meet the provisions of 1-3-2, and helmets that meet the provisions of 1-5-1 and are free of cracks and damage (4-1-3b). On detected violations of 4-1-3b for the use of a damaged helmet, the helmet shall be immediately removed from play (4-1-3b PENALTY).

⬜ Rationale

Starting in 1983, the committee decided to match other rules codes by putting the responsibility of proper equipment being worn by players on the head coach. The "good sporting behavior" part of this rule was added 2001 because the committee wanted to emphasize the importance of sportsmanship to the educational values of baseball.

Confirm Players are Properly Equipped: Caseplays

4.1.3 SITUATION A: During the pregame conference, the umpire-in-chief asks the respective coaches if their players are properly equipped according to rule. The home team coach verifies that his players are properly equipped. The visiting team coach states that he is not sure. **RULING:** The game shall not begin until both coaches verify to the umpire-in-chief that all participants are properly equipped.

4.1.3 SITUATION B: As the pre-game conference concludes, the umpire-in-chief emphasizes to both coaches that all participants are expected to exhibit good sporting behavior throughout the game. The home coach questions why this was mentioned. **RULING:** By rule, the umpire-in-chief should emphasize the importance of sportsmanship to both coaches and captains.

Legality of Lineup

Lineups become official after they have been exchanged, verified and then accepted by the umpire during the pregame conference (1-1-2). A player is designated on the lineup card and in the scorebook by name, shirt number, batting order position and fielding position (1-1-3). Each team's lineup card shall list a minimum of nine players to start the game. The substitution regulations are then in effect (4-1-3).

After the umpire has received the official lineup card prior to the game, the player listed as pitcher shall pitch until the first opposing batter has been put out or has advanced to first base. In any other case, a substitute may replace a player of his team when the ball is dead and time has been called (3-1-1).

Legality of Lineup: Caseplays

1.1.2 SITUATION A: During the pregame conference, head coaches of Team A and Team B hand in their lineup cards to the umpire-in-chief. Team A's starting players as well as all eligible substitutes are listed on the lineup card properly, but Team B's lineup card lists only starting players. During the first inning, Team B wishes to pinch hit with a substitute player who is not listed on the lineup card. **RULING:** The name and the shirt number of each eligible substitute shall be listed. The plate umpire accepts Team B's lineup card but encourages the head coach to list the eligible substitutes. Later, if Team B wishes to substitute a player who was not listed on the lineup card, it may do so without penalty.

1.1.2 SITUATION B: Team A's JV team has returned to join the varsity team during the sixth inning of the varsity game. A member of Team

A's JV team attempts to enter the game as a pinch runner, but Team B's coach notices that Team A's JV player was not listed on the starting lineup card and argues he should not be allowed to enter the game. **RULING:** There is no penalty if the names are not listed on the lineup card. However, it is suggested that all players who might possibly enter the game be listed with their proper names and shirt numbers.

1.1.3 SITUATION: F4, Brown, listed in the batting order as wearing uniform No. 4, is wearing No. 21. After reaching base in the third inning, defensive coach appeals to the umpire that Brown is batting out of order. **RULING:** While Brown is in technical violation of the rule that requires that player's name, shirt number and position be on the lineup card, there is no penalty, since the batting-out-of-order rule requires only that the name be in the proper order. If the number was correct but the player batting was not Brown, the batting-out-of-order penalty would be imposed. Listing of both numbers and positions provides easier recordkeeping for scorekeepers and umpires.

3.1.1 SITUATION K: (a) Before the pregame conference, or (b) after the pregame conference, Team A's coach decides not to start F1. **RULING:** Lineups become official after they have been exchanged, verified and then accepted by the umpire-in-chief during the pre-game conference. In (a), lineup changes may be made without penalty. In (b) unless F1 is injured, ill or ejected, or removed by his coach for disciplinary reasons, F1 shall pitch to one batter. If F1 does not pitch to one batter, F1 shall not pitch for the remainder of the game, but he may play another position (1-1-1, 3-1-2).

Topic:
__Designated Hitter__

A hitter may be (not mandatory) designated for any one starting play- er (not just pitchers) and all subsequent substitutes for that player in the game. A designated hitter for said player shall be selected prior to the start of the game, and his name shall be included on the lineup cards presented to the umpire-in-chief and to the official scorer. A team forfeits the use of a designated hitter if it fails to declare a designated hitter prior to the game. If a pinch hitter or pinch runner for the designated hitter is used, that player becomes the new designated hitter. The player who was the designated hitter may re-enter as the designated hitter under the re-entry rule. A designated hitter and the player for whom he is batting are locked into the batting order. No multiple substitutions may be made that will alter the batting rotation. A designated hitter may be used in one of the two scenarios:

• The designated hitter may be a 10th starter hitting for any one of the nine starting defensive players. If the designated hitter (DH) is used in this manner, the role of the DH is terminated for the remainder of the game when the defensive player, or any previous defensive player for whom the designated hitter batted, subsequently bats, pinch-hits or pinch-runs for the designated hitter; or the designated hitter or any previous designated hitter assumes a defensive position.

• The starting designated hitter may be any one of the starting defensive players. In this manner, the starting defensive player has two positions: the defensive player and the designated hitter. The role of the defensive player may be substituted for by any legal substitute. If the defensive player has been substituted for, the original player/DH may re-enter one time. The role of the DH is terminated for the remainder of the game when a substitute or former substitute for the defensive role subsequently participates in an offensive role; or the starting defensive player/DH is substituted for either as a hitter or a runner (3-1-4).

Fundamental #3

The designated hitter, no matter how utilized, is locked into that spot in the batting order.

Designated Hitter: Caseplays

3.1.4 SITUATION A: DH Jones, who has been batting for F3 in the fourth position in the batting order, hits a triple in the fifth inning and sprains his ankle sliding into third base. His coach has S1 enter the game to be a pinch runner for DH Jones. How does that affect the playing status of DH Jones and F3? **RULING:** When a pinch runner or pinch hitter replaces the DH, that player becomes the DH. F3 would not be affected by the substitution. However, if the DH were to play defense, F3 would have to leave the game.

3.1.4 SITUATION B: DH, batting in the second position in the lineup for starter F5, safely reaches first base, where pinch runner S1 replaces him. **RULING:** The DH has been out of the game once. S1 may become the new DH or the original DH may re-enter as DH or may play defense. If he plays defense, the role of DH is terminated. Whenever any current or former DH enters the game on defense, the role of the DH is terminated.

3.1.4 SITUATION C: F4, for whom the DH is batting, pinch hits or pinch runs for the DH. **RULING:** The DH position is eliminated for the remainder of the game. However, the starting DH could re-enter as a player but not in the role of DH. If he does re-enter, he must re-enter in the same position in the batting order, replacing F4.

3.1.4 SITUATION D: The starting DH, who is batting for F4, goes on defense for F4 at the end of the second inning. **RULING:** This eliminates the DH position for the remainder of the game.

*3.1.4 SITUATION E: Prior to the start of the game at the pre-game conference meeting, the (a) home team's coach presents the plate umpire a lineup card with Holaday the DH for Feldhausen the RF and the (b) visiting team's coach presents a lineup card with Sullivan listed as the RF/DH. **RULING:** Legal in both (a) and (b). Teams may choose to use either DH option or no DH for a particular game as long as they declare their intentions prior to the start of the game.

*3.1.4 SITUATION F: Sanders is listed as the P/DH, hitting in the third position in the batting order. (a) In the fifth inning, McNeely enters the game as pitcher with Sanders reaching his pitch count limit. Sanders continues as DH for McNeely; (b) in the sixth inning, substitute Jackson enters to pitch replacing McNeely. Sanders remains the DH for Jackson; and (c) in the seventh inning, Sanders returns to de- fense as the catcher and is still listed as the DH. **RULING:** Legal in (a), (b) and (c).

*3.1.4 SITUATION G: Kruger is listed as the RF/DH, hitting third in the batting order. In the fifth inning, substitute Brodell enters as the right fielder with Kruger still the DH, hitting for Brodell. **RULING:** This is legal.

*3.1.4 SITUATION H: With Dolan listed in the starting lineup as the 2B/ DH and batting fourth in the order, the coach wants to bring in Tatelman to hit for Dolan. **RULING:** If substitute Tatelman comes in to hit (or run) for Dolan, the role of the DH is terminated for the game. If eligible, Dolan may re-enter the game on defense and bat in the same spot in the batting order.

*3.1.4 SITUATION I: In the fourth inning, Montalbo replaces Colgate as the start- ing P/DH as pitcher. In the fifth inning, Colgate sprains his ankle as he slides into second base on a double. Colgate cannot continue and requires a pinch-runner. **RULING:** If an eligible substitute enters the game to pinch-run for Colgate, the role of the DH is terminated and Colgate is removed from the game. The coach may substitute another player, but this will end Montalbo as the pitcher since the substitute enters the game in the batting order spot already occupied by Montalbo. However, if the coach has Montalbo pinch-run for Colgate, Montalbo may continue to pitch and hit for himself.

*3.1.4 SITUATION J: In the fourth inning, Federico, who is listed fourth in the batting order as P/DH and hitting fourth, sprains his ankle running the bases and is taken out of the game replaced and by McGinnis, who later has an at bat. Later in the six inning, Federico re-enters to (a) pinch-hit for McGinnis or (b) play defense for Russell at first base with McGinnis still pitching. **RULING:** Legal in (a); illegal in (b). Federico and McGinnis are locked into the same lineup spot and cannot be in the game on defense at the same time.

Topic:
Speed-up Rules

Rule modifications to speed up the game may be adopted by state associations (2-33-1). Those modifications include rules for courtesy runners and defensive procedures after putouts.

Speed-up Rules: Caseplay
2.33.1 SITUATION: By mutual agreement, coaches of both teams decide to allow a courtesy runner for the catcher for the duration of the game. **RULING:** Suggested speed-up rules may be used in part or their entirety only if the state association has approved their use.

Speed-up Rules: After Putouts
If the state association has adopted speed-up rules, the defensive team must limit its throws after putouts.

After a putout in the outfield and with no runners on base, the ball shall be thrown to a cutoff man and, if desired, to one additional infielder before being returned to the pitcher for delivery to the next batter.

After a putout in the infield and with no runners on base, the ball shall be returned directly to the pitcher.

Following the final out in any inning, the ball shall be given to the nearest umpire. The plate umpire shall give the ball to the catcher. The base umpire shall place the ball on the pitcher's plate (Suggested Speed-Up Rules).

> # Did You Know ?
>
> Speed-up rules were first allowed in 1978 by state association adoption, but none were actually listed in the book. "Suggested speed-up rules" did not appear until 1982.

Speed-Up Rules: Courtesy Runners

By state association adoption any, all, or any part of the suggested speed-up rules may be used.

At any time, the team at bat may use courtesy runners for the pitcher and/or the catcher. The same individual runner may not be used for both positions (pitcher and catcher) during the game. In the event that the offensive team bats around, the pitcher and/or catcher who had a courtesy runner inserted on their behalf may bat in their normal position in the batting order.

Neither the pitcher nor the catcher will be required to leave the game under such circumstances.

Players who have participated in the game in any other capacity are ineligible to serve as courtesy runners.

A player may not run as a courtesy runner for the pitcher or the catcher and then be used as a substitute for another player in that half inning. If an injury, illness or ejection occurs and no other runners are available, the courtesy runner may be used as a substitute.

The umpire-in-chief shall record courtesy runner participation and also announce it to the scorer.

A player who violates the courtesy-runner rule is considered to be an illegal substitute. Should an injury, illness or ejection occur to the courtesy runner, another courtesy runner for the pitcher or catcher may run (Suggested Speed-Up Rules).

Speed-Up Rules: Courtesy Runners Caseplays

3.1.1 SITUATION R: In the first inning, C1 is a courtesy runner for the pitcher. In the second inning, C1 is a courtesy runner for the catcher. **RULING:** Upon discovery, C1 is called out and restricted to the dugout for the remainder of the game.

CR 1 SITUATION: Team A's courtesy runner runs for F1 and later in that same half-inning runs for F2. **RULING:** The courtesy runner can run for one or the other, but not both. This is an illegal substitution and shall result in the courtesy runner being declared out and restricted to the bench/dugout.

CR 2 SITUATION: Jones runs for F2 in the first inning, but Smith comes out to run for F2 in the third inning. **RULING:** This is legal if Jones and

Smith are both eligible courtesy runners and have reported to the umpire-in-chief as they enter as courtesy runners.

CR 3 SITUATION: The coach of Team A sends out a courtesy runner for F2 in the third inning with one out. After the second out, he sends F2 back out to run for himself. **RULING:** Illegal. Once the courtesy runner replaces F2, F2 cannot re-enter for the courtesy runner in that half-inning unless the offensive team bats around. However, in case of injury with no other courtesy runner available, F2 may re-enter.

CR 4 SITUATON: The coach of Team B sends out a courtesy runner for F1 in the fifth inning with no outs. In the same half-inning, after the offensive team bats around, F1 returns as a batter. **RULING:** Legal. While F1 may not return in the half-inning as a runner on the bases, he may return as a batter.

CR 5 SITUATION: F2 doubles with no outs. Two outs later the coach sends out a courtesy runner for F2. **RULING:** A courtesy runner does not have to be entered when the catcher first reaches base. A courtesy runner may be entered at any time.

CR 6 SITUATION: McCormick is a courtesy runner for F2 in the first inning. He then is a courtesy runner for F1 in the sixth inning. **RULING:** Illegal. The same player cannot be a courtesy runner for both positions. The illegal substitute is declared out and restricted to the bench/dugout.

CR 7 SITUATION: Herrmann is a courtesy runner for F2 in the top half of the sixth inning. He then enters to pinch-hit for F4 later in that half-inning. **RULING:** Illegal. A courtesy runner is not eligible to enter the game as a substitute during the same half-inning in which he has served as a courtesy runner. Therefore, Herrmann is declared out and restricted to the bench/dugout.

CR 8 SITUATION: Harty pinch-runs for F7 in the second inning, and then leaves the game. He is inserted as a courtesy runner for F2 in the eighth inning. **RULING:** Illegal. Harty is out and restricted to the bench/dugout.

CR 9 SITUATION: The coach of Team A sends out a courtesy runner for F1 and fails to report the change to the umpire-in-chief. **RULING:** Upon entering the game, the courtesy runner became an official substitute. There is no penalty. F1 has been replaced and may only return if he has re-entry eligibility. Since Team A's coach did not inform the umpire that the substitute was a courtesy runner for F1, the umpire shall treat the change as a normal substitution. Therefore, F1 is out of the game.

CR 10 SITUATION: F1 singles and is replaced at first by a courtesy runner. On the next pitch, the courtesy runner steals second base and sprains his ankle, but is safe on the slide. Does F1 have to replace the courtesy runner? **RULING:** No. Any legal substitute may become the courtesy runner. In this case, if no legal substitute is available, F1 shall return to run.

CR 11 SITUATION: F2 singles and is replaced by a courtesy runner. B2 walks. Before the next pitch, the courtesy runner is replaced by another courtesy runner. **RULING:** Legal. A courtesy runner may be replaced by another legal courtesy runner at any time.

CR 12 SITUATION: Thompson enters the game as the courtesy runner for F2 in the bottom half of the first inning. In the bottom half of the fourth inning F2 walks. Must Thompson or another player be the courtesy runner for F2? **RULING:** No. Each team has the option of using a courtesy runner each time the pitcher or catcher reaches base.

CR 13 SITUATION: In the top of the sixth inning with two outs, B3, who is the catcher, singles. The coach sends out a courtesy runner for F2 (a) before the first pitch to B4 or (b) with a count on B4 of three balls and two strikes. **RULING:** Legal in (a) and (b).

CR 14 SITUATION: Cook is a courtesy runner for the pitcher. He then pinch hits for the uninjured shortstop in the same half-inning. **RULING:** Cook is an illegal substitute and is declared out. He is restricted to the dugout for the remainder of the game. If he had previously been restricted to the dugout, he is out and ejected.

CR 15 SITUATION: Munoz was a courtesy runner for the catcher and enters the game to courtesy run for the uninjured pitcher. **RULING:** Munoz is out and restricted to the dugout for the remainder of the game.

CR 16 SITUATION: Adams courtesy runs for F1 (Jones) in the 1st inning. Baker courtesy runs for F2 (Smith) in the 3rd inning. In the 4th inning, Jones and Smith swap defensive positions. Which person can Adams courtesy run for? **RULING:** Adams may only courtesy run for F1 who is now Smith not Jones.

*CR 17 SITUATION: Adams is the catcher for Team A and is to leadoff in the bottom of the fifth inning. The coach has Smith to pinch-hit for him (first time in the game Adams has had a substitute for him) and Smith leads off with a single. The coach re-enters Adams into the game and then requests to have a courtesy runner for Adams. The coach of

Team B protests that is not legal. **RULING:** It is legal. Since Smith is not the catcher of record in the last half inning (top of the fifth), a courtesy runner may not run for Smith. But if the coach decides to reenter Adams, he may do so and have a courtesy runner run for him.

Topic:
Start of Game

The visiting team shall be the first to take its turn at bat. On a neutral field or by agreement, either team may be designated as home team (4-1-4). The umpire-in-chief's duties include calling "Play" and using the correct hand signal to start the game (10-2-3b). The game begins when the umpire calls "Play" after all infielders, pitcher, catcher and batter are in position to start the game (4-1-5).

Topic 2
Pitching

PlayPic®

Key Terms

The pitcher is the player who is designated in the lineup as being responsible for delivering (pitching) the ball to the batter (2-28-1). A pitch is a live ball delivered to the batter. The term implies a legally delivered ball unless otherwise stated (2-28-2).

A legally delivered pitch that is not put into play must be a ball or a strike. A pitch is a strike if it passes through the strike zone in flight. The strike zone is the space over home plate, the top of which is halfway between the batter's shoulders and the waistline, and the bottom being the knees, when he assumes his natural batting stance (2-35-1). If the pitch is not a strike and not touched by the bat, it is a ball (2-4-1).

A foul is a batted ball which settles on foul territory between home and first base or between home and third base; or that bounds past first or third base on or over foul territory; or that first falls on foul territory beyond first or third base; or that, while on or over foul territory, touches the person of an umpire or a player or any object foreign to the natural ground; or is inadvertently being declared foul by an umpire; or that hits the batter in the batter's box; or that hits the ground or home plate and then hits the batter or the bat which is held by the batter, while he is in the batter's box (2-16-1a through g).

A foul tip is a batted ball that goes directly to the catcher's hands and is legally caught by the catcher. It shall be called a strike and the ball is in play (2-16-2).

An illegal pitch is an illegal act committed by the pitcher with no runner on base, which results in a ball being awarded the batter. When an illegal pitch occurs with a runner, or runners, on base, it is ruled a balk (2-18-1). A balk is an illegal act committed by the pitcher with a runner(s) on base which entitles each runner to advance one base (2-3-1).

The pitch ends when the pitched ball is secured by the catcher, comes to rest, goes out of play, becomes dead or the batter hits the ball (other than a foul tip) (2-28-4).

The strike zone is the space over home plate, the top of which is halfway between the batter's shoulders and the waistline, and the bottom being the knees, when he assumes his natural batting stance (2-35-1).

Topic:
Pitching Regulations _____

After the umpire has received the official lineup card prior to the game, the player listed as pitcher shall pitch until the first opposing batter has been put out or has advanced to first base (3-1-1). The starting pitcher may warm up by using not more than eight throws, completed in one minute (timed from the first throw). At the beginning of each subsequent inning, the pitcher may warm up by using not more than five throws, completed in one minute (timed from the third out of the previous half-inning). In either case, the umpire-in-chief may authorize more throws because of an injury, ejection or inclement weather (6-2-2c exception).

Each state association shall have a pitching restriction policy based on the number of pitches thrown to afford pitchers a required rest period between pitching appearances (6-1-6).

In Simple Terms

Umpires have no jurisdiction over any teams pitching restrictions. That is up to the state association.

◪ Rationale

The rule requiring states to have a pitching restriction came about in 1990 after numerous reports of perceived overuse and abuse of pitchers. The committee left it up to each state to determine what limit was best for its situations.

Pitching Regulations: Caseplays

3.1.1 SITUATION K: (a) Before the pregame conference, or (b) after the pregame conference, Team A's coach decides not to start F1. **RULING:** Lineups become official after they have been exchanged, verified and then accepted by the umpire-in-chief during the pregame conference. In (a), lineup changes may be made without penalty. In (b) unless F1 is injured, ill or ejected, or removed by his coach for disciplinary reasons, F1 shall pitch to one batter. If F1 does not pitch to one batter, F1 shall not pitch for the remainder of the game, but he may play another position (3-1-2).

3.1.2 SITUATION C: In the top half of the first, S1 pinch hits for F1. In the bottom half of the first inning, F1 (a) re-enters to face the first batter or (b) does not re-enter until later. **RULING:** A substitute may replace F1 while his team is at bat without penalty. Since F1 is a starter, he shall re-enter and pitch to the first batter in the bottom of the first inning. In (a) F1 has complied with the rule. In (b), since F1 did not pitch to the first batter, F1 may not return to pitch. He may, however, play another position (3-1-1, 3-1-3).

6.1.6 SITUATION A: The coach of Team A has an ambidextrous pitcher and wants to know if the player can pitch the limitation both left-handed and right-handed. **RULING:** Pitching limitations are to apply to the player as an individual, not as a left-handed and right-handed pitcher.

6.1.6 SITUATION B: F1 is a replacement relief pitcher. He attempts to pick off R1 from first base. The offensive team's coach realizes that F1 has exceeded his number of pitched innings per the state association pitching restrictions and requests from the umpire-in-chief that his opponent forfeit the game. The defensive team argues that F1 has not thrown a pitch and therefore replaces him with a legal substitute. **RULING:** The forfeit is not honored. F1's attempt to pick off R1 by definition is not considered to be a pitch (2-28-2). The defensive coach is allowed to replace him with an eligible pitcher.

 COMMENT: During the pregame conference, the coach of Team A tells the umpire that he is going to allow his best pitcher to throw as many innings as necessary to ensure a win or that he is authorizing the pitcher to pitch both games of the doubleheader since the pitcher's family and friends have traveled so far to see him pitch. **RULING:** The amount a pitcher may pitch is determined by the state associations, not the coaches or umpires. Limitations may vary from state to state. However, limitations are to ensure that pitchers are not overused and that they have had reasonable rest between pitching appearances (6.1.6 comment).

6.2.2 SITUATION B: S1 replaces F1. How much time or how many throws are permitted for his warm-up? **RULING:** S1 is permitted eight pitches completed in one minute. The umpire is authorized to allow more when the weather is inclement or if F1 is removed because of injury and S1 did not have time to warm up before entering.

6.2.2 SITUATION C: F1, who was a baserunner in his half of the inning, is slow in coming out to take his warm-up pitches. The umpire refuses to permit him to warmup, stating he used up his one-minute allotted time. **RULING:** The umpire is correct. The one-minute time limit begins at the conclusion of the final out of the previous half-inning. However, in the above situation, the umpire should use good judgment in enforcing this rule (6-2-2).

6.2.2 SITUATION E: Prior to the start of the third inning, starter F1 is late in getting to the mound to take his warm-up throws. **RULING:** The starter may take five warm-up throws, if he can get them in within the one-minute time limit, which begins at the conclusion of the final out of the previous half-inning.

Replacing the Pitcher

A player may change to a different fielding position at any time except that a pitcher, after being listed as such on the official lineup card handed the umpire, cannot change until certain conditions are met (1-1-5). The starting pitcher shall pitch until the first opposing batter has been put out or has advanced to first base (3-1-1). If the starting pitcher does not face one batter, he may play another position, but not return to pitch (3-1-1 penalty).

If a pitcher is replaced while his team is on defense, the substitute pitcher shall pitch to the batter then at bat, or any substitute for that batter, until such batter is put out or reaches first base, or until a third out has been made. To ensure that the requirements of this article be fulfilled, the umpire will deny any coach-defensive player conference that will violate the rule. If a pitcher is incapacitated or guilty of flagrant unsportsmanlike conduct, this rule is ignored. A player may be removed as pitcher and returned as pitcher only once per inning, provided the return as pitcher does not violate either the pitching, substitution or charged conference rule.

If the pitcher, because of an injury or being incapacitated, is replaced as pitcher and the above rule is not satisfied, or if his replacement requires more warm-up throws than permitted in 6-2-2 exception, he cannot return to the game as a pitcher (3-1-2).

When a pitcher is replaced during an inning or prior to an inning, the relief pitcher may not use more than eight throws, completed in one minute (timed from the first throw) (6-2-2c). The umpire-in-chief may authorize more throws because of an injury, ejection or inclement weather (6-2-2c exception). Should there be no announcement of a substitution, a substitute pitcher is considered to have entered the game when the ball is live and the pitcher takes his place on the pitcher's plate (3-1-1b).

If the pitcher, because of an injury or being incapacitated, is replaced as pitcher before meeting the requirements of facing one batter or recording the third out, or if his replacement requires more warm-up throws than permitted in 6-2-2 exception, he cannot return to the game as a pitcher (3-1-2 note).

Replacing the Pitcher: Caseplays

3.1.2 SITUATION A: F1 is replaced by S1. The catcher or coach of the defensive team indicates to the umpire-in-chief that his team wishes to grant an intentional base on balls. Following the intentional base on balls, S1 is replaced by S2. **RULING:** That is legal, since S1 has faced the necessary one batter.

3.1.2 SITUATION B: While taking his warm-up pitches prior to the start of the fourth inning, F1 develops a blister on the tip of his index finger and is replaced as pitcher. F1's replacement takes (a) the remaining number of warm-up pitches due starter F1, or (b) more warm-up pitches than starter F1 was entitled. **RULING:** As a substitute for the pitcher, S1 is allowed eight warm-up pitches. If S1 only takes eight warm-up pitches, F1 may return to pitch later in the game provided all other aspects of pitcher substitution have been met. If S1 needs to take more than eight warm-up pitches, that may be allowed by PU, but F1 could no longer return to pitch in this game.

6.2.2 SITUATION A: F1 intentionally throws at B4 and is ejected from the contest. The opposing coach feels that S1 is only allowed five warm-up pitches. **RULING:** Incorrect interpretation. S1 is allowed the same number of warm-up pitches (8) as if the pitching change was a result of injury or inclement weather.

6.2.2 SITUATION E: Prior to the start of the third inning, starter F1 is (a) late in getting to the mound to take his warm-up throws or (b) is replaced by a relief pitcher. **RULING:** In (a), the starter may take five warm-up throws, if he can get them in within the one-minute time limit. In (b), the pitcher may take up to eight warm-up throws. The one-minute time limit at the start of each half-inning begins at the conclusion of the final out of the previous half-inning.

Topic:
Defensive Conferences

A charged conference is a meeting which involves the coach or his non-playing representative and a player or players of the team (2-10-1). Play is suspended when a player or coach requests "Time" and it is granted by the umpire for a substitution, conference with the pitcher or for similar cause (5-2-1e).

Number of Defensive Conferences

Each team, when on defense, may be granted not more than three charged conferences during a seven-inning game, without penalty, to permit coaches or their non-playing representatives to confer with a defensive player or players. In an extra-inning game, each team shall be permitted one charged conference each inning while on defense without penalty. The number of charged conferences permitted is not cumulative. A request for time for this purpose shall be made by a coach, player, substitute or an attendant. Time granted for an obviously incapacitated player shall not constitute a charged conference. Prior to accumulating three charged conferences in seven innings or less, a conference is not charged if the pitcher is removed as pitcher. After three charged conferences in a seven-inning game, or for any charged conference in excess of one in each extra inning, the pitcher shall be removed as pitcher for duration of the game (3-4-1).

Did You Know? The limits on defensive conferences in 1959 were meeting with a pitcher more than twice in an inning or more than four times in a game.

Number of Defensive Conferences: Caseplays

3.4.1 SITUATION A: The coach of the defensive team moves to the pitcher's mound in the eighth inning (a) after having used his three allowable defensive charged conferences in the first seven innings or (b) not having used any of his three allowable defensive charged conferences in the first seven innings. **RULING:** There is no penalty in either (a) or (b). A team is permitted three defensive charged conferences in a seven-inning game, and if a game goes into extra innings, that team is permitted only one charged defensive conference in each of the extra innings. Unused defensive charged conferences in the first seven innings are not accumulative.

3.4.1 SITUATION C: The coach of the defensive team has used his three charged conferences. In the seventh inning the coach (a) stops play to confer with his infielders about a bunt r (b) goes to the mound to check his pitcher who has just been hit by a batted ball. **RULING:** In (a), F1 must be removed as pitcher for the remainder of the game. In (b), this is not a charged conference.

3.4.1 SITUATION D: In the third inning the coach of the defensive team, who has yet to have a charged conference, goes to the mound to talk to his pitcher. He (a) changes pitchers or (b) does not change pitchers. The next inning he receives time to visit with his catcher. How many charged conferences has the coach accumulated? **RULING:** The meeting with the catcher is one charged conference. In (a), there is no charged conference, so the coach still has two charged conferences remaining. In (b), he has accumulated two charged conferences: one for the visit with the catcher and one for the pitcher who was not removed. Therefore, the coach would have one charged conference remaining.

3.4.1 SITUATION E: Team A has had two charged conferences. The coach of Team A is granted time to visit with his pitcher. At the same time his assistant coach goes out to talk to the first baseman. The opposing team's coach claims that another conference also should be assessed and that the pitcher would have to be removed, since it would be that team's fourth. **RULING:** As long as the assistant coach does not delay the game when play is to resume, there is no penalty. If he does delay, his team is subject to an additional charged conference being called, which then would require the pitcher to be removed as pitcher for the rest of the game.

3.4.1 SITUATION F: In the top of the fifth inning (a) the defensive team's head coach asks for "Time" to check on his center fielder who appeared to be ill. At the same time (b) the assistant coach goes to the pitcher's mound to visit with the pitcher. Has a charged conference occurred? **RULING:** A conference is not charged when "Time" is called for an obviously incapacitated player. In (a), if the umpire judged the player the coach went to check on was ill and unable to continue, then no conference would be called. In (b), since "Time" is out, the assistant coach is permitted on the field to talk to any defensive player. When play is to resume, if he is not off the field, he shall be charged a conference for delay. NOTE: If the umpire believes that a player is faking an injury so that a coach can talk to the pitcher or another defensive player without being charged a conference, the umpire may prohibit additional conferences from taking place at that time.

3.4.1 SITUATION G: Team A has had three charged conferences by the fifth inning. With the game tied in the sixth inning, the coach of Team A informs the umpire that (a) F6 and F1 are going to trade positions or (b) that S1 is replacing F1. Can the pitcher who is being replaced return to pitch later in the game, or is this considered a charged conference? **RULING:** In (a) and (b), the pitcher being replaced may return to pitch as long as he has not been replaced and returned to pitch previously in the same inning. Also, if his removal is because of an injury and he has not faced at least one batter or if (a) F6 or (b) S1 needs more warm-up pitches than permitted, then F1 is not permitted to return to pitch. The umpire shall permit the coach to switch players or substitute, provided the coach does not take advantage of the situation by having a conversation with any of the players. A violation shall result in a charged conference being assessed, which would be more than allowed, resulting in the pitcher not being able to return to pitch (3-1-2 Note).

3.4.1 SITUATION H: Between innings the coach of Team A walks from the third base coach's box to the pitcher's mound and proceeds to visit with F1. **RULING:** F1 has one minute in which to complete his warmup throws. At that point, the coach should leave the field. The umpire should not allow play to begin until the coach is off the field. The umpire may assess the coach a charged conference if he delays leaving the field (6-2-2c exception).

3.4.1 SITUATION I: The coach of the defensive team, just after the ball is returned to F1, yells from the dugout: (a) giving instructions to F4 and F6; or (b) to have F6 and F9 switch positions. **RULING:** Situations (a) and (b) do not warrant a charged conference being called (3-4-1, 3-4-3).

Defensive Conference Ends

A defensive charged conference is concluded when the coach or non-playing representative crosses the foul line if the conference was in fair territory. If the conference was in foul territory, the conference concludes when the coach or non-playing representative initially starts to return to the dugout/bench area (3-4-3). If a coach who has been restricted to the dugout/bench area is involved in a charged conference, that conference shall end when the players involved initially start to return to their positions on the field (3-4-3 note). The coach shall be given a reasonable amount of time for the charged conference as determined by the umpire-in-chief (3-4-3 note).

Defensive Conference Ends: Caseplay

3.4.3 SITUATION: A coach goes to the pitcher's mound for a defensive charged conference. He (a) starts to return to his dugout but does not cross the foul line and returns to the pitcher's mound to continue the charged conference or (b) starts to return to his dugout, crosses the foul line, and then returns to the pitcher's mound. **RULING:** In (a) the coach is not charged for a second conference unless the umpire has told him previously his time was up. In (b), the coach is charged with a second conference as he ended the initial charged conference when he crossed the foul line unless he removes the pitcher after returning to the mound.

Topic:
Pitching Positions

The pitcher shall pitch while facing the batter from either a windup position or a set position. The position of his feet determine whether he will pitch from the windup or the set position. He shall take his sign from the catcher with his pivot foot in contact with the pitcher's plate. The pitching regulations begin when he intentionally contacts the pitcher's plate. He shall not make a quick-return pitch in an attempt to catch a batter off balance. The catcher shall have both feet in the catcher's box at the time of the pitch (6-1-1). If a pitcher is ambidextrous, the umpire shall require the pitcher to face a batter as either a left-handed pitcher or right-handed pitcher, but not both (6-1-1 note).

The pitcher's pivot foot is that foot with which the pitcher contacts the pitcher's plate when he delivers the ball. For example, the pivot foot is the left foot for a left-handed pitcher (2-28-6).

> ## Fundamental #4
> A pitcher may deliver from either the windup or set position at any time.

Pitching Positions: Caseplays

6.1.1 SITUATION F: Switch-hitting B1 steps in against ambidextrous F1. B1 assumes a position in the batter's box as a left-handed hitter, prompting F1 to prepare to pitch left-handed. B1 quickly changes to the other batter's box to bat right-handed. F1 then switches to pitch right-handed. How is this situation prevented? **RULING:** The umpire shall call "Time" and require the pitcher to face B1 as either a left-hander or right-hander, but not both. Only after B1 is put out, reaches base, is replaced by a substitute, or a third out ends the inning, may F1 change to the other hand to face the next batter.

6.1.3 SITUATION L: With R3 on third, F1 assumes his windup position, and takes his sign from the catcher. He now desires to pitch from the set position. **RULING:** It is legal for F1 to assume his windup position and then change to the set position. After he assumes either position he must step backward from the plate with his pivot foot first to become an infielder, before again assuming either pitching position. As long as F1 has not made a preliminary motion he may step backward off the pitcher's plate (6-1-1, 6-1-2).

◰ Rationale

Pitching restrictions used to begin as soon as the pitcher took his signal from the catcher. However, some pitchers were not taking signals, making it difficult for umpires to determine when to enforce the restrictions.

Pitcher as an Infielder

When a pitcher is attempting to field a batted or thrown ball or is throwing to a base while his pivot foot is clearly off his plate, his status is that of an infielder except that if a batted ball passes but does not touch him and then strikes an umpire or a runner, the ball may become dead because of interference (6-1-5).

In Simple Terms

A ball thrown by a pitcher when his pivot foot is not on the rubber is treated as if it was thrown by an infielder.

Pitcher as an Infielder: Caseplay

6.1.5 SITUATION: With R3 on third base and R1 on first base, F1 legally steps off the pitcher's plate and feints to third and then steps and throws to first attempting to pick off R1. The throw goes into dead-ball territory.

The offensive team's coach wants a balk to be called because the pitcher never threw the ball toward third. **RULING:** When the pitcher stepped off the pitching plate in his feint to third, he became an infielder. Hence, when his throw goes into dead-ball territory, all runners are awarded two bases. R3 gets home and R1 gets third. Had F1 stayed on the pitching plate during his feint to third and his throw to first, all runners would be awarded one base. R3 would get home and R1 would get second. This would not be a balk as F1 made a legal feint and a legal pickoff attempt with no prior motion to pitch.

Set Position

For the set position, the pitcher shall have the ball in either his gloved hand or his pitching hand. His pitching hand shall be down at his side or behind his back. Before starting his delivery, he shall stand with his entire non-pivot foot in front of a line extending through the front edge of the pitcher's plate and with his pivot foot in contact with or directly in front of and parallel to the pitcher's plate. He shall go to the set position without interruption and in one continuous motion. He shall come to a complete and discernible stop (a change of direction is not considered an acceptable stop) with the ball in both hands in front of the body and his glove at or below his chin. Natural preliminary motions such as only one stretch may be made. During these preliminary motions and during the set position until a delivery motion occurs, the pitcher may turn on his pivot foot or lift it in a jump turn to step with the non-pivot foot toward a base while throwing or feinting, or he may lift his pivot foot in a step backward off the pitcher's plate which must be in or partially within the 24-inch length of the pitcher's plate (6-1-3). A feint is a movement which simulates the start of a pitch or throw to a base and which is used in an attempt to deceive a runner (2-28-5). If there is a runner or runners, any feinting toward the batter or first base while the pitcher is touching the pitcher's plate is a balk (6-2-4a).

In order to change to the wind-up position, he must first step clearly backward off the pitcher's plate with his pivot foot first. After the pitcher has placed his pivot foot on the ground clearly behind the plate, he then has the right to throw or feint to a base the same as that of any other infielder (6-1-3).

Turning the shoulders to check runners while in contact with the pitcher's plate in the set position is legal. Turning the shoulders after bringing the hands together during or after the stretch is a balk (6-1-1).

Rationale

The discussion in 2013 concerning the hybrid pitching position — one in which the pitcher's feet do not meet the qualifications of either the windup or set positions — sparked tremendous discussion. One year later, the committee added wording specifically spelling out the physical position of the pivot foot in the set position to eliminate confusion of the pitching rule.

Set Position: Caseplays

*6.1.1 SITUATION A: F1 pitches with the toe of his pivot foot (right foot for right-handed pitcher) in contact with the pitcher's plate but his heel is outside a line through the end edge of the plate. He pitches from the set position. **RULING:** Legal, provided that F1's pivot foot is parallel to the pitcher's plate.

6.1.1 SITUATION D: F1 takes his sign in the (a) windup position or (b) set position. R3 at third attempts to steal home. F1 steps forward off the pitcher's plate and throws to F2. **RULING:** This is a balk in (a) and (b).

COMMENT: After assuming a windup or set position stance on the plate, the pitcher must step clearly backward off the plate with the pivot foot in order to play on R1 at the plate (6-1-2, 6-1-3).

6.1.1 SITUATION G: The bases are loaded. F1, while on the pitcher's plate and from the set position prior to beginning the stretch, turns his shoulder and glances at the runner. **RULING:** This is legal.

6.1.1 SITUATION H: From the set position, F1, while in the stretch, slowly brings his hands to his belt and then delivers a pitch. **RULING:** Unless F1 came to a complete stop, one that is clearly recognizable, he has committed a balk.

6.1.1 SITUATION I: When is a pitcher permitted to step backward off the pitching plate in the set position? **RULING:** While in the set position stance, he may step backward off the pitcher's plate prior to the start of the pitch (2-28-3).

6.1.1 SITUATION J: With R1 on first base, F1, from the set position and prior to bringing his hands together while in contact with the pitcher's plate, (a) abruptly and quickly turns his shoulders toward first base in an attempt to drive back the runner; or (b) casually turns his shoulders to observe the runner at first base. **RULING:** Legal in both (a) and (b).

*6.1.3 SITUATION A: F1 takes the set position with his pivot foot entirely in front of and parallel with the pitcher's plate. F1's non-pivot foot is entirely in front of his pivot foot (toward home plate) but is not within the plane of each end of the pitcher's plate. **RULING:** This is legal, since only part of the pivot foot is required to be parallel to the pitcher's plate, within the plane of each end of the pitcher's plate, and in contact with it. The non-pivot foot is required to be entirely in front of the front plane of the pitcher's plate but does not have to be within the plane of the pitcher's plate.

6.1.3 SITUATION B: F1 is in a set position and the heel of the pivot foot is in contact with the pitcher's plate. The rest of the pivot foot is on an angle towards home plate. **RULING:** Illegal. The pivot foot is required to be parallel to the pitcher's plate in a legal set position.

6.1.3 SITUATION C: Left-handed F1 assumes a set position with R1 on first. F1 steps back off the pitcher's plate with his pivot foot and throws to first base without stepping to the base. **RULING:** This is legal, provided F1's pivot foot touches the ground prior to separating his hands.

6.1.3 SITUATION D: With R1 at first, F1, while in the set position, takes his sign with ball in his glove and pitching hand at his side or behind his back, and begins his stretch. Before he is set, F2 changes sign and F1 (a) stops without stepping backward off the pitcher's plate or (b) steps backward off the pitcher's plate and stops. **RULING:** This is a balk in (a). F1 must come set without interruption and in one continuous motion. This is legal in (b).

6.1.3 SITUATION E: With R1 on first, F1, in a set-position stance with the ball in his gloved hand and his pitching hand at his side, takes his sign. He removes the ball from his glove and goes to a set position. **RULING:** This is a balk.

6.1.3 SITUATION F: With R1 on first, F1 receives the ball from F2 and with his feet in set position stance and in contact with the pitcher's plate (a) nervously tosses the ball in his glove two or three times, or (b) removes the ball from his glove. **RULING:** This is a balk in (a) and (b). Restrictions on F1's movements begin when he intentionally contacts the pitcher's plate with his pivot foot.

6.1.3 SITUATION G: With R2 on second (a) F1 stretches and comes to a stop, or (b) he stretches a second time and comes to a stop. In both (a) and (b), he then steps toward third and throws there in an effort to put out R2 who is attempting to steal. **RULING:** Legal in (a), provided F1 did not start a pitch after coming set. In (b), the umpire shall declare the ball dead as soon as the second stretch occurs. R1 is awarded third on balk by F1 (6-1-3).

6.1.3 SITUATION H: With R1 on first, F1 is in set position in a wide stance. He lifts his nonpivot foot to shorten his stance and then returns to his wide stance (a) during his stretch and before his stop or (b) after his stop. **RULING:** This is legal in (a), but is a balk in (b). If nonpivot foot is lifted after the stop, he must immediately pitch or step directly toward base and throw to that base.

6.1.3 SITUATION I: With R1 on first, F1 is in set position. He stretches his arms and, without stopping, steps toward and throws to first. **RULING:** This is legal. Stopping is required only before a pitch.

6.1.3 SITUATION J: R2 is on second. From the set position, F1 uses a jump turn. He comes down astride the pitching plate with his non-pivot foot toward second base and throws or feints there. **RULING:** Legal.

 COMMENT: F1's pivot foot shall contact the ground before he releases the ball.

6.1.3 SITUATION M: With R2 on second base, F1, a right-handed pitcher, assumes the set position stance as a left-handed pitcher to keep R2 close. **RULING:** Balk. The pitcher's pivot foot is his right foot since he is right-handed. If he takes the pitcher's plate with the left foot, he is in violation of the rules.

6.1.3 SITUATION N: With the bases loaded, F1 takes the set position with the ball in both hands in front of his body and comes to a complete stop with the glove over his head. **RULING:** This is not legal. This is a balk. F1 must come to a complete stop with his glove at or below his chin.

6.1.3 SITUATION O: With R3 at third and R1 at first, F1 comes to a complete stop with his glove partially above his chin. Is this legal? **RULING:** This is legal.

6.1.3 SITUATION Q: With a runner on first, Team A right-handed pitcher is in the set position, bent at the waist and his pitching arm naturally hangs down slightly in front or to the side away from his body. As he looks to the catcher for a signal, a) the pitchers arm is stationary or b) the pitching arm rocks slightly from side to side. **RULING:** In a)

the position of the arm is natural and can be considered by his side in meeting the rule. Any movement would then start the pitch. In b) any movement of the arm is considered the start of the pitching motion and a pitch must be delivered to the plate so this motion results in a balk.

Rationale

Because runners were placed at a disadvantage by not being able to tell when a pitcher was committed to pitch, the committee eliminated the provision that a change of direction would be considered a stop in 1989. A stop must now be recognizable and observable and whether those conditions are met or not is left to umpire's judgment.

Wind-up Position

For the wind-up position, the pitcher is not restricted as to how he shall hold the ball. A pitcher assumes the windup position when his hands are: (a) together in front of the body; (b) both hands are at his side; (c) either hand is in front of the body and the other hand is at his side. The pitcher's non-pivot foot shall be in any position on or behind a line extending through the front edge of the pitcher's plate. He is limited to not more than two pumps or rotations. After he starts his movement to pitch, he must continue the motion without interruption or alteration.

With his feet in the wind-up position, the pitcher may only deliver a pitch or step backward off the pitcher's plate with his pivot foot first. After the pitcher has placed his pivot foot clearly behind the plate, he has the right to change to the set position or throw or feint to a base the same as that of any infielder. During delivery, he may lift his non-pivot foot in a step forward, a step sideways, or in a step backward and a step forward, but he shall not otherwise lift either foot (6-1-2).

Wind-up Position: Caseplays

* **6.1.1 SITUATION A:** F1 pitches with the toe of his pivot foot (right foot for right-handed pitcher) in contact with the pitcher's plate but his heel is outside a line through the end edge of the plate. He pitches from the windup position. **RULING:** Legal, provided that F1's pivot foot is parallel to the pitcher's plate.

6.1.1 SITUATION D: F1 takes his sign in the (a) windup position or (b) set position. R3 at third attempts to steal home. F1 steps forward off the pitcher's plate and throws to F2. **RULING:** This is a balk in (a) and (b).

COMMENT: After assuming a windup or set position stance on the plate, the pitcher must step clearly backward off the plate with the pivot foot in order to play on R1 at the plate (6-1-2, 6-1-3).

6.1.1 SITUATION E: With the bases loaded, F1 pitches from the windup position. After F1 intentionally contacts the pitcher's plate, he (a) fakes a throw to first, or (b) steps forward off the rubber. **RULING:** This is a balk in (a) and (b). F1 must step clearly backward off the pitcher's plate with his pivot foot first to disengage the pitcher's plate or make a play. The umpire shall declare the ball dead immediately when the infraction occurs.

6.1.1 SITUATION G: The bases are loaded. F1, while on the pitcher's plate, fakes a throw to first while in the windup position. **RULING:** This is a balk.

6.1.1 SITUATION I: When is a pitcher permitted to step backward off the pitching plate in the windup position? **RULING:** The pitcher can legally step backward off the pitcher's plate in the windup position stance at any time prior to the start of any motion indicating the start of the windup.

6.1.2 SITUATION A: With no runners on base, F1 starts his windup or preliminary motion and the ball slips from his hand. **RULING:** There is no infraction provided F1 delivers a pitch within 20 seconds after he received the ball. If F1 fails to do so, the batter is awarded a ball. If there had been a runner or runners on base, dropping the ball while in contact with the pitcher's plate is a balk if the ball did not cross the foul line. Each base runner shall be awarded one base.

6.1.2 SITUATION B: What is meant by a pump or rotation? **RULING:** A pump or rotation is a movement of the arms, by a pitcher when in the windup position, immediately prior to delivering a pitch to the batter. The pump is an alternate downward and upward motion of the arms generally terminated by placing both hands together. A rotation is a circular movement of the pitching arm immediately prior to delivery to the batter during the windup position. The rules limit a pitcher to not more than two pumps or rotations when using the windup position.

6.1.2 SITUATION C: With a runner on third base, F1 steps on to the pitcher's plate in the windup position and his glove hand in front of his body and his pitching hand at his side (a) immediately brings his hands together for the purpose of taking the sign but does not begin his delivery, or (b) gets the sign and then brings his hands together and stops before delivering a pitch, or (c) gets the sign, brings his hands together and continues his pitching motion. **RULING:** In (a), (b) and (c), these are all legal moves.

6.1.2 SITUATION D: F1, while on the pitcher's plate in either the windup or set position, (a) adjusts his cap or (b) shakes off the signal with his glove, or (c) shakes off the signal with his head. **RULING:** In (a) through (c), these are legal actions if these movements of the arms and legs are not associated with the pitch.

6.1.2 SITUATION E: With the bases loaded, F1 steps on the pitcher's plate in the windup position with the ball in his glove hand in front of his body and his pitching hand at his side. F1 then brings his pitching hand to his glove and adjusts the ball after receiving the sign from the catcher. He then (a) delivers the pitch or (b) steps back off the pitcher's plate with his pivot foot. **RULING:** Legal in (a) and (b).

6.1.2 SITUATION F: With R3 on third base, F1 steps on the pitcher's plate and his hands already together in front of his body. F1 then drops his pitching hand to his side and stops. **RULING:** This is a balk and R3 is awarded home. F1 separated his hands without delivering the pitch.

6.1.2 SITUATION G: From the windup position, F1 steps onto the pitcher's plate with both hands together. As he moves his non-pivot leg behind the pitcher's plate, he completely stops his motion. **RULING:** Balk. This is an illegal pitch.

6.1.2 SITUATION H: F1, with both arms at his side in the wind-up position, first moves his glove to a position in front of his chest, stops his momentum, and then moves his pitching hand into the glove. **RULING:** This is an illegal move. He must intentionally contact the pitcher's plate with one of the three legal positions: (a) hands together in front of the body; (b) with both hands at his side; (c) with either hand in front of the body and his other hand at his side.

6.1.2 SITUATION I: With one hand at his side and the other hand in front of his body, F1 looks into the catcher for a sign from the wind-up position. He then brings his hands together and pauses. The opposing coach yells that this is a balk and that the runner on third base should score. **RULING:** This is not a balk. This is a legal pitching position. The pitcher is permitted to have one hand forward prior to bringing the other hand forward.

Topic:
The Pitch

A live ball delivered to the batter is a pitch. The term implies a legally delivered ball unless otherwise stated. When a pitcher commits a balk and completes his delivery to the batter, or delivers an illegal pitch, it is not considered a pitch, because the ball became dead at the time of the infraction (2-28-2).

Did You Know?	The rule concerning a pitch dropped during delivery was clarified in 1982 to provide the specific guidelines that exist today.

Each legal pitch shall be declared by the umpire as a strike, ball, fair or foul hit or a dead ball. A pitch dropped during delivery and which crosses a foul line shall be called a ball. Otherwise, it will be called no pitch. A pitch dropped during delivery with at least one runner on base would be a balk if it does not cross a foul line (6-1-4).

In Simple Terms
A coach or catcher can request an intentional base on balls, which can be awarded at any time.

Ball
A ball is credited to the batter when a pitch is not touched by the bat and is not a strike or when there is an illegal pitch (7-2-2). A base on balls is an award of first base (often referred to as a "walk") if a batter receives four balls. The batter must go immediately to first base before time-out is called (2-4-2). An intentional base on balls may be given by the defensive team by having its catcher or coach request the umpire to award the batter first base. This may be done before pitching to the batter or on any ball-and-strike count. The ball shall be declared dead before making the award (2-4-3).

Ball: Caseplay
6.1.1 SITUATION C: When is a pitch a ball even if it goes through the strike zone? **RULING:** An illegal pitch, such as pitching with pivot foot off the pitcher's plate, is a ball if there is no runner on base. A pitch that hits the ground and then bounces through the strike zone is a ball unless the batter strikes at it.

Dead Ball

A pitch becomes a dead ball when the pitch touches a batter or his clothing or a runner (5-1-1a); a pitch is touched by a spectator, a non-participating squad member; goes into a stand or other dead-ball area or players' bench (even if it rebounds to the field), or over or through or wedges in the field fence; lodges in an umpire's, catcher's or offensive player's equipment or uniform (5-1-1g 1-4); or the pitcher balks or delivers an illegal pitch (5-1-1k).

After a dead ball, the ball becomes live when it is held by the pitcher in a legal pitching position, provided the pitcher has engaged the pitcher's plate, the batter and the catcher are in their respective boxes, and the umpire calls "Play" and gives the appropriate signal (5-1-4).

Dead Ball: Balks

If there is a runner or runners, any of the following acts by a pitcher while he is touching the pitcher's plate is a balk:

Any feinting toward the batter or first base, or any dropping of the ball (even though accidental) and the ball does not cross a foul line (6-1-4, 6-2-4a).

Failing to step with the non-pivot foot directly toward a base (occupied or unoccupied) when throwing or feinting there in an attempt to put out, or drive back a runner; or throwing or feinting to any unoccupied base when it is not an attempt to put out or drive back a runner (6-2-4b).

Making an illegal pitch from any position (6-1, 6-2-1a-e, 6-2-4c).

Fundamental #5

No action by the offense can cause a balk.

Taking a hand off the ball while in a set position, unless he pitches to the batter or throws to a base or he steps toward and feints a throw to second or third base (6-2-4e).

Failing to pitch to the batter when the entire non-pivot foot passes behind the perpendicular plane of the back edge of the pitcher's plate, except when feinting or throwing to second base in an attempt to put out a runner (6-2-4f).

It is also a balk if the pitcher fails to pitch to the batter in a continuous motion immediately after any movement of any part of the body such as he habitually uses in his delivery (6-2-4d).

If the pitcher, with a runner on base, stops or hesitates in his delivery beause the batter steps out of the box (a) with one foot or (b) with both feet or (c) holds up his hand to request "Time," it shall not be a balk. In (a) and (c), there is no penalty on either the batter or the pitcher. The umpire shall call "Time" and begin play anew. In (b), a strike shall be called on the batter for violation of Rule 7-3-1, the rule requiring the batter to stay in the box. In (a), (b) and (c), if the pitcher legally delivers the ball, it shall be called a strike and the ball remains live. Thus, two strikes are called on the batter in (b). If the umpire judges the batter's action to be a deliberate attempt to create a balk, the batter shall be ejected (3-3-1o, 6-2-4d-1).

◪ Rationale

After working for several years to simplify the administration of the balk/illegal pitch rule, the committee decided to make all balks and illegal pitches immediate dead balls in 1985. Since the ball is dead immediately, the one-base award is automatic because there are no circumstances for the offense to gain more than one base. Also, nothing can happen even if a pitcher delivers a pitch or attempts to pick a runner off base.

Dead Ball: Balks: Caseplays

6.1.1 SITUATION B: With R3 on third, B2 has three balls and two strikes. F1 balks, but then delivers a pitch. The pitch is over F2's head and B2 (a) swings at it or (b) does not swing. In either case, R3 goes home. **RULING:** The ball is dead immediately when the balk occurs, and the balk penalty is enforced (6-2-4, 6-2-5 Penalty).

6.1.3 SITUATION P: With R3 at third and R1 at first, F1 is in contact with the pitcher's plate but has not yet come set. He brings his pitching hand to his mouth and distinctly wipes it off. **RULING:** Balk, award R3 home and R1 second. The pitcher cannot bring his hand to his mouth because the pitcher is required to go to the set position without interruption and in one continuous motion.

6.2.4 SITUATION A: With R3 on third and R1 on first, F1 stretches and comes set. He then swings his entire non-pivot foot behind the back edge of the pitcher's plate, steps toward second and (a) throws the ball to second in an attempt to retire R1, who is advancing there or (b) feints throw to second to drive R1 back to first, who has neither attempted nor feinted an advance to second. **RULING:** In (a), this is legal. In (b), it is a balk.

6.2.4 SITUATION B: With R1 on first, F1 attempts a pickoff while stepping at an angle but to the home plate side. **RULING:** Balk. To comply with the requirement to "step directly toward," F1 must step to the first-base side of a 45-degree angle between center of pitcher's plate and between home and first base (6-2-4b).

6.2.4 SITUATION C: With R3 on third and R1 on first, F1 comes set. He then feints toward third, or he removes one hand from the ball and makes an arm motion toward third but does not step toward third. He follows with a throw to first base. **RULING:** This is a balk. F1 must step toward third base when feinting there. F1 may not feint to first base. He must step toward the base and throw. He might, while he is on the plate, step toward occupied third and feint a throw, and then turn to step toward first and throw there with or without disengaging the pitcher's plate. If F1 steps and feints to first, he must first disengage the pitcher's plate or he is guilty of a balk.

6.2.4 SITUATION D: With a runner or runners on base, F1 assumes the set position. He stretches his arms above his head, brings them down together and pauses with the ball in both hands in front of the body after which he (a) separates hands and then steps back off pitcher's plate with pivot foot or (b) steps back off pitcher's plate with pivot foot and feints throw to unoccupied first. **RULING:** In (a), this is a balk. In (b), this is legal.

 COMMENT: There is a distinction between "stepping off" the pitcher's plate and "stepping toward" a base. "Stepping off" means that pitcher has removed his pivot foot backward from the plate and has become an infielder. "Stepping toward" indicates movement of the nonpivot foot toward a base (6.2.4 Comment A).

6.2.4 SITUATION E: With R2 on second base, F1 wheels and fakes a throw to second on a pickoff attempt. As R2 dives back to the base, F4 and F6 run into short center field as if chasing an errant throw. R2 seeing this, takes off for third base where he is thrown out by F1. **RULING:** This is legal and is not considered unsportsmanlike conduct. R2's base coaches have the responsibility to keep R2 informed.

6.2.4 SITUATION F: With R2 and R1 on second and first bases, respectively, F1, who is a left-handed pitcher, is in the set position. He stretches and comes to a complete stop with the ball in the glove completely below his chin in front of the body. He then lifts his entire non-pivot foot and swings it behind the perpendicular plane of back edge of the pitcher's plate and (a) throws to F3 in an attempt to pick off R1 or (b) continuing through, throws or feints a throw to second base. **RULING:** This is a balk in (a). Action in (b) is legal, provided the non-pivot foot movement was not interrupted nor stopped prior to completion of the action.

6.2.4 SITUATION G: R2 is on second and R1 is on first. After F1 has come set, he steps with his non-pivot foot (a) toward second or (b) toward first or home. He does not throw the ball. **RULING:** In (a), the act is legal. In (b), F1 has committed a balk.

6.2.4 SITUATION J: With R1 on first base and two outs, F1 attempts to pick off R1. As F1 pivots to throw, he realizes that F3 is not on the base, but is in his normal defensive position. F1 completes the throw without interruption. The coach of the offensive team wants a balk called on F1. **RULING:** As long as F3 is in the proximity of the base, F1 would not be guilty of a balk. Proximity is umpire judgment and is based on whether the fielder is close enough to the base to legitimately make a play on the runner.

6.2.5 SITUATION A: With R1 at first, F1, in the stretch position, steps quickly backward off the pitcher's plate and with a motion much like his pitching delivery throws to the plate where (a) B2 hits the throw or (b) R1 is thrown out stealing by F2 on a pitchout. **RULING:** In (a) and (b), it is a balk. F1, while he is not touching the pitcher's plate, shall not make any movement naturally associated with his pitch.

6.2.5 SITUATION B: With R1 on first base, the umpire calls "balk" just as F1 delivers the pitch. B2 hits the ball over the outfield fence for a home run. **RULING:** The ball becomes dead the moment the balk occurs. Therefore, B2 does not have the opportunity to hit the pitch in this case; R1 is awarded second base and B2 remains at the plate.

8.3.4 SITUATION E: R1, R2 and R3 are on third, second and first bases, respectively. There are two outs and a count of three balls, two strikes on B6. As F1 starts pumping, runners begin to advance. F1 pumps three times and umpire signals dead ball. The violation occurs after R2 and R3 each have advanced one base. F1 delivers following his violation and B6 swings and misses a third strike. **RULING:** Balk. Each runner is awarded one base from where he was at the time of the pitch when F1 started his pumping motion. Count remains three balls, two strikes on B6.

COMMENT: How does an illegal pitch differ from a balk? A pitch is illegal if it does not conform to the requirements of the windup position or the requirements of the set position. An illegal pitch can occur with or without a runner(s). If there is a runner(s), it is one type of balk. If the pitch is illegal and there is no runner, a ball is awarded to the batter's count, whether or not it is pitched. A balk can occur only when there is a runner(s). When a balk is called, it never includes the awarding of a ball in addition to an advance by the runner(s). As an example of the differences, with no runner(s), a quick pitch is an illegal pitch and is called a ball whether or not it goes through the strike zone. If there is a runner(s), a quick pitch is a balk. The ball is dead immediately when an illegal pitch is called (6.2.4 Comment B).

Dead Ball: Hit Batters, Runners

A batter becomes a runner with the right to attempt to score by advancing to first, second, third and home bases in the listed order when a pitched ball hits his person or clothing, provided he does not strike at the ball (8-1-1d). If he makes no effort to avoid being hit (7-3-4), or if the umpire calls the pitched ball a strike, the hitting of the batter is disregarded except that the ball is dead. It is a strike or ball depending on location of the pitch. Each runner other than the batter-runner is awarded one base when pitch strikes a runner.

Dead Ball: Hit Batters, Runners: Caseplays

5.1.1 SITUATION E: On the third strike, B1 swings at and misses a pitch. The ball touches his arm or person. **RULING:** B1 is out. The ball becomes dead immediately (5-1-1a, 8-1-1d).

7.3.4 SITUATION A: With R1 on first, B2 has two strikes. He swings at the next pitch, which touches him. R1 steals second. **RULING:** B2 is out. The ball becomes dead and R1 must return to first.

7.3.4 SITUATION B: B1 is at bat with a three-ball, two-strike count. He swings at the next pitch and the ball hits his right fist and, without contacting the bat, goes into foul territory. F2 retrieves the ball and throws to F3 who is covering first base and tags B1 with the ball. **RULING:** As soon as the ball hit the batter it became dead. B1 is declared out. To have the play ruled a foul ball, the ball would have to have hit the bat of B1 before it touched his hand.

8.1.1 SITUATION Q: A 1-1 pitch, which is just off the plate, strikes an armband-type placard device used for play situations, which is loosely attached to the batter's waist. **RULING:** The umpire shall call the pitch and declare a dead ball. The batter shall not be awarded first base.

COMMENT: The armbland placard is not designed to be worn on the waistband of the uniform pants. It was intended to be properly worn on the wrist/forearm of the player.

Dead Ball: Illegal Pitches

An illegal pitch is an illegal act committed by the pitcher with no runner on base, which results in a ball being awarded the batter. When an illegal pitch occurs with a runner, or runners, on base, it is ruled a balk (2-18-1).

Dead Ball: Illegal Pitches: Caseplay

6.1.3 SITUATION K: Does a quick pitch or other illegal pitch always result in a ball being called? **RULING:** Not always. If there is a runner, it is a balk and no ball is called.

Dead Ball: Other Pitches

The ball becomes dead immediately when a pitch is touched by a spectator; is intentionally touched by a non-participating squad member; goes into a stand or other dead-ball area or players' bench (even if it rebounds to the field), or over or through or wedges in the field fence or lodges in an umpire's, catcher's or offensive player's equipment or uniform (5-1-1g).

Strike

A strike is a charged to the batter when a pitch enters any part of the strike zone in flight and is not struck at; a pitch is struck at and missed (even if the pitch touches the batter); a pitch becomes a foul when the batter has less than two strikes; a pitch becomes a foul tip (even on third strike) or a foul from an attempted bunt; a batter delays; or a batted ball contacts the batter in the batter's box (foul ball) (7-2-1a-f).

The umpire-in-chief sometimes asks for aid from the base umpire when there is a question as to whether a batter's "half swing" is such as to be called a strike. As an aid in deciding, the umpire may note whether the swing carried the barrel of the bat past the body of the batter, but final decision is based on whether the batter actually struck at the ball (10-1-4a).

If the pitcher, with a runner on base, stops or hesitates in his delivery because the batter steps out of the box with both feet, a strike shall be called on the batter for violation of the Rule 7-3-1, which requires the batter to remain in the box. If the pitcher legally delivers the ball, it shall be called a strike and the ball remains live. Thus, two strikes are called on the batter (6-2-4d note).

If the third strike is not caught, provided a runner occupies first base and there are less than two outs (7-4-1b) or if the third strike is caught (7-4-1c), the batter is out.

Strike: Caseplays

2.16.2 SITUATION A: B1 swings and tips the ball, (a) the ball goes directly to the catcher's glove and then rebounds to the catcher's chest protector then the ball is caught by the catcher, or (b) the ball goes directly to the catcher's chest protector and then is caught by the catcher. **RULING:** In (a) the pitch is a strike and remains alive. In (b) this is a foul ball.

2.16.2 SITUATION B: With R1 on first base, B2 attempts to hit on the first pitch, which goes directly from his bat to F2's mitt, then rebounds to F1, who catches the ball in flight as R1 is advancing. **RULING:** This is a foul ball. The ball is dead and R1 returns to first base.

2.16.2 SITUATION C: With R1 on first base, B2 has a one-and-one count and attempts to bunt. The ball goes from his bat high into the air with a perceptible arc to F2's glove, and rebounds toward F1, who catches the ball while R1 is advancing. **RULING:** This is not a foul tip, but a caught foul fly. R1 is in jeopardy of being out if he does not return to properly retouch first base.

2.35.1 SITUATION: The pitch is across home plate and at the batter's arm pits. **RULING:** This is a ball. Had the pitch been halfway between the batter's shoulders and his waistline, the pitch would have been a strike.

 COMMENT: It is not necessary that the entire ball, when legally pitched and before it has touched the ground but not swung at, pass through the batter's strike zone to be called a strike. It is a strike when any part of the ball on a legal pitch enters the strike zone. The umpire shall determine a batter's strike zone according to the usual stance of the batter.

6.2.4 SITUATION H: R3 is on third base. There are two outs and B4 has a count of 3-2. While F1 is in motion, B4 requests time-out, which is not granted, and steps out of the box with (a) one foot or (b) both feet. F1 delivers a pitch that sails over F2's head. B4 advances to first while R1 scores. **RULING:** In (a) and (b), the run counts. B4 is credited with a strikeout and remains on first base. Since B4 did not intentionally try to cause F1 to balk or throw a wild pitch, the umpire shall not eject him. The ball remains live (7-3-1 Penalty).

Did You Know?

The dimensions of the strike zone have undergone several changes through the years.

Prior to 1974, the strike zone was between the top of the batter's shoulders and his knees when he assumed his natural batting stance.

Today's rule — with the top of the zone being halfway between the batter's shoulders and waistline, and the bottom being the knees — came about in 1998.

6.2.4 SITUATION I: With R3 on third base, F1 starts his pitching motion and B2 requests "Time," but the umpire does not grant "Time." B2 steps out of the batter's box with both feet and (a) F1 delivers a pitch, (b) does not deliver the pitch or (c) throws a wild pitch. **RULING:** (a) The umpire shall call two strikes on B2, one on the pitch, and one for stepping out of the box. In (b), the umpire shall call a strike on B2 for stepping out of the batter's box. The balk is nullified. In (c), two strikes shall be called on B2, one on the pitch and one for stepping out. The ball remains live (7-3-1 Penalty).

7.2.1 SITUATION A: With F1 having a hard time throwing strikes, the coach of the team at bat instructs B1 to assume an exaggerated crouch stance to lessen his strike zone. F1's first pitch is directly over the plate, but approximately chin high, which the umpire calls a strike. The coach of the team at bat requests time to ask the umpire how he is determining the batter's strike zone. **RULING:** The umpire informs the coach that the strike zone is the space over home plate which is halfway between the batter's shoulders and his waistline and the knees when B1 assumes his natural batting stance. If a batter assumes an exaggerated stance, such as crouching, the umpire shall use his judgment to determine what a natural batting stance would be for the batter (2-35-1).

7.2.1 SITUATION B: B1 starts to swing at the pitch but attempts to hold back on it or it appears as though he attempts to bunt the ball. In either case, B1 misses the ball. How does umpire determine what to call the pitch? **RULING:** A call of that nature is based entirely upon the umpire's judgment. Therefore, the umpire must, in order to be consistent, have criteria to guide him in making the decision. The rule that most umpires follow is that if the bat is swung so it is in front of the batter's body or ahead of it, it is a strike. In bunting, any movement of the bat toward the ball when the ball is over or near the plate area, is a strike. The mere holding of the bat in the strike zone is not an attempt to bunt (10-1-4 Note).

10.1.3 SITUATION: B1, attempting to check his swing at a pitch, carries the barrel of the bat past his body. **RULING:** The umpire should note whether or not the batter's movement carried the barrel of the bat past the batter's body in an attempt to strike the ball.

Time of Pitch

The time of the pitch is when the pitcher has committed himself to delivering the pitch to the batter (2-28-3, 2-28-3 Comment).

For the windup position, the "time of the pitch" occurs when the pitcher, (a) first starts any movement of his arm(s) or leg(s) after stepping onto the pitcher's plate with his hands already together in front of his body; (b) with both hands at his side, first starts any movement with both arms or leg(s) prior to the pitch; (c) with either hand in front of the body and the other hand at his side, after bringing his hands together, first starts any movement of his arm(s) or leg(s) prior to the pitch.

For the set position, the "time of the pitch" occurs the instant the pitcher, after coming to a complete and discernible stop, starts any movement with arm(s) and/or leg(s) that commits him to pitch.

Time of Pitch: Caseplays

2.28.3 SITUATION A: R3 is on third and R1 on first with no outs. F1 contacts the pitcher's plate and assumes the set position stance. As he begins his stretch, R1 advances toward second base attempting to steal. F1 realizes R1 is stealing but he does not throw to second, fearing that R3 will break for home and score. F1 completes his stretch, coming to a pause with the ball in both hands in front of his body. R1 reaches second and rounds it, after which F1 delivers the ball to B3, who fouls a pitch into the stands. **RULING:** R1 is allowed to remain on second because he was there prior to the time of the pitch. The definition of "time of the pitch" determines the base to which R1 is entitled.

2.28.3 SITUATION B: R3 is on third base with two outs. F1 contacts the pitcher's plate and assumes the wind-up position with his glove hand in front of his body and his pitching hand by his side. As he brings his pitching hand to his glove hand, R3 takes off for home. F1 steps legally off the pitcher's plate with his pivot foot and throws to F2 to tag out R3. **RULING:** This is not a balk. With the pitcher's glove hand in front of his body and the pitching hand by his side, the act of bringing the two hands together does not constitute the "time of the pitch." The out stands.

2.28.3 SITUATION C: With R3 on third base, F1 steps on the pitcher's plate to take a sign from F2. After taking the sign, F1 brings both hands up together in front of his body and then stops to adjust the ball. **RULING:** This is a balk. R3 is awarded home. The time of the pitch occurred when F1 moved both arms.

Topic:
Other Pitching Violations

Defacing the Baseball
Illegal acts include applying a foreign substance to the ball (6-2-1a), spitting on the ball or glove (6-2-1b), rubbing the ball on the glove, clothing or person if the act defaces the ball (6-2-1c) or discoloring the ball with dirt (6-2-1d).

Defacing the Baseball: Penalty
In each of the violations, the ball is dead immediately. The umpire may eject the pitcher. If such defaced ball is pitched and then detected, it is an illegal pitch (6-2-1 penalty).

If the pitcher brings the pitching hand in contact with his mouth without distinctly wiping off the pitching hand before it touches the ball, a ball shall be awarded each time a pitcher violates and subsequently engages the pitching plate (6-2-1e, 6-2-1 penalty).

◪ Rationale
This change, made for 2007, was instituted to make the penalty less severe.

Defacing the Baseball: Caseplays
6.2.1 SITUATION A: With no runners on base, F1 places his pitching hand on his mouth and distinctly wipes off his pitching hand prior to touching the ball, (a) while not touching the pitcher's plate, (b) while touching the pitcher's plate. **RULING:** (a) Legal; (b) illegal, and a ball shall be awarded to the batter's count.

6.2.1 SITUATION B: With R1 at first, F1 places his pitching hand on his mouth and distinctly wipes off his pitching hand prior to touching the ball (a) while not touching the pitcher's plate or (b) while touching the pitcher's plate in the set position. **RULING:** Legal in (a). In (b), the pitcher has balked and R1 is awarded second base.

6.2.1 SITUATION D: With R2 at second, F1 is not on the pitcher's plate. He goes to his mouth and goes directly to the ball with his pitching hand. (a) F1 calls time and requests a new ball or (b) F1 legally engages the pitching plate. **RULING:** Legal in (a). In (b), time is called and a ball is added to the count.

Delaying the Game

Delay of the game includes:

• Throwing to any player other than the catcher, when the batter is in the batter's box, unless it is an attempt to retire a runner (6-2-2a). The pitcher shall be ejected from the game after a warning (6-2-2a penalty).

• Consuming time as the result of the coach or his representative conferring with a defensive player or players after being charged with three defensive conferences (6-2-2b). For violation, the pitcher shall be replaced as pitcher for the duration of the game (6-2-2b penalty).

• Failing to pitch or make or attempt a play, including a legal feint, within 20 seconds after he has received the ball (6-2-2c). The penalty is that the batter shall be awarded one ball (6-2-2c penalty). Umpires shall require that the ball be returned promptly to the pitcher.

▨ Rationale

The committee was concerned about the length of games, in particular pitchers that were taking extended periods of time between pitches. This change came at the same time that the warmup pitches in between innings were reduced from eight to five, with a one-minute maximum.

Delaying the Game: Caseplays

6.2.2 SITUATION D: With R2 on second base, F1, in the set position, suddenly turns and makes a legal feint to F4 in an effort to drive R2 back to the base. **RULING:** Even though the 20-second period may have elapsed during the play, there is no penalty. The count restarts once F1 returns to his position on the pitcher's plate.

6.2.2 SITUATION F: With R1 at first, F1 (a) looks at the runner four or five times in an effort to hold him close and 20 seconds elapse or (b) makes repeated throws to first base at about 10-second intervals in an effort to hold the runner. **RULING:** In (a), umpire will call time and call a ball on B2. In (b), this is legal. F1 must pitch or make a play or a legal feint within the 20-second time period. After such a play or feint, the 20-second count is restarted.

COMMENT: This rule is intended to maintain the flow of the game with continuous action and to eliminate "dead" periods of inactivity. While it may be argued that the delay is still present if F1 makes the throw, action is continuing and there is still the element of risk for the defense of making an errant throw or committing a balk.

6.2.2 SITUATION G: With R1 at first and B2 in the batter's box, F1 steps back off the pitcher's plate after having the ball for 18 seconds. **RULING:** The pitcher is required to pitch, or make/attempt a play, including a legal feint, within 20 seconds. Stepping backward off the pitcher's plate can be considered part of a feint, if in the umpire's judgment there is accompanying action. However, if this is not the case, a ball shall be awarded the batter.

Hidden Ball Trick

If a runner or runners are on base and the pitcher, while he is not touching the pitcher's plate, makes any movement naturally associated with his pitch, or he places his feet on or astride the pitcher's plate, or positions himself within approximately five feet of the pitcher's plate without having the ball, the pitcher is guilty of a balk (6-2-5).

Hidden Ball Trick: Caseplay

5.1.4 SITUATION B: B1 goes to first because (a) he is hit by a pitched ball, or (b) of ball four, or (c) he hits a single to the outfield and he returns to first base. After B1 has touched first, he steps off the base and F3 tags him by use of the "hidden ball" trick. **RULING:** In (a), the runner is safe. The ball remains dead until held by pitcher on his plate, B2 and F2 are in their respective boxes and the umpire then calls "Play." In (b) and (c), B1 is out.

Illegal Clothing, Glove

A pitcher may not wear any items on the hands, wrists or arms that may be distracting to the batter (6-2-2f). The umpire has sole authority to judge whether or not an item is distracting and shall have that item removed (6-2-2f penalty).

A pitcher may not wear or place tape, bandages or other foreign material (other than rosin) on the fingers or palm of his pitching hand that could come in contact with the ball (6-2-2g). Under umpire supervision, the pitcher may dry his hands by using a finely meshed cloth bag of powdered rosin. He may rub the ball with his bare hands to remove any extraneous coating (6-2-1 note).

The pitcher may not wear a glove/mitt that includes the colors white or gray (1-3-6, 6-2-2h) or have exposed undershirt sleeves that are white or gray (1-4-2, 6-2-2i). The glove/mitt worn by the pitcher that includes the colors white and/or gray shall be removed from the game upon discovery by either team and/or umpire (1-3-6).

A pitcher shall not wear any item on his hands, wrists or arms which may be distracting to the batter (1-4-2).

Rationale

The 2008 rule change concerning the color of the pitcher's glove ensured the penalty enforcement would be consistent across the country. The only penalty for a pitcher wearing a glove that contains white and/or gray is for the pitcher to remove the glove.

Illegal Clothing, Glove: Caseplays

1.4.2 SITUATION A: Team A wears the new vest type jersey. The school's colors are red and white. Their road uniform top is red, with a white undershirt. The pitcher is wearing this uniform. A) The sleeve of the white shirt does not extend beyond his elbow or B) He is wearing a long sleeved white compression shirt which extends beyond the elbow. **RULING:** A) This is legal. In B) this would be illegal.

1.4.2 SITUATION B: Team A wears their gray road traditional sleeved jerseys. The sleeves of the jersey extend beyond the pitcher's elbow. **RULING:** This is an illegal jersey for the pitcher.

10.2.3 SITUATION C: F1's cap frequently falls off his head and in the umpire's judgment, it is either distracting to the batter or delaying the game. **RULING:** The umpire shall instruct the defensive team's coach that F1's cap must be secured. If this situation is not corrected, F1 will be removed as pitcher.

Pitching at a Batter

A pitcher may not intentionally pitch close to a batter (6-2-3).

Pitching at a Batter: Penalty

The pitcher shall be ejected if the act is judged to be intentional. In case of doubt, the umpire may first warn the pitcher (6-2-3 penalty).

Pitching at a Batter: Caseplay

6.2.2 SITUATION A: F1 intentionally throws at B4 and is ejected from the contest. The opposing coach feels that S1 is only allowed five warm-up pitches. **RULING:** Incorrect interpretation. S1 is allowed the same number of warm-up pitches (8) as if the pitching change was a result of injury or inclement weather.

Topic 3
Fielding

PlayPic®

Key Terms

A fielder is any one of the nine players of the defensive team (2-13-1). The catcher is the player to whom the pitcher throws when delivering the ball to the batter (2-9-2).The players who play left field, right field and center field are outfielders (2-13-2). The others are infielders (2-13-3). The pitcher and catcher are the battery (2-13-4).

A catch is the act of a fielder in getting secure possession in his hand or glove of a live ball in flight and firmly holding it, provided he does not use his cap, protector, mask, pocket or other part of his uniform to trap the ball. The catch of a fly ball is not completed until the continuing action of the catch is completed (2-9-1).

Obstruction is an act (intentional or unintentional, as well as physical or verbal) by a fielder, any member of the defensive team or its team personnel that hinders a runner or changes the pattern of play or when a catcher or fielder hinders a batter (2-22-1). A fake tag is an act by a defensive player without the ball that simulates a tag. A fake tag is considered obstruction (2-22-2). A fielder without possession of the ball who denies access to the base the runner is attempting to achieve is also guilty of obstruction (2-22-3).

An out is one of the three required retirements of players of the team at bat (2-24-2).

A play is a unit of action which begins when a pitcher has the ball in his possession in pitching position and ends when ball becomes dead or pitcher again holds the ball while in pitching position (2-29-1). A defensive appeal of a runner failing to touch a base or tag up is not a play (2-29-6).

A throw is the act of voluntarily losing possession through having the ball leave the hand for a purpose other than a pitch. It may result in the ball being bounced, handed, rolled, tossed or thrown (2-37-1).

Topic:
Outs

The team in the field attempts to end each turn at bat of the opponent by causing three of its batters or base runners to be out (1-1-1). A half-inning ends when there is a third out or when, in the last inning, the winning run is scored. In either case if there is a delayed out declared by the umpire for a baserunning infraction, a possible fourth out may be recognized (2-20-2).

There are multiple types of outs: a catch of a batted ball, a force-out, strikeout, tag out and throw out.

The batter-runner is out when his fair hit or foul (other than a foul tip which is not a third strike) is caught by a fielder, or such catch is prevented by a spectator reaching into the playing field (8-4-1b).

A force-out is a putout during which a runner who is being forced to advance is tagged out, or is put out by a fielder who holds the ball while touching the base toward which the forced runner is advancing (2-24-1).

A strikeout is the result of the pitcher getting a third strike charged to a batter. This usually results in the batter being out, but does not so result if the third strike is not caught and the batter-runner legally reaches first base (2-24-3).

A tag out is the put out of a runner, including the batter-runner, who is not in contact with his base when touched with a live ball, or with the glove or hand when the live ball is held securely therein by a fielder. The ball is not considered as having been securely held if it is juggled or dropped after the touching, unless the runner deliberately knocks the ball from the hand of the fielder (2-24-4).

A throw out is a putout caused by a throw to first base to retire a batter-runner, or to any other base to which a runner is forced or is required to retouch (2-24-5).

When the ball becomes dead, no action by the defense can cause a player to be put out (unless it is a dead-ball appeal) (5-2-2a).

◪ Rationale

This rule was rewritten in 1982 to clear up confusion. Specifically, it means the defense can do nothing during a dead ball to put a runner out. If a runner misses a base and touches a succeeding base and the ball becomes dead, the runner may not return to the missed base and is subject to being called out on appeal.

Outs: Caseplays

5.2.2 SITUATION A: B1 hits a ground ball to F6 and continues to run as F6 overthrows first. The ball goes out of play. B1 continues to second and stops at third. The umpire rules that B1 must return to second because the throw by F6 went out of play and B1 had not reached first base at the time of the throw, which was the first play by an infielder. The defense tags B1 with the ball while he is returning to second, stating that because B1 touched a succeeding base (third), he may not return. **RULING:** No action by the defense during the time the ball is dead can cause a player to be put out. The defense may make a legal dead-ball appeal.

5.2.2 SITUATION B: R1, while advancing to second, interferes with a ground ball or F4 to prevent a double play. If the umpire declares batter-runner out as well as R1, is that in conflict with the statement that a player may not be put out during dead ball? **RULING:** No. The two outs occurred at the time of the interference, (i.e., while ball was live, even though the announcement was made after ball became dead) (5-1-1e).

Topic:
Position of the Fielders _____

At the time of the pitch, all fielders shall be on fair ground except the catcher who shall be in the catcher's box. A fielder is in fair ground when at least one foot is touching fair ground (1-1-4). The penalty for this is an illegal pitch.

The catcher's box is an area 43 inches by 8 feet (2-9-3).

Position of the Fielders: Caseplay

1.1.4 SITUATION: With R1 on first, (a) F9 cuts in behind R1 for a throw from F1, who is in contact with the pitcher's plate, and receives a pickoff throw in foul territory; or (b) F3 has one foot in foul territory when he receives a pickoff throw; or (c) F3, in contact with the base, has one foot in foul territory as the throw is received. **RULING:** Legal in (a), (b) and (c). In (a), since F1 had not committed himself to pitch to the batter, the play is legal. In (a), (b), and (c) F3 is permitted to have a foot in foul territory, even at the time of the pitch.

> **COMMENT:** Rule 1-1-4 requires all defensive players except the catcher to be in fair territory at the time of the pitch. By definition and interpretation, at least one foot must be in fair territory to comply with this rule.

Topic:
Equipment _____

Catcher's Equipment

The catcher shall wear, in addition to a head protector, a mask with a throat protector, body/chest protector that meets the NOCSAE standard (effective January 1, 2020), protective cup (male only), and baseball protective shin guards (1-5-3). The SEI/NOCSAE mark is required on all body/check protectors that meet the NOCSAE standard that will be used in high school competition. Please see the accompanying mark.

The catcher's helmet and mask combination shall meet the NOCSAE standard. Any helmet or helmet and mask combination shall have full ear protection (dual ear flaps). A throat protector, which is either a part of or attached to the catcher's mask, is mandatory. A throat protector shall adequately cover the throat. The

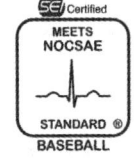

commercially manufactured catcher's head, face and throat protection may be a one-piece or multi-piece design. While in a crouch position, any non-adult warming up a pitcher at any location shall wear a head protector, a mask with a throat protector and a protective cup (male only). Failure by a player to wear proper equipment after being so ordered by the umpire, shall result in ejection (1-5-4). Defective equipment must be repaired or replaced immediately (1-5-6).

Catcher's Equipment: Caseplays

1.5.4 SITUATION A: The home team catcher takes his position behind the plate in the top of the first inning with a skull cap helmet-and-mask combination. **RULING:** This is illegal. A catcher will be required to wear head protection with double ear flaps that meets the NOCSAE standard. He will be told to get a legal helmet-and-mask combination. If he does not comply, he will be ejected.

1.5.4 SITUATION B: The visiting team catcher has a hockey-style helmet. **RULING:** This is legal. The hockey-style helmet is legal, provided it meets the NOCSAE standard.

1.5.4 SITUATION C: F1 and a player are playing catch. F1 begins throwing hard. The player playing catch with the pitcher is standing up. Is that player required to wear a catcher's mask? **RULING:** No. Until a player playing catch with the pitcher or other player or substitute assumes a crouch position, he is not required to wear protective equipment, no matter how hard the pitcher throws.

Did You Know?

Until 1972, catchers were not required to wear a head protector. Baseball protective shin guards became required in 1981, and throat protectors (either attached to or part of the mask) became required a year later. Starting in 1983, any player warming up a pitcher at any location was required to wear a protective cup and mask with throat protector. Finally, in 2003, NOCSAE certification was required, and that included dual-ear flap protection on the helmet.

1.5.4 SITUATION D: The visiting team's catcher's one-piece hockey-style mask breaks, causing the catcher to use a traditional Brewer mask-and-Acme helmet combination, which have not been tested together. **RULING:** The umpire requests that the visiting coach provides documentation that the Brewer/Acme components were tested together. He is unable to comply. The Brewer mask-and-Acme helmet combination is not allowed to be used. The catcher's helmet-and-mask combination shall meet the NOCSAE standard of being tested together.

Defensive Helmets

Defensive players are permitted to wear face/head protection in the field. If a pitcher or any defensive player wears face/head protection, its outer covering shall have a non-glare surface (1-5-5).

Defensive Helmets: Caseplays

1.5.5 SITUATION A: The umpire notices F6 is wearing a head or face protector with a glared surface. **RULING:** Illegal, defensive players are allowed to wear a head or face protector as long as the outer surface is non-glare.

1.5.5 SITUATION B: The umpire notices F9 is wearing a non-glare head or face protector. **RULING:** Legal, the rule allows defensive players to wear non-glare head or face protector.

1.5.5 SITUATION C: F1 is wearing a non-glare hard skull cap. The offensive team coach complains to the umpire-in-chief that it is illegal to wear a skull cap. **RULING:** It is legal for any defensive player to wear a head or face protector as long as the outer surface is non-glare and does not need dual earflaps.

Gloves

Gloves/mitts made of leather shall be worn by all fielders and not be altered to create an adhesive, sticky, and/or tacky surface. The glove/mitt worn by the catcher may be any size. The glove/mitt worn by the pitcher that includes the colors white and gray shall be illegal.

The glove/mitt worn by all fielders except the catcher shall conform to the following maximum specifications:

- Height (measured from the bottom edge or heel straight up across the center of the palm to a line even with the highest point of the glove/mitt): 14 inches.

- Width of palm (measured from the bottom edge of the webbing farthest from the thumb in a horizontal line to the outside of the little finger edge of the glove/mitt): 8 inches.

- Webbing (measured across the top end or along any line parallel to the top): 5 -3/4 inches.

Gloves: Caseplays

1.3.6 SITUATION A: F1 prepares to pitch and the offensive team protests that he is wearing a multi-colored pitcher's glove. **RULING:** The multi-colored glove is legal, as long as it does not include the colors white or gray, and it is determined not to be distracting.

1.3.6 SITUATION B: F3 catches a routine fair fly ball. The offensive coach in the first-base coaching box notices something dark on his glove. After bringing it to the attention of the base umpire, it is discovered that F3 (a) has excess glove conditioning lotion or (b) has tacky pine tar on the glove near the pocket area. **RULING:** Legal in (a), illegal in (b). The runner will be awarded third base (8-3-3b).

1.3.6 SITUATION C: F9 catches a fly ball with a first baseman's mitt. While leaving the playing field after the third out, the coach of Team B detects this. **RULING:** There is not a distinction between a glove or mitt. Therefore, the catch is legal. Gloves/mitts that meet the maximum specifications are legal.

1.3.6 SITUATION D: F1 prepares to pitch and is wearing a glove that has (a) white laces, (b) gray piping, (c) manufacturer's white logo. **RULING:** Illegal in (a), (b), (c). Gloves/mitts worn by pitchers shall not include the colors white or gray.

1.3.6 SITUATION E: F1's glove is (a) red, (b) green, (c) multi-color with no white or gray or (d) black with white laces. **RULING:** Legal in (a), (b) and (c); in (d), upon discovery, the glove must be removed from the game. The pitcher may resume wearing the glove if the white and/or gray is covered up or removed. The umpires shall not allow the game to be delayed while the equipment is being fixed. EXCEPTION: Any glove ruled distracting by the umpire-in-chief would not be allowed for the pitcher.

1.3.6 SITUATION F: F1 is wearing a glove that contains a white manufacturer's logo. The glove has not been discovered by the umpires. B1 bunts to the pitcher, who fields the ball and throws B1 out at first base. The offensive coach brings the glove to attention of the umpire-in-chief and wants the penalty for an illegal glove enforced. **RULING:** Although a pitcher is not allowed to wear a glove that includes white and/or gray, the only penalty is that the glove shall be removed from play upon discovery. There is no additional penalty (base award).

Topic:
Defensive Actions

A Catch
A catch is the act of a fielder in getting secure possession in his hand or glove of a live ball in flight and firmly holding it, provided he does

not use his cap, protector, mask, pocket or other part of his uniform to trap the ball.

The catch of a fly ball by a fielder is not completed until the continuing action of the catch is completed. A fielder who catches a ball and then runs into a wall or another player and drops the ball has not made a catch. A fielder, at full speed, who catches a ball and whose initial momentum carries him several more yards after which the ball drops from his glove has not made a catch.

In Simple Terms

The fielder must demonstrate complete control of the ball and that his release is voluntary and intentional in order for there to have been a catch.

When the fielder, by his action of stopping, removing the ball from his glove, etc., signifies the initial action is completed and then drops the ball, will be judged to have made the catch. The same definition of a catch would apply when making a double play.

It is considered a catch if a fielder catches a fair or foul ball and then steps or falls into a bench, dugout, stand, bleacher or over any boundary or barrier, such as a fence, rope, chalk line, or a pregame determined imaginary boundary line from the field of play. Falling into does not include merely running against such object.

It is not a catch when a fielder touches a batted ball in flight which then contacts a member of the offensive team or an umpire and is then caught by a defensive player (2-9-1).

In Simple Terms

Defensive players are not protected when reaching over a fence to make a play on the ball.

When a batted ball or a pitch is involved, the above definition of a catch applies. For any other thrown ball, the term is used loosely to also apply to a pick-up or to the trapping of a low throw which has touched the ground. A fielder may have the ball in his grasp even though it is touching the ground while in his glove (2-9-1 note).

The batter-runner is out when his fair hit or foul (other than a foul tip which is not a third strike) is caught by a fielder, or such catch is prevented by a spectator reaching into the playing field (8-4-1b). The batter-runner is also out when a third strike is caught by the catcher (8-4-1e).

A Catch: Caseplays

2.9.1 SITUATION A: B1 hits a ground ball to F5. The throw to F3 is wide causing him to stretch for the catch. The ball arrives in time, but as F3 attempts to regain his balance, he drops the ball. Is the runner out? **RULING:** Attempts to regain balance after receiving the ball are considered a part of the act of catching; and if the fielder does not come up with the ball in his possession, it is not considered a catch. In all such cases, judgment is a factor. If the ball is clearly in the fielder's possession and if some other new movement not related to the catch is then made, and if the ball is fumbled during such new movement, the umpire will declare it a catch followed by a fumble.

2.9.1 SITUATION B: B1 hits ground ball to F6 who throws to first. F3 juggles the ball so that it rolls up his arm and is clamped to his body by an elbow or forearm when B1 touches first. **RULING:** B1 is safe. It is not a catch until the ball is secured by the bare hand or glove hand.

2.9.1 SITUATION C: B1 hits a fly to F8. F8 gets the ball in his hands but it is dropped (a) when he falls to the ground and rolls over; or (b) when he collides with a fielder or a wall; or (c) when he starts to throw to the infield. **RULING:** In (a) and (b), it is not a catch. In (c), it is a legal catch if an umpire rules that the ball was dropped as the fielder voluntarily removed the ball from the glove.

 COMMENT: The playing field includes both fair and foul playing territory. Any other areas beyond the playing field are defined as being outside the playing field (dead-ball area). Any wall, fence, barricade, rope, wire, marked or imaginary line is considered a part of the playing field. Any areas beyond those boundaries are outside the playing field. A fielder's status, generally, is determined by the location of his feet, and when a foot is touching a boundary line or the playing field inside the boundary line, he has not left the playing field, even though his other foot might be in contact with the area beyond the boundary line. Umpires may use the following guidelines to determine the status of a fielder following the catch of a batted or thrown live ball:
(1) It is a catch when he has one or both feet touching the playing field, or with both feet in flight prior to his touching any dead-ball area.
(2) If after making the catch both feet are entirely in a dead-ball area, the ball becomes dead.
(3) If the ball is caught after he has established his position outside the playing field, it is not a legal catch (2.9.1 Comment).

Also remember that whenever a dead ball follows a catch, there are instances when one or more runners may be awarded bases (5-1-1i, 8-3-3d).

2.9.1 SITUATION D: B1 hits a two hopper back to the pitcher. F1 gloves the bat- ted ball but cannot get the ball out of his glove. He quickly removes the glove with ball that is securely stuck inside the webbing of the glove and shovels the glove to the first baseman who is in contact with first base. The first baseman catches the glove with the ball in it, just before B1 touches first base. Is B1 out? **RULING:** B1 is out, because F3 had secure possession of the glove and ball.

A Tag
The batter-runner is out when after a dropped third strike or a fair hit, if the ball held by any fielder touches the batter before the batter touches first base (8-4-1f).

A runner is out when he is touched by a live ball securely held by a fielder or is touched by a fielder's glove or hand with the live ball held therein, while the runner is not touching his base (8-4-2f). The ball is not securely held if it is dropped or juggled after the runner is touched (8-4-2f note).

In Simple Terms
The tag must include the ball. If the ball isn't in the glove, the glove touching the runner has no effect.

If a batter-runner safely touches first base and then overslides or overruns it, except on a base on balls, he may immediately return to first base without liability of being tagged out, provided he did not attempt to run or feint to second. Also, if any base comes loose from its fastening when any runner contacts it, such runner cannot be tagged out because the base slides away from him (8-4-2h-1).

A Throw
A throw is the act of voluntarily losing possession through having the ball leave the hand for a purpose other than a pitch. It may result in the ball being bounced, handed, rolled, tossed or thrown (2-37-1).

Any thrown ball that is touched by a spectator, is intentionally touched by a non-participating squad member, goes into a stand or other dead-ball area or player' bench (even if it rebounds to the field), or over or through or wedges in the field fence or lodges in an umpire's, catcher's or offensive player's equipment or uniform is a dead ball (5-1-1g).

It is umpire interference when he inadvertently moves so as to hinder a catcher's attempt to throw (2-21-2). It is a delayed dead ball when the umpire interferes with the catcher who is attempting to throw (5-1-2c). If the runner is not put out, the runner must return to the base occupied at the time of the pitch (Dead Ball Table).

A Throw: Caseplays

2.21.2 SITUATION: With R2 on second base, the umpire inadvertently interferes with catcher's throw back to F1 and R2 advances to third base. **RULING:** If, in the umpire's judgment, his interference permitted R2 to reach third base safely, the umpire shall send R2 back to second base (5-1-2c).

5.1.1 SITUATION K: A ball thrown wildly to third base continues toward Team A's dugout and is intentionally touched by the (a) bat boy for Team A or (b) photographer. **RULING:** The ball becomes dead immediately.

5.1.2 SITUATION B: With runners on third and first base, a double steal is called. R3 attempts to steal home, and the umpire interferes with F2's throw to second base. **RULING:** The umpire gives the dead-ball signal. If R1 is not put out on F2's throw, the umpire shall declare the ball dead, and R3 and R1 must return to the base they occupied before the interference (5-1-2c, 8-2-9).

5.1.2 SITUATION C: With R3 on third, R1 on first and no outs, R1 attempts to steal second. F2 is obstructed on his throw to second base by the plate umpire. The throw is cut off by the shortstop and relayed back to the plate in time to retire R3 trying to score. **RULING:** If an out was not made at the end of F2's throw, the umpire shall call the ball dead immediately. Both runners shall return to the bases occupied at the time of the interference.

A Touch

The batter-runner is out if any fielder, while holding the ball in his grasp, touches first base or touches first base with the ball before the batter-runner touches first base (8-4-1f).

Fundamental #7
All forces are removed when the batter-runner is ruled out.

A runner is out when he fails to reach the next base before a fielder either tags the runner out or holds the ball while touching such base, after runner has been forced from the base he occupied because the batter became a runner (with ball in play) when other runners were on first base, or on first and second, or on first, second and third. There shall be no accidental appeals on a force play. No runner may be forced out if a runner who follows him in the batting order is first put out, including a batter-runner who is out for an infield fly (8-4-2j).

A Touch: Caseplay

2.29.3 SITUATION: With one out and R1 on first base, B3 hits a fly ball to short left field. R1 rounds second, but retreats toward first base when he thinks the ball will be caught. The ball drops, but F7 retrieves the ball and throws it to second base. R1 is between first and second. **RULING:** R1 is out, as the force was reinstated when he retreated past second base.

Topic:
__ Appeals _____

The defense may appeal when a runner misses a base or leaves a base on a caught fly ball before the ball is first touched (8-2-6a).

If the ball is live, an appeal may be made by any fielder in possession of the ball touching the base missed or left too soon on a caught fly ball, or by tagging the runner committing the violation if he is still on the playing field (8-2-6b). Runners may advance during a live-ball appeal play. If a time out is requested for an appeal, the umpire should grant it, and runners may not advance until the ball becomes live again (8-2-6e).

In Simple Terms
Appeals by tagging a base or runner can happen any time during a play. A verbal appeal can only happen when the ball is dead.

For a dead ball appeal, once all runners have completed their advancement and time has been called, a coach or any defensive player, with or without the ball, may make a verbal appeal on a runner missing a base or leaving a base too soon on a caught fly ball. The administering umpire should then make a decision on the play. If the ball has gone out of play, runners must be given the opportunity to complete their base-running responsibilities before the dead-ball appeal can be made (8-2-6c).

If any situation arises which could lead to an appeal by the defense on the last play of the game, the appeal must be made while an umpire is still on the field of play (8-2-6j). An appeal may be made after the third out as long as it is made properly and the resulting appeal is an apparent fourth out (8-2-6i). Multiple appeals are permitted as long as they do not become a travesty of the game (8-2-6f).

▧ Rationale

In 2002, the committee restored the burden of responsibility for the appeal to the defense. They modified the rule to allow for coaches to make a verbal appeal, to "improve upon a traditional element in baseball."

Appeals: Caseplays

2.29.6 SITUATION A: B1 hits a ground ball to F5, who throws the ball into the dugout. B1 misses first base while advancing to second. The coach of the offensive team says an appeal cannot be honored because the act of throwing the ball into a dead-ball area was a play. **RULING:** An appeal can be made for the missed base by the defensive team. The throw by F5 was part of the initial play and did not end his team's right to appeal.

2.29.6 SITUATION B: Following a base hit by B2, the visiting team wishes to appeal R1 missing third base as he advanced to home. After all playing action is over, the pitcher throws the ball to the third baseman while claiming that R1 missed the base. F5 is not watching and the throw goes into a dead-ball area. **RULING:** After B2 has been awarded two bases, the visiting team may now verbally appeal R1's missed base. Because an appeal is not a play, the visiting team retains its ability to appeal the baserunning error.

8.2.2 SITUATION A: The runner on second base misses third base and subsequently scores on a double by the batter. There is no appeal by the defense, and a pitch is made to the next batter. **RULING:** The run counts.

8.2.2 SITUATION B: With the bases loaded and one out, a fly ball is hit to deep center field and caught. The runner on third legally tags and advances to home plate. The runner on second leaves before the ball is touched by the center fielder. With runners now standing on third and second base, and before a pitch, the defense is granted time and verbally appeals that the runner on second left the base too early. **RULING:** This is a valid appeal and the runner is declared out. The run scoring on the proper tag-up from third base will count.

8.2.2 SITUATION C: The runner from first base misses second base on his way to third. He is: (a) standing on third base; or (b) halfway between second and third base when the throw from the outfield sails into the bleachers. **RULING:** In (a), all the defense needs to do is verbally state that the runner missed second base. He would be ruled out. He cannot legally attempt to return to touch second, since he was on a subsequent base when the ball became dead. In (b), the runner may attempt to return and touch second base since he has not yet gained third base. The defense cannot appeal the missed base if the runner has initiated an attempt to return to the base or until all playing action is over.

8.2.2 SITUATION D: The runner from first base misses second base on his way to third. With the ball still live and all playing action over, the defense: (a) touches the runner standing on third base with the ball; (b) touches second base while holding the baseball; (c) the coach verbally states that the runner missed second base; or (d) requests and is granted time and then states the runner missed second base. **RULING:** In (a), (b), and (d), these are legal appeals, and the runner would be declared out. In (c), since the coach can only verbally appeal when the ball is dead, this appeal would not be honored by the umpire.

8.2.2 SITUATION E: The runner misses second base and, with the ball still in play, attempts to return and touch second base. The defense simply announces that he missed the base. **RULING:** Since the runner has initiated action to return, the defense must tag him unless it is a force play, in which case all they would need to do is touch the base with the ball.

8.2.2 SITUATION F: Following a pitch to the next batter, the defensive coach states that the runner scoring from third left too early on a caught fly ball. **RULING:** The appeal is not valid, since it came after the next pitch (legal or illegal) and the coach cannot make a live-ball appeal. The run will count.

8.2.2 SITUATION G: Having missed second base, the runner is standing on third. The pitcher, before any pitch, legally attempts to pick off the runner standing on first. The coach then requests time and verbally states that the runner on third missed second base. **RULING:** The defense forfeits its right to appeal by making an attempted play on the runner on first. The appeal is denied and the runner remains on third base.

8.2.2 SITUATION H: Following an inside-the-park home run, the defense appeals that both runners on base and the batter missed third base as they advanced to home. **RULING:** This is a legal appeal. The umpire will rule depending on his judgment of the play.

8.2.2 SITUATION I: With bases loaded and two outs, the batter hits an extra base hit, scoring the runner from third. The runner from second is thrown out at home for the third out as the runner from first advanced to third, but missed second base. With time called and the teams beginning to change positions on the field, the defensive shortstop stays in fair territory. The defensive coach then verbally appeals the missed base. **RULING:** This is a legal appeal. The runner who missed second base would be declared out. While this is a fourth out, it would be granted and used as a third out. Since it would be a force play, no runs would score.

8.2.2 SITUATION J: With the winning run scoring in the bottom of the seventh inning, the umpires attempt to leave the field. While one umpire has stopped for a drink of water at the dugout, the visiting team appeals that the runner who scored missed third base. **RULING:** This is a valid appeal since there is at least one umpire still on the field of play.

8.2.2 SITUATION K: B1 hits a ground ball to F6, who throws the ball into the dugout. B1 had legally touched first base before the throw. The umpire awards B1 third base, but B1 misses second base as he advances on the award. Once B1 is standing on third, the defense appeals that he missed second base. **RULING:** This is a legal appeal, and the batter would be declared out.

8.2.2 SITUATION L: R3, R2 and R1 are on third, second and first bases, respectively, with no outs when B4 flies out to F9. R2 leaves second before F9 touches the ball and R3 advances to home after the catch. F9 throws to home but R3 scores. F2 then throws the ball to F4 who tags out R1 at second. F4 returns the ball to F1 who is standing off the pitcher's plate. **RULING:** The defense may appeal during a live- or dead-ball situation. If a proper appeal is made, the umpire would declare R2 out for leaving second base before F9 touched the ball and one run would score.

8.2.2 SITUATION M: With R2 on second, B2 hits a grounder to left field. R2 touches third base but misses the plate in attempting to score. F7 having thrown home, F2 steps on the missed base to retire R2 and throws to F6 in an attempt to put out B2: (a) before R1 attempts to return home; or (b) after R2 attempts to return to touch home plate. **RULING:**

(a) Upon proper defensive appeal, R2 would be ruled out. (b) Since R2 initiated action prior to the defense touching the plate, R2 must be tagged to record the out. R2 may legally return to touch home if he has not touched the steps of the dugout and if a subsequent runner has not yet scored.

8.2.5 SITUATION A: With R1 on first and no outs, B2 hits a long fly ball over the head of F8. R1 thinks the ball will fall in for a hit and attempts to advance to third. However, F8 makes the catch. F8 throws to first base, but the ball goes into dead-ball territory. R1, who is attempting to return to first base, is between second and third base when the ball becomes dead. **RULING:** A runner may not return to a base that he left too soon on a caught fly ball if he was on or beyond a succeeding base when the ball became dead, or if he advances and touches a succeeding base after the ball became dead. Upon a proper appeal, R1 shall be called out. If no proper appeal is made by the defense, R1 will be awarded third base (5-2-2b, 8-2-5).

8.2.5 SITUATION B: With two outs, B3 misses first base on his way to second. With B4 up to bat, the defensive coach requests to walk him intentionally. The plate umpire grants the request. The coach then appeals B3's missed base for the third out. **RULING:** The inning continues with B3 on second and B4 on first base. Once the request for the intentional base on balls to B4 was granted, the defense can no longer appeal B3's baserunning error.

Did You Know?	Appeals rules have changed for various reasons. Prior to 1981, the appeals rule was similar to other levels of baseball. The defense had to initiate the appeal by tagging the player or the base where the infraction occurred. Starting in 1981, appeals fell to the responsibility of umpires. The committee felt that baseball was the only sport where obvious rule violations were not penalized when observed by officials. It was felt that this was not consistent with other sports or the rules of good sportsmanship. Some felt that the umpire, by ignoring the infraction, was condoning cheating.

8.2.5 SITUATION C: With R1 on first and one out, B3 hits a single to right field. R1 misses second on his way to third base. At the end of the playing action, (a) the defensive coach verbally appeals that R1 missed second base; (b) the defensive coach requests and is granted time and then verbally appeals that R1 missed second base. **RULING:** In (a), a coach cannot appeal during a live ball. In (b), the umpire will call R1 out on the appeal.

8.2.5 SITUATION D: R2 is on second base with one out. B3 hits a single to right field. R2 misses third base and continues on to touch home plate. The defensive coach is granted time to confer with his pitcher. With the ball back in play, B3 attempts to steal second base and the pitcher legally throws to second. Following this play, the pitcher throws the ball to third while appealing that R2 missed the base. RULING: This is a legal appeal. The play made on B3's attempted steal of second was initiated by the offense and does not deny the defense the right to appeal R2 missing third base.

8.2.5 SITUATION E: R1 is on first base. B2 hits a single to the outfield. As R1 nears second base he is obstructed by F6 causing him to miss second base. R1 is safe at third base. The defense then appeals that he missed second base. **RULING:** R1 is not out on appeal if, in the umpire's judgment, the obstruction caused him to miss second base.

8.2.6 SITUATION C: R1 is on first when B2 hits a fly ball to F9 who overthrows first in an attempt to double up R1. The throw goes wild and into the dugout. R1 is awarded second and third (a) R1 fails to retouch first, or (b) R1 fails to touch second on his way to third. **RULING:** Upon proper defensive appeal, the umpire will declare R1 out in (a) and (b).

Topic:
Defensive Violations

Equipment Violations
Loose equipment, such as gloves, bats, helmets or catcher's gear, of either team may not be on or near the field (1-3-7).

Illegal use of detached player equipment or an illegal glove/ mitt does not cause ball to immediately become dead. If each runner advances to or beyond the base which he would reach as a result of the award, the infraction is ignored. Any runner who advances beyond the base he would be awarded does so at his own risk and may be put out (8-3-4). It is a delayed dead ball when a ball touches an illegal glove/ mitt (5-1-2f).

▨ Rationale
Prior to 1987, there was no penalty for use of an illegal glove. The glove was simply replaced. The committee didn't feel this was a severe

enough penalty. Now, along with the penalty, the defender is still required to secure a legal glove.

Equipment Violations: Penalties

If loose equipment interferes with play, the umpire may call an out(s), award bases or return runners, based on his or her judgment and the circumstances concerning the play (1-3-7).

Each runner is awarded two bases if a live thrown ball, including a pitch, is touched by an illegal glove or mitt, or by detached player equipment which is thrown, tossed, kicked or held by a fielder (8-3-3c).

Each runner is awarded three bases if a batted ball (that is not a prevented home run) is touched by an illegal glove or mitt, or by detached player equipment which is thrown, tossed, kicked or held by a fielder, provided the ball when touched is on or over fair ground, or is a fair ball while on or over foul ground, or is over foul ground in a situation such that it might become a fair ball (8-3-3b).

Each runner is awarded four bases (home) if a fair ball is prevented from going over the fence is touched by an illegal glove/mitt or detached player equipment which is thrown, tossed, kicked or held by a fielder (8-3-3a).

If a ball is touched with an illegal glove or mitt, that is discovered by the umpire, the coach or captain of the team at bat has the choice of taking the result of the play or having the award for use of an illegal glove or mitt. The illegal glove or mitt must be replaced immediately. A foul fly caught with an illegal glove/mitt shall be nullified and treated as a foul ball, unless the team at bat elects to take the result of the play (1-5-7).

Equipment Violations: Caseplays

1.3.7 SITUATION A: With R2 on second base and one out, B3 gets a base hit line drive to short center field. As R2 advances to third base, F8 throws to F5 in an attempt to put out R2. The ball gets by F5 and is prevented from entering the dugout by a shinguard left on the field by the defense. **RULING:** The plate umpire, based on the circumstances of the play, judges that the ball would have entered the dead-ball area had it not been for the shinguard left outside the dugout. He awards R2 home and B3 second base.

1.3.7 SITUATION B: B1 hits a high pop-up and Team A's F2 stumbles over some batting helmets near Team B's dugout and misplays the ball and it becomes foul. **RULING:** The umpire may award the out, may award base(s) or may return runner(s) of Team B's because of Team B's loose equipment near the dugout. Umpires are expected to enforce this rule for equipment that should not be in live-ball area. An example would be bats or helmets of the defensive team near a dugout or catcher's equipment or gloves of the offensive team near a dugout.

1.5.7 SITUATION: R1 is at first base and the outfield is shading left field. After the pitch, F2 attempts to pick off R1, but overthrows F3. The ball rolls to the outfield fence after touching F9's glove. R1 is between first and second. R1 continues to third and attempts to score, but is thrown out on a throw by F9. Before the next pitch, F9's glove is determined to be illegal by the umpire. **RULING:** The award for use of an illegal glove is two bases from the time the ball touched the illegal glove. Therefore, R1 would have been awarded third base. Since R1 advanced beyond the base that would have been awarded, R1's out stands and the infraction is ignored. The illegal glove shall be replaced.

8.3.3 SITUATION C: R2 is on second and R1 is on first when B3 hits ground ball to F6. F6 fields the ball, steps on second for a force on R1 advancing from first, and then throws wildly to F3. F3 tosses his glove into the air, intentionally hitting the ball. **RULING:** R1 is out. Both R2 and B3 are awarded two bases from their positions on base when the detached mitt or glove of F3 touched the thrown ball. In this situation or any other situation where a detached glove or mitt touches a ball, prior to the ball becoming dead because of going into a dead-ball area, the rule that applies to detached player equipment prevails. If the detached glove or mitt touches the ball after the ball has become dead because of going into a dead-ball area, the ruling governing detached player equipment has no bearing.

8.3.3 SITUATION F: B1 hits a fair line drive over the head of F5, who jumps high attempting to field the ball. As he jumps upward, his glove accidentally dislodges from his hand and touches the ball. **RULING:** If the umpire decides the detached glove was not thrown or tossed intentionally, there is no penalty. If the umpire should decide the act was deliberate, he shall advance B1 to third.

Fake Tags

A player shall not fake a tag without the ball (3-3-1b). A fake tag is an act by a defensive player without the ball that simulates a tag (2-22-2).

Fake Tags: Penalties

A fake tag is considered obstruction (2-22-2). When a runner is obstructed while advancing or returning to a base by a fielder, who without the ball, fakes a tag, the umpire shall award the obstructed runner and each other runner affected by the obstruction the bases they would have reached, in his or her opinion, had there been no obstruction. If the runner achieves the base he was attempting to acquire, then the obstruction is ignored. The obstructed runner is awarded a minimum of one base beyond his position on base when the obstruction occurred (8-3-2).

At the end of playing action following a fake tag, the umpire shall issue a waring to the coach of the team involved and the next offender on that team shall be ejected (3-3-1 penalty).

Fake Tags: Caseplays

8.3.2 SITUATION B: While (a) B1 is moving toward second base on a hit to right-center field, F6, who does not have the ball in his possession, fakes a tag on B1 or (b) B1 is returning to first base and F3, who does not have the ball, fakes a tag on B1. **RULING:** In both cases it is ruled obstruction, and B1 is awarded second base or if, in the umpire's judgment, the runner could have advanced farther had obstruction not occurred, the umpire could award additional bases.

8.3.2 SITUATION E: R1, who is on first base, attempts to steal second base. (a) F2 does not make throw or (b) F2 throws the ball into center field. In both cases F6 fakes a tag on R1. **RULING:** In (a), R1 is awarded second base on the obstruction call. In (b), the umpire shall call an obstruction. Make the ball dead and award bases that in his judgment the runner would have obtained had the obstruction not occurred. The umpire shall issue a warning to the defensive coach for F6 faking a tag.

Did You Know?

The penalty for a fake tag used to be an ejection with no warning. Also, when the rule was initially written, it covered fake tags on advancing runners, but not on runners returning to bases. Preventing fake tags was a point of emphasis for many years.

Fielder Leaves Field With Ball

The ball becomes dead immediately when a fielder, after catching a fair or foul ball (fly or line drive), leaves the field of play by stepping with both feet or by falling into a bench, dugout, stand, bleacher, or over any boundary or barrier such as a fence, rope, chalk line, or a pregame determined imaginary boundary line (5-1-1i).

Fielder Leaves Field With Ball: Caseplays

5.1.1 SITUATION L: F7, while attempting to catch a fly ball near dead-ball area (a) makes the catch with one foot on the dead-ball area line and the other foot in dead-ball area, or (b) makes the catch with both feet in the dead-ball area, or (c) makes the catch with both feet in the playing area and then steps with both feet or falls into the dead-ball area. **RULING:** In (b) and (c), the ball becomes dead. In (a) and (c), it is a legal catch, but in (c), F7 has left the playing area and if there are any runners on base, they each are awarded one base. In (b), it is not a catch (8-3-3d).

5.1.1 SITUATION P: F7 makes a diving catch. As he slides over the line designating dead-ball territory, his feet remain in live-ball territory. Is the ball dead? **RULING:** No. F7 must be entirely in dead-ball territory before the ball shall be declared dead. As long as any part of F7's body is touching the designated dead-ball line, the ball remains live (5-1-1i).

Hitting Balls to Players Once Game Started

A coach, player, substitute, attendant or other bench personnel shall not hit the ball to players on defense after the game has started (3-3-1e).

◪ Rationale

In the interest of safety and possible delay of game, hitting infield between innings or during charged conferences was prohibited in 1990.

Hitting Balls to Players
Once Game Started: Penalty

The umpire shall issue a warning to the coach of the team involved and the next offender on that team shall be ejected (3-3-1 penalty).

Hitting Balls to Players
Once Game Started: Caseplays

K: During a charged conference, the coach or other bench personnel (a) hits or (b) throws fly balls to a substitute outfielder, F8. **RULING:** Illegal in (a) and legal in (b).

10.2.3 SITUATION B: The coach of Team A hits balls to the infield or the outfield while F1 is warming up at the start of an inning. **RULING:** There shall be no balls hit to any fielders following pregame infield/outfield practice.

Intentionally Dropped Ball

The ball becomes dead immediately when an infielder intentionally drops a fair fly, fair line drive or fair bunt in flight with at least first base occupied and with less than two outs. This rule does not apply if the infield fly rule is in effect (5-1-1j).

In Simple Terms

Rules that cover the infield fly, dropped third strikes and intentionally dropped balls are in place to protect the offense and prevent undeserved double plays.

The ball is dead and the runner or runners shall return to their respective base(s) (8-4-1c). In this situation, the batter is not out if the infielder permits the fair fly, fair line drive or fair bunt in flight to drop untouched to the ground, except when the infield fly rule applies (2-19, 5-1-1j, 8-4-1c-1).

Intentionally Dropped Ball: Caseplays

5.1.1 SITUATION M: R1 is on first base with less than two outs when (a) B2 hits a line drive to F4 or (b) B2 hits a fair pop fly to F3. In both (a) and (b), the infielder intentionally drops the ball. **RULING:** In both (a) and (b), B2 is out and R1 returns to first base. The ball becomes dead immediately when it is intentionally dropped by an infielder except in the case of an infield fly (5-1-1j, 8-4-1c).

7.4.1 SITUATION C: Is it a "delayed dead ball" when a fair fly, fair line drive or fair bunt in flight is declared intentionally dropped by an infielder? **RULING:** No. The ball is declared dead as soon as infielder intentionally drops the ball. All runners return to bases occupied at the time of the pitch.

8.4.1 SITUATION F: With R1 on first and no outs, B2 bunts the ball in the air and it is intentionally dropped by F5. **RULING:** The ball is declared dead immediately and B2 is declared out. R1 remains at first.

8.4.1 SITUATION G: With the bases loaded and one out, B5 bunts a ball in the air. F3 uses the back of his glove to gently knock the ball to the ground where he picks it up and throws to F2 who touches the plate and then throws out B5 at first. **RULING:** The ball is dead. B5 is out and the runners return. Manipulating the ball to the ground is prohibited. Allowing the ball to drop to the ground untouched is not considered an intentionally dropped ball.

8.4.1 SITUATION J: B1 bunts the ball down the first-base line, the catcher comes out from behind the plate and (a) the batter/runner intentionally drops/throws his bat and contacts the batted ball prior to any fielder having an opportunity to field the ball; (b) without contacting the ball intentionally, the batter/runner drops/throws his bat or other batter/player equipment which impedes a fielder's opportunity to field the ball. **RULING:** The ball becomes dead immediately in both (a) and (b), the batter/runner is ruled out and all runners return to the base they occupied at the time of the pitch. The batter may not use a bat or any other personal equipment to hinder the defense.

Malicious Contact

A coach, player, substitute, attendant or other bench personnel shall not initiate malicious contact on offense or defense. If the defense commits the malicious contact, the player is ejected, the umpire shall rule either safe or out on the play and award the runner(s) the appropriate base(s) he or she felt the runners would have obtained if the malicious contact had not occurred (3-3-1m). Malicious contact always supersedes obstruction (8-4-2e note).

Malicious Contact: Caseplays

3.3.1 SITUATION JJ: With two outs, and R2 on second base and R1 on first base, B5 hits the ball in the gap. R2 touches and rounds third, R1 touches and rounds second. B5 touches and rounds first, F3 initiates malicious contact with B5 as a play is developing at third base on R2 a) before a tag, or b) after a tag. **RULING:** In (a), the ball is dead, and in the umpires judgment R2 scores, R1 is awarded third base, B5 is awarded second base, and F3 is ejected for malicious contact. In (b) the ball is dead, the out at third base is recorded, thus making R2's score a timing play. F3 is also ejected for malicious contact.

8.3.3 SITUATION O: With R3 at third and R1 at first with one out, B4 hits a ground ball to F4. While attempting to tag R1 advancing to second, F4 applies intentional excessive force to R1's head. On the play R3 is (a) advancing to the plate, or (b) R3 holds at third. **RULING:** In both (a) and (b), F4 is guilty of malicious contact. The play becomes dead immediately, and F4 is ejected. Since F4 tagged R1 out simultaneously with the malicious contact, the out stands; B3 is awarded first. In (a) R3 will be awarded home, scoring the run. In (b) R3 will stay at third since he was not advancing on the play.

8.3.3 SITUATION P: With R1 at first, B2 hits a sharp line drive down the line into the right-field corner. As he rounds second base, F6 reaches out and clotheslines R1, bringing him to the ground. **RULING:** F6 is guilty of not only of obstruction, but of malicious contact. The play becomes dead immediately, and F6 is ejected. R1 will be awarded at least third base and B2 at least first base. If in the umpire's judgment both R1 and B2 could have attained additional bases had the malicious contact not occurred, those additional bases will be awarded.

Obstructing Batter or Runner

When a runner is obstructed while advancing or returning to a base, the umpire shall award the obstructed runner and each other runner affected by the obstruction the bases they would have reached, in his opinion, had there been no obstruction. If the runner achieves the base he was attempting to acquire, then the obstruction is ignored. The obstructed runner is awarded a minimum of one base beyond his position on base when the obstruction occurred. If any preceding runner is forced to advance by the awarding of a base or bases to an obstructed runner, the umpire shall award this preceding runner the necessary base or bases. Malicious contact supersedes obstruction. When obstruction occurs, the umpire points and calls "obstruction." If an award is to be made, the ball becomes dead when time is taken to make the award (8-3-2).

A batter becomes a runner with the right to attempt to score by advancing to first, second, third and home bases in the listed order when the catcher or any other defensive player obstructs him. The coach or captain of the team at bat, after being informed by the umpire-in-chief of the obstruction, shall indicate whether or not he elects to decline the obstruction penalty and accept the resulting play. Such election shall be made before the next pitch (legal or illegal), before the award of an intentional base on balls, or before the infielders leave the diamond. Obstruction of the batter is ignored if the batter-runner reaches first and all other runners advance at least one base (8-1-1e).

Fundamental #8
The fielder has an absolute right to make an initial play on a batted ball.

Any runner attempting to advance (i.e., steal or squeeze) on a catcher's obstruction of the batter shall be awarded the base he is attempting. If a runner is not attempting to advance on the catcher's obstruction, he shall not be entitled to the next base, if not forced to advance because of the batter being awarded first base. If obstruction is enforced, all other runners on the play will return to base occupied at time of the pitch. The batter is awarded first base, if he did not reach base. If obstruction is not enforced, all other runners advance at their own risk (8-1-1e notes).

It is a delayed dead ball when a catcher or any fielder obstructs a batter or runner (5-1-2b).

Obstructing Batter or Runner: Caseplays

2.22.1 SITUATION A: R1 attempts to steal second. F2, upon receiving the pitch, throws a pop-up to F6. F5 yells "get back, get back." R1 thinks B2 has hit a pop-up and starts back to first where he is tagged out. **RULING:** This is verbal obstruction and R1 shall be awarded second base.

2.22.1 SITUATION B: B1 hits the ball into the gap. He rounds first and heads to second base. F6 blocks the base (a) while the outfielder still has the ball, (b) after F6 catches the ball, or (c) the ball is in motion from the outfield and F6 will probably make a play on B1. **RULING:** Obstruction in (a); legal in (b); obstruction in (c) if F6 denies access to the base without possession of the ball.

2.22.1 SITUATION C: A runner is advancing to score when F7 throws home. F2 completely blocks home plate with his lower leg/knee while (a) in possession of the ball or (b) while juggling and attempting to secure the ball or (c) before the ball has reached F2. **RULING:** Legal in (a); obstruction in (b) and (c) if the catcher denied access to home plate prior to securely possessing the ball.

8.1.1 SITUATION E: R2 is on second. F2 obstructs B2 but he hits and reaches first safely but R2, who was not moving on the pitch, is thrown out at home plate. **RULING:** Obstruction is ignored since R2 advanced one base and B2 reached first base safely. R2's advance past third was at his own risk and he is out (5-1-2b, 8-3-3d).

8.1.1 SITUATION F: R2 is on second base. After B2 takes his position in batter's box, F2 clearly reaches out over home plate (a) prior to; (b) after F1 has made a movement that has committed him to pitch; or (c) to receive the pitch. **RULING:** It is catcher obstruction in both (b) and (c), and B2 is awarded first base and R2 is awarded third base only if he was stealing on the pitch. F2 may not catch the pitch until it has passed home plate. In (a), there is no violation provided F2 and his equipment are removed from the area over home plate before pitcher has made a movement that committed him to pitch (8-3-1c).

In Simple Terms

Obstruction is an infraction by the defense and is always a delayed-dead ball, while interference is an infraction by the offense and is almost always an immediate dead ball.

8.1.1 SITUATION G: R3 is on third. After F1 winds up, R3 starts home as in a squeeze play. F3, who is playing close for a bunt, cuts off the pitch and tags R3. **RULING:** This is a defensive obstruction. The ball becomes dead when touched by F3. R3 is awarded home and batter is awarded first (5-1-2b, 8-1-1e, 8-3-1c).

8.1.1 SITUATION H: R2 is on second with one out. F2 obstructs B3, but he hits a ground ball to F4 who throws him out. F3 overthrows third in attempt to retire R2 who scores on overthrow. **RULING:** The coach of the offense may elect to take the result of the play, scoring R2, or he may accept the catcher's obstruction penalty, placing R2 on second and B3 on first.

8.1.1 SITUATION I: R2 is on second base with one out. B3 hits a long fly ball to F8 after his swing was obstructed by F2. R1 tags up and scores after the catch. **RULING:** The coach or captain of the offense may advise the umpire-in-chief that he elects to decline the obstruction penalty and accept the resulting play. Such election shall be made before the next pitch, legal or illegal, before the award of an intentional base on balls, or before the infielders leave the diamond.

*8.1.1 SITUATION J: With R2 on second, F2 tips the bat of B2 who swings and misses the pitch. R1 was stealing on the pitch. F2 attempts to throw out R2 at third in which case R2 is called (a) out or (b) safe. **RULING:** The umpire signals dead ball. In (a), R2 is awarded third base and the batter is awarded first base. In (b), the batter is awarded first base. Since R2 is stealing at the time of the pitch, he is awarded third base and may remain there.

8.1.1 SITUATION K: With the bases loaded and the infield-fly rule in effect, F2 obstructs the batter's swing which results in a high fly ball. Umpires invoke the infield-fly rule. The ball is caught. **RULING:** Because of the result of the batter being awarded first base, each runner will be awarded one base because of the force situation.

8.1.1 SITUATION L: With R3 on third base and trying to score on a steal or squeeze play, F2 obstructs the batter's swing. **RULING:** This is defensive obstruction and R3 is awarded home. The batter is awarded first base.

 COMMENT: If the catcher, or any other defensive player, obstructs the batter before he has become a batter-runner, the batter is awarded first base. If on such obstruction a runner is trying to score by a steal or a squeeze from third base, the play will be a delayed dead ball which results in the runner on third scoring and the batter being awarded first base. Runners not attempting to steal or not forced to advance remain on the bases occupied at the time of the obstruction.

8.1.1 SITUATION M: With R2 on second base, B2 is obstructed by F2 but he hits to F6 who throws B2 out at first base. F3 throws to third base to retire R2 who overslides third base. R2 was not attempting to steal on the pitch. **RULING:** This is defensive obstruction. B2 is awarded first base. R2 is returned to second base.

8.1.1 SITUATION N: R3 is on third base and R2 on second base, with one out. F2 obstructs B4 who hits a ground ball to F4. R2 was attempting to steal third, even though third was occupied. B4 is thrown out at first on the play. **RULING:** B4 did not reach first safely, so the coach has the option of taking the play or the penalty. If he takes the penalty, B4 is awarded first. R2 is awarded third because he was attempting to steal on the pitch, and R3 is forced to advance to home.

8.1.1 SITUATION O: With two outs, R2 attempts to steal third. F2 obstructs B4 as B4 swings. F2 overthrows F5 at third trying to get R2. R2 attempts to score and is thrown out at the plate by F7. **RULING:** The coach of the team at bat, after being informed of F2's obstruction, elects to have the penalty for defensive obstruction enforced. Therefore, B4 is awarded first base and R2 is awarded third base (8-1-1e).

8.1.1 SITUATION P: With R2 on second and R1 on first and one out, B4 hits a pop fly to the second baseman that is declared a legal infield fly. During B4's swing, F2 obstructed the swing with his mitt. The defense does not catch the ball, and R2 scores with R1 advancing to third base. B4 ends up on second base. **RULING:** U1 announced "That's Obstruction" when B4, in his attempt to hit the ball, makes contact with F2's glove by his bat. Although U1 declared "Infield fly, batter's out," the offense may choose to take the result of the play or the penalty. If the play stands, R2 will score, R1 will remain at third and B4 will be out due to the infield fly. If the offense chooses to have the penalty for the obstruction enforced, R2 will be returned to third base, R1 will return to second base and B4 will be awarded first base. B5 will come to bat with the bases loaded and one out.

8.3.2 SITUATION A: R2 and R1 are on second and first, respectively, when B3 beats out an infield hit. R1 advances to and past third toward home. In a rundown, F5 obstructs R2. However, R2 gets back to third safely and finds R1 there. F5 tags R1 with the ball. **RULING:** Umpire shall call "Obstruction!" when the infraction by F5 occurs. At the conclusion of playing action, he declares the ball dead, then awards home to R2 and allows R1 to remain at third. When a runner is obstructed, the obstructed runner is awarded a minimum of one base beyond his position on base when the obstruction occurred.

8.3.2 SITUATION C: F2 is in the path between third base and home plate while waiting to receive a thrown ball. R3 advances from third and runs into the catcher, after which R3 is tagged out. **RULING:** Obstruction. F2 cannot be in the base path without the ball in his possession, nor can he be in the base path waiting for a ball to arrive without giving the runner some access to home plate.

8.3.2 SITUATION D: With one out, R2 on second and R1 on first, B4 hits ground ball directly to F1 who throws to F5 for force on R2 at third. F5 then throws to F3 in time to put out B4. F6 holds R2, preventing him from advancing to third. **RULING:** The umpire will signal obstruction when it occurs, and then call time after runners have advanced as far as possible, which in this situation would probably be second for R1. R2 will then be awarded third. Because of the obstruction of F6, the out at first stands. B5 will come to bat with two outs and R2 is on third and R1 is on second base.

8.3.2 SITUATION F: With R1 on first base, B2 illegally hits a pitch that goes toward F6 and F4 obstructs R1 advancing to second base. **RULING:** The ball became dead at the time of B2's violation. B2 is out and R1 must return to first base.

8.3.2 SITUATION G: F1 attempts to pick off R1 at first base. As F3 is about to receive the throw, he drops his knee and (a) blocks the entire base prior to possessing the ball or (b) blocks part of the base prior to possessing the ball or (c) blocks the entire base while being in possession of the ball. **RULING:** Obstruction in (a); legal in (b) and (c).

8.3.2 SITUATION H: With no outs, R2 is obstructed rounding third. R1 had advanced beyond second. B3 then interferes with F3. **RULING:** The umpire shall deal with obstruction and then interference, since this is the order in which the infractions occurred. If R2 was obstructed after he rounded third, he would be awarded home. If he was obstructed before reaching third, the umpire may award him home if, in the umpire's judgment, R2 could have scored had he not been obstructed. The umpire then shall enforce the interference penalty, which would place R1 at second base and declare B3 out (8-4-2g).

8.3.2 SITUATION I: R3 is attempting to score from third and F8 throws the ball to F2. F2 is four or five feet down the line between home and third, but is not actually able to catch the ball in order to make the tag. R3, rather than running into F2, slides behind F2 into foul territory and then touches home plate with his hand. After R3 slides, F2 catches the ball and attempts to tag R3 but misses. The coach of the offensive team coaching at third base claims that obstruction should have been called even though there was no contact. **RULING:** Obstruction. Contact does not have to occur for obstruction to be ruled. F2 cannot be in the baseline without the ball if it is not in motion and a probable play is not going to occur, nor can he be in the baseline without giving the runner access to home plate.

8.3.2 SITUATION J: F1 feints a throw to first base. Someone in the defensive team's dugout throws a ball against the fence alongside first base, making R1 think an overthrow took place. **RULING:** The umpire shall call obstruction and award R1 second base. He shall also eject the offender from the game and issue a warning to the coach (2-22-1, 8-3-2, 3-3-1g(4)).

8.3.2 SITUATION K: F6 fields a ground ball and throws to F3 in attempt to retire B1 at first. The ball is thrown wide. As F3 lunges towards the ball, F3 collides with B1, knocking him to the ground prior to possessing the ball (a) while the runner is short of first base or (b) after the runner has contacted first base. **RULING:** (a) Obstruction; (b) legal.

8.3.2 SITUATION L: R1 is advancing on the pitch and F6 drops to a knee while taking the throw, partially blocking the inside edge of the base. R1 slides to the inside edge of the base, contacts F6's knee, and is then tagged out. The head coach of Team A argues this should be called obstruction. **RULING:** This is not obstruction as F6 did provide access to part of second base, even though it was not the part of the base that R1 wanted or believed was most advantageous.

Topic 4
Hitting

Key Terms

The batter is the player of the team at bat who is entitled to occupy either of the two batters' boxes (2-7-1). The batter's box is the 4-foot-by-6-foot area in which the batter shall stand when batting. The lines are part of the box (2-7-2).

A batter-runner is a player who has finished a time at bat until he is put out or until playing action ends (2-7-3).

A batted ball is in flight until it has touched the ground or some object other than a fielder (2-6-1).

A foul tip is a batted ball that goes directly to the catcher's hands and is legally caught by the catcher. It shall be called a strike and the ball is in play (2-16-2).

A bunt is a fair ball in which the batter does not swing to hit the ball, but holds the bat in the path of the ball to tap it slowly to the infield (2-8-1).

Follow-through interference is when the bat hits the catcher after the batter has swung at a pitch and hinders action at home plate or the catcher's attempt to play on a runner (2-21-4, 7-3-5c).

Backswing interference is when a batter contacts the catcher or his equipment prior to the time of the pitch (2-21-5, 7-3-7).

An on-deck circle for each team is a circle five feet in diameter located 37 feet to the side and away from home plate if space permits. Otherwise, it should be a safe distance to the side and away from home plate (2-23-1).

Topic:
— Equipment _____

The Bat

The bat shall have the following characteristics and components.

Each legal wood, aluminum or composite bat shall be one piece, multi-pieces and permanently assembled, or two pieces with interchangeable barrel construction (1-3-2a-1); shall not have exposed attachments, rivets, pins, rough or sharp edges or any form of exterior fastener that would present a potential hazard (1-3-2a-2); shall be free of rattles, dents, burrs, cracks and sharp edges. Bats that are broken, altered or that deface the ball are illegal. Materials inside the bat or treatments/devices used to alter the bat specifications and/or enhance performance are prohibited and render the bat illegal (1-3-2a-3).

Each legal wood, aluminum or composite bat shall have the following components. The bat knob shall protrude from the handle. The knob may be molded, lathed, welded or permanently fastened. Devices, attachments or wrappings are permitted except those that cause the knob to become flush with the handle. A one-piece rubber knob and bat grip combination is illegal (1-3-2b-1).

The bat handle is the area of the bat that begins at, but does not include, the knob and ends where the taper begins (1-3-2b-2).

The barrel is the area intended for contact with the pitch. The barrel shall be round, cylindrically symmetric and smooth. The barrel may be aluminum, wood or composite (made of two or more materials). The type of bat (wood, aluminum or composite) shall be determined by the composition of the barrel (1-3-2b-3).

The taper is an optional transition area which connects the narrower handle to the wider barrel portion of the bat. Its length and material may vary but may not extend more than 18 inches from the base of the knob (1-3-2b-4).

The end cap is made of rubber, vinyl, plastic or other approved material. It shall be firmly secured and permanently affixed to the end of the bat so that it cannot be removed by anyone other than the manufacturer, without damaging or destroying it. By definition, a one-piece construction bat does not have an end cap (1-3-2b-5).

Each bat not made of a single piece of wood shall have a safety grip made of cork, tape (no smooth, plastic tape) or commercially manufactured composition material. The grip must extend a minimum of 10 inches, but not more than 18 inches, from the base of the knob. Slippery tape or similar material shall be prohibited. Resin, pine tar or any drying agent to enhance the hold are permitted only on the grip. Molded grips are illegal (1-3-2c-1); must be 2-5/8 inches or less in diameter at thickest part and 36 inches or less in length (1-3-2c-2); not weigh, numerically, more than three ounces less than the length of the bat (e.g., a 33-inch-long bat cannot be less than 30 ounces) (1-3-2c-3).

Bats that are not made of a single piece of wood shall meet the Batted Ball Coefficient of Restitution (BBCOR) performance standard, and such bats shall be labeled with a silkscreen or other permanent certification mark. No BBCOR label, sticker or decal will be accepted on any non-wood bat. The certification mark shall be rectangular, a minimum of one inch on each side and located on the barrel of the bat in any contrasting color to read: "BBCOR .50" (1-3-2d). The NFHS has been advised that certain manufacturers consider alteration, modification and "doctoring" of their bats to be unlawful and subject to civil and, under certain circumstances, criminal action (1-3-2d Note).

A bat made of a single piece of wood may be roughened or wound with tape not more than 18 inches from the handle end of the bat. No foreign substance may be added to the surface of the bat beyond 18 inches from the end of the handle. Each bat made of a single piece of wood shall be 2-3/4 inches or less in diameter at the thickest part and 36 inches or less in length (1-3-3a-b).

Only bats may be used in warming up (including weighted bats used for this purpose) at any location. Only bats and items designed to remain part of the bat, such as weighted bats, batting donuts, and wind-resistant devices are legal at any location (1-3-4).

☑ Rationale
While foreign substances such as pine tar are still illegal on bats beyond the 18-inch mark, NFHS rules no longer require the 18-inch encircling mark on bats. The encircling mark requirement was removed in 1990 when the committee felt the rule had served its purpose and abuse of the rule was virtually non-existent.

Bats that are altered from the manufacturer's original design and production, or that do not meet the rule specifications, are illegal (1-3-5, 7-4-1a). No artificial or intentional means shall be used to control the temperature of the bat. No foreign substance may be inserted into the bat. Bats that are broken, cracked or dented or that deface the ball, i.e., tear the ball, shall be removed without penalty. A bat that continually discolors the ball may be removed from the game with no penalty at the discretion of the umpire (1-3-5).

The ball becomes dead immediately when the batter enters the batter's box with an illegal bat (5-1-1c).

Illegal Bat: Penalty
On the first violation for entering the box with an illegal bat, the penalty for an illegal bat is applied (7-4-1a) and the head coach shall be restricted to the bench/dugout for the remainder of the game. On the second violation for entering the box with an illegal bat, the penalty for an illegal bat is applied and the head coach shall be ejected. On subsequent violations for entering the box with an illegal bat, the penalty for an illegal bat is applied and the designated head coach shall be ejected.

☑ Rationale
The NFHS is aware that the incidence of bat altering is on the rise. In addition, the bat manufacturers are also aware and extremely concerned about their products being misrepresented and altered. Modifying a bat from its original manufactured form is viewed as unlawful and, under specific circumstances, civil and criminal action could be taken.

The Bat: Caseplays
1.3.2 SITUATION A: In the third inning, the batter comes to the plate with (a) a wood bat that has no certification mark; or (b) a non-wood bat with a visible certification mark. **RULING:** The wood bat, provided

it is no thicker in diameter than 2-3/4 inches or longer than 36 inches in length, is legal and is not required to be BBCOR-certified. All non-wood bats shall meet the BBCOR standard and shall be labeled with a completely visible silkscreen or permanent certification mark.

Accordingly, the bat in (b) is legal if the BBCOR certification is completely visible.

1.3.2 SITUATION B: B1 appears at bat with a bat that is (a) wood, (b) aluminum, (c) bamboo, (d) composite, (e) fiberglass or (f) titanium. All have the BBCOR certification mark. **RULING:** Not needed in (a). Legal in (b) – (f).

1.3.2 SITUATION C: In the top half of the fifth inning, a player enters the batter's box with a bat that has manufactured holes or ridges in the taper of the bat. **RULING:** Provided the bat meets all other bat requirements, it is a legal bat. Only the barrel is required to be round, cylindrically symmetric and smooth.

1.3.2 SITUATION D: During the game, B1 enters the batter's box with a wood composite bat without the BBCOR certification mark, or a bat made of a grass, such as bamboo. The umpire-in-chief questions the coach. It is the coach's opinion that since the bats are partially made of wood, the bats are not subject to the BBCOR standard and do not require the BBCOR certification mark. **RULING:** The coach is incorrect. A bat is either solid wood or non-wood. Any bat that is not solid wood is considered a non-wood bat and is subject to the BBCOR requirements. The bat is illegal, BI is out and the penalties of 4-1-3b are applied to the head coach.

1.3.2 SITUATION E: The batter enters the box with a non-wood bat (a) that has the BESR certification mark and appeared on the 2011 approved bat list, but does not have a BBCOR certification mark, or (b) that has a BBCOR certification mark. **RULING:** In (a), the bat is illegal and the penalty for an illegal bat shall apply, including the provisions of 4-1-3b applied to the head coach; in (b) the bat is legal for play.

1.3.2 SITUATION F: A batter enters the box with a non-wood bat that has a post-production sticker labeling it as BBCOR certified. **RULING:** The bat is illegal since BBCOR post-production labels, stickers or decals are not allowed. The batter is out and the penalties of 4-1-3b are applied to the head coach.

1.3.2 SITUATION G: A batter enters batting box with an illegal bat in the first inning. The umpire detects the illegal bat. In the third inning, another player for the same team enters the box with an illegal bat and it is detected. In the fifth inning, a third player from the same team enters the box with an illegal bat and it is detected. **RULING:** For the offense in the first inning, the batter is out (7-4-1a) and the head coach is restricted to the dugout. For the offense in the third inning, the batter is out (7-4-1a) and the head coach is ejected. For the offense in the fifth inning, the batter is out (7-4-1a) and the person who is now acting as head coach is ejected.

1.3.5 SITUATION A: The umpire notices that B1's bat has a "tacky" substance extending beyond the 18-inch limit (a) before he steps into the batter's box or (b) after he hits a long foul ball. **RULING:** In (a), B1 may obtain a legal bat without penalty. In (b), B1 would be declared out for using an illegal bat and the penalties of 4-1-3b are applied to the head coach.

1.3.5 SITUATION B: With a runner on first base and one out, the batter enters the batter's box with a non-wood bat that is 2-3/4 inches in diameter. **RULING:** The bat is illegal. The batter is declared out. The coach is restricted to the bench/dugout if this is the first violation (4-1-3b, 7-4-1a).

1.3.5 SITUATION C: In the second inning, the pitcher shows the plate umpire a baseball that was fouled off by the batter. The ball has a dark smudge mark on it from the bat. **RULING:** Unless the umpire feels the bat needs to be removed, the bat is legal and may continue in play. If the plate umpire were to feel that it needed to be removed, it would be done so with no penalty to the offense.

Did You Know? Bat length was limited to 36 inches (the current standard) in 1992. Bat weight/length ratio was first set at minus-5 in 1993, and changed to the current minus-3 ratio in 2001.

1.3.5 SITUATION D: The first baseman hits a home run with the bases empty using a bat that, while otherwise legal, has a small crack in the barrel. The plate umpire notices the crack: (a) as the batter enters the box; or (b) when the defense complains before the next pitch that it is an illegal bat. **RULING:** In (a), the bat is illegal upon detection as the head coach had verified that all equipment was legal. The first baseman is declared out and the penalties of 4-1-3b are applied to the head coach. In (b), the home run stands. The bat will be removed from the game. If the same bat were subsequently to be used later in the game, it would be subject to the illegal bat rule.

NOTE: In (a), if the plate umpire feels that the damage to the bat was done during the course of play during that game, the bat may be removed from the game, and replaced with no penalty to the offense. If the same bat were subsequently used later in the game, it would be subject to the illegal bat rule.

1.3.5 SITUATION E: Bases are loaded with two outs, B6 hits a home run, and while he is circling the bases F2 hands the bat to the umpire-in-chief to examine the barrel. It is discovered that the bat's end cap has been removed and the bat has been stuffed with ping-pong balls. **RULING:** The bat is illegal, B6 is called for the third out and no runs score and the penalties of 4-1-3b are applied to the head coach (1-3-5, 4-1-3b, 7-4-1a).

The Helmet

It is mandatory for on-deck batters, batters, runners, retired runners, players/students in the coaches boxes as well as non-adult bat/ball shaggers to wear a batting helmet that has a non-glare (not mirror-like) surface and meets the NOCSAE standard at the time of manufacture. The batting helmet shall have extended ear flaps that cover both ears and temples and also display the NOCSAE stamp and the exterior warning statement. The warning statement may be affixed to the helmet in sticker form, or it may be embossed at the time of manufacture (1-5-1).

A face mask/guard may be attached to batting helmets at the time of manufacture. All face mask/guards shall meet the NOCSAE standard. A face mask/guard specifically designed for a particular helmet model may be attached after manufacture, provided that procedure is approved by the manufacturer and meets the NOCSAE standard (1-5-2).

The umpire shall call "Time" and play is suspended when a player is ordered to secure protective equipment (5-2-1c).

The Helmet: Caseplay

1.5.2 SITUATION: A player wants to wear a face mask when he bats. The coach provides (a) a helmet with attached mask that is commercially manufactured, came assembled from the manufacturer and is NOCSAE approved, (b) a football helmet with a lineman's mask, (c) NOCSAE helmet that has been drilled out by the school shop instructor and assembled, but not NOCSAE nor manufacturer approved, (d) NOCSAE approved helmet and a face mask that requires assembly or (e) non-traditional face mask or eye protection attached to NOCSAE approved helmet which is NOCSAE and helmet manufacturer approved. **RULING:** Legal in (a), (d) and (e). Illegal in (b) and (c). In (d), even though assembly is required, as long as the face mask is designed specifically for that helmet, there is no violation.

COMMENT: In all cases, the umpire has the final say as to whether equipment is legal and/or minimizes risk to the player(s).

Did You Know ?	In 1965, a batter or runner not wearing a helmet would be declared out if the infraction was discovered by anyone, including the official scorekeeper. If the offensive team noticed the infraction, it could get a helmet with no penalty.

Topic:
On-Deck Circle

The on-deck circle should be to the side and away from home plate, 37 feet if space allows. Neither team's players shall warm up in the other team's on-deck circle. The on-deck circle does not have to be occupied, but if a player wishes to warm up, he shall do so only in his team's on-deck circle, provided the on-deck circle is located safely away from home plate (1-2-3).

Players loosening up to bat shall remain in the area of their team's on-deck circle while the pitcher is warming up (3-3-3).

On-Deck Circle: Caseplays
1.3.4 SITUATION: Team A is using a donut on a legal bat as a warmup device for on-deck batters. The umpire notices the donut fly off the barrel of the bat. The inside layer of the donut may have chipped away, making the device unsafe and illegal. Many devices that attach to bats are legal when new, but may become illegal due to wear or damage. **RULING:** The device shall be declared illegal in its present state.

In Simple Terms
Only bats (even weighted ones) may be used to warm up within the confines of the field.

3.3.3 SITUATION: As a pitcher is warming up, the coach of the team at bat calls the next batter over to him for a visit near home plate. **RULING:** A member of the team at bat should not be allowed to be any nearer home plate than the on-deck circle when a pitcher is warming up.

COMMENT: When it is apparent the pitcher has completed his warmup or when summoned by the umpire, the next batter may come to the plate. A player may report to the umpire, who is near home plate, but the player must return to the area of the on-deck circle.

7.4.1 SITUATION I: Team A has a runner on second base, B2 hits a high foul fly ball in the vicinity of the on-deck circle. The on-deck batter, while watching the catcher coming toward him, backs away from the ball but into the path of F5 and makes contact. **RULING:** B2 is out.

Topic:
Batted Ball in Play

A foul ball or a fair hit (which may be a bunt) occurs when a pitch is touched by the bat of the batter who is in his box (7-2-3).

A batted ball is either a fly ball, line drive or ground ball. A fly ball is a batted ball which rises an appreciable height above the ground (2-6-2). A line drive is a batted ball which travels parallel, or nearly so, with the ground through most of its flight (2-6-3). A ground ball is neither a fly ball or a line drive (2-6-4).

Fair Ball

A fair ball is a batted ball which meets any of the following conditions:

• It settles on fair territory between home and third base or between home and first base.

• It contacts fair ground on or beyond an imaginary line between first and third base.

• It is on or over fair ground when bounding to the outfield past first or third base.

• It first falls on fair ground on or beyond first or third base.

• It touches first, second or third base.

• While on or over fair territory, it touches the person of an umpire or player, their clothing or equipment.

• While over fair ground, it passes out of the playing field in flight.

NOTE: A fly ball or line drive, which passes over or inside first or third base in flight and curves to foul ground beyond such base, is not a fair hit. However, a hit which goes over or through the fence is a fair hit if it is over fair ground when it leaves the field (2-5-1).

It is umpire interference when he inadvertently moves so as to hinder a catcher's attempt to throw, or when a fair ball touches an umpire as in 5-1-1f, or thrown ball as in 5-1-1g (2-21-2). When a plate umpire hinders, impedes or prevents a catcher's throw attempting to prevent a stolen base or retire a runner on a pickoff play, if an out is not made at the end of the catcher's initial throw, the ball shall be dead and all runners shall return to the bases occupied at the time of the interference (8-4-6). A fair ball becomes dead immediately when it touches a runner or an umpire before touching any fielder and before passing any fielder other than the pitcher, touches a runner after passing through or by an infielder and another infielder could have made a play on the ball, touches a spectator, goes over or through or wedges in the field fence, or lodges in players equipment or uniform (5-1-1f).

In Simple Terms

For purposes of declaring a batted ball that hits a runner or umpire dead, the pitcher does not count as an infielder.

Fair Ball: Caseplays

2.5.1 SITUATION A: B1 hits a fair line drive that is touched in flight by F4, after which it hits an umpire standing behind F4. The ball is then caught by F6 before it touches the ground. **RULING:** B1 is not out. The ball remains live because it has been touched by a defensive player before it hit the umpire. Any batted ball that stays in play cannot be caught for an out if it hits an umpire.

2.5.1 SITUATION B: B1 hits a ground ball that rolls along third baseline and touches both outside and inside the foul line. The ball bounces directly over third or touches third. It lands on foul or fair ground. **RULING:** The ball is fair.

2.5.1 SITUATION C: B1 hits a fly ball that comes down on foul ground (a) between home and first or (b) beyond first. In each case, before it has touched anyone, it rolls to fair ground first, where it is then fielded or lies on the ground. **RULING:** In (a), it is a fair ball. In (b), it is a foul ball.

2.5.1 SITUATION D: B1 hits a line drive that is inside the foul line when it passes over the fence in front of the stands but which is blown by the wind or curves so it hits the back of the stands outside the foul line extended. **RULING:** This is a fair ball.

2.5.1 SITUATION E: The batter hits the ball, drops the bat and it unintentionally hits the ball a second time in (a) fair territory and is either touched by a fielder and/or comes to rest in fair territory; (b) foul territory and is either touched by a fielder and/or comes to rest in either fair or foul territory; or (c) fair territory and is either touched by a fielder and/or comes to rest in foul territory. **RULING:** In (a), the ball is fair. In (b) and (c), the ball is foul.

5.1.1 SITUATION H: With R2 on second, B2 hits between F5 and F6, both of whom are playing in for a bunt in front of R2. The batted ball touches R2 and is deflected to foul ground. F6 was in such a position he had no chance to play the ball. **RULING:** If the touching by R2 is accidental, it is ignored because the batted ball has passed a fielder other than the pitcher and no other fielder has a play on the ball. If R2 intentionally deflected the batted ball, the umpire shall rule interference and declare the ball dead. R2 is declared out. B2 is credited with a base hit and placed on first (8-4-2k).

5.1.1 SITUATION I: With R3 on third and R1 on first, a ball batted by B3 hits the umpire who is (a) on fair territory behind F5 or (b) behind the pitcher but in front of F4. **RULING:** In (a), the ball remains live since it has passed a fielder. In (b), unless the ball touches F1, it becomes dead and each runner is sent to the base he occupied or to which he was being forced when the ball became dead i.e., R3 remains on third and R1 and B3 go to second and first (8-1-2b).

Fundamental #9

The position of the ball, not the fielder, determines fair or foul.

5.1.1 SITUATION J: With a fielder in position to make a play, R1 is on first and R2 is (a) between second and third or (b) touching second. R2 is hit by ball batted by B3. **RULING:** The ball becomes dead immediately in (a) and (b). In (a), R2 is out. He is also out in (b), unless it is declared an infield fly. In (a) and (b), unless B3 is out because it is an infield fly, he is entitled to first base. R1 is awarded second base.

5.1.1 SITUATION N: With R3 at third and F5 playing deep, B2 hits a ball that caroms off the base into foul territory where it touches R3. **RULING:** A runner who is hit by a batted fair ball in foul territory is not out and the ball remains live.

Foul Ball

A foul is a batted ball which settles on foul territory between home and first base or between home and third base; or that bounds past first or third base on or over foul territory; or that first falls on foul territory beyond first or third base; or that, while on or over foul territory, touches the person of an umpire or a player or any object foreign to the natural ground; or is inadvertently being declared foul by an umpire; or that hits the batter in the batter's box; or that hits the ground or home plate and then hits the batter or the bat which is held by the batter, while he is in the batter's box (2-16-1a through g).

In Simple Terms
A batted ball declared foul is dead when it hits the ground.

The ball becomes dead immediately when a foul ball touches any object other than the ground or any person other than a fielder, goes directly from the bat to the catcher's protector, mask or person without first touching the catcher's glove or hand or becomes an uncaught foul (5-1-1d).

A batter is also out when a foul ball (other than a foul tip not a third strike) is caught by a fielder or such catch is prevented by a spectator reaching into the playing area (7-4-1d) or an attempt to bunt on third strike is a foul (7-4-1e).

Foul Ball: Caseplays

2.16.1 SITUATION A: On a count of 1-ball, 2-strikes, B1 hits a fly ball down the right field line. While the ball is in the air, the umpire inadvertently declares, "Foul ball;" (a) F9 catches the ball in flight, (b) the ball falls to the ground in fair territory, (c) the ball falls to the ground in foul territory. **RULING:** (a) The batter is out and the ball remains live, (b) and (c) the ball is immediately dead as soon as it touches the ground, the batter returns to bat with a count of 1-2.

2.16.1 SITUATION B: On a count of 1-ball, 2-strikes, B1 hits a ground ball down the third base line and the umpire inadvertently declares, "Foul ball." F5 fields the ball in fair territory and throws to F3. **RULING:** The ball is dead immediately once it hits the ground, B1 returns to bat with a count of 1-2.

2.16.1 SITUATION C: B1 hits a fly ball down the left-field line. F7 goes over near foul line and is in fair territory when he reaches over foul line and drops an attempt to catch the ball. **RULING:** Even though F7 is in fair territory when he touches the ball, the ball is foul because it is the position of the ball and not the player that determines whether a ball is fair or foul.

2.16.1 SITUATION D: B1's bunt rolls up the first-base line where it hits B1's bat that was lying on the ground in fair territory. The ball deflects into foul territory. Is the ball fair or foul? **RULING:** The ball is foul, provided the bat was not placed there intentionally. The bat is considered to be part of the playing field (2-5-1, 2-8-1, 8-4-1d).

2.16.1 SITUATION E: While B1 is batting, he hits the ball and the ball strikes him (a) while he is in the batter's box, (b) when he is outside the batter's box. **RULING:** (a) declared a foul ball, (b) runner is declared out. In both situations, the ball is immediately dead once it touches the batter.

5.1.1 SITUATION A: With runners on first and third base and no outs, R3 and R1 proceed with a double steal, B3 hits a high pop fly over foul territory and the wind starts to carry the ball into fair territory. The umpire-in-chief prematurely calls foul ball as F2 attempts to make the catch and drops the ball in fair territory. **RULING:** The fact that the ball touches the ground has made the ball dead and the umpire sends R3 and R1 back to their respective bases.

5.1.1 SITUATION B: On an 0-1 pitch, B1 hits a high pop fly on the foul line just past first base. F3 attempts to make a play, but drops the ball. The plate umpire signals fair ball but the base umpire verbalizes foul ball. **RULING:** This conflicting play would have been eliminated with better pregame planning of the officials. The foul ball call of the first base umpire would prevail. However, the ball touched the ground and that rendered it dead. B1 would return to the plate with a 0-2 count.

5.1.1 SITUATION C: On a 1-1 pitch, B1 hits a line drive down the left field line that goes out of play. The ball clearly kicked up chalk when it landed. The plate umpire, because he was blocked by F5, mistakenly ruled a foul ball. The offensive team requests that the plate umpire ask for help. **RULING:** Even though this was a fair ball, because the umpire inadvertently called it foul and it touched the ground, the ball is dead and B1 will return to the plate with a count of 1-2.

 COMMENT: Determining when the ball becomes dead on a foul is sometimes tricky. With R2 on second and no one out, consider the following:

(1) An attempted bunt on third strike by B2 is a foul fly that is caught by F2. B2 would have been out without the catch, but because of the catch, F1 is not credited with a strikeout and R2 may attempt to advance after the catch.

(2) The first strike on B2 is a result of a foul fly that comes down near the backstop with F2 attempting a catch. While reaching into the field of play a spectator deflects it and (a) prevents the catch or (b) F2 gets the deflected ball in his glove and holds it. In (a) and (b), the ball shall be dead at the moment of spectator interference. B2 is declared out and R2 will be awarded the bases he would have reached in the judgment of the umpire had there been no spectator interference (8-3-3e).

(3) B2 hits high foul fly to right field. It is not caught. R2, who was on second base, has passed third before the ball becomes dead. R2 must return to second.

(4) A pitch touches the bat of B2. In (a), it goes directly to F2's glove, then to his protector and rebounds into his hand or glove or (b) it goes directly to F2's protector or mask and rebounds into his hand or glove. In (a), it is a foul tip and a catch. In (b), the ball becomes dead when it touches the body of F2 and is an uncaught foul. In a related situation, a foul ball rises and comes down to strike the catcher's mask or protector and then rebounds into his hand. It is a caught foul. B2 is out and the ball remains live.

Care must be taken with premature rendering a "foul ball" situation considering that a foul call renders the ball dead that touches the ground (2.16.1 Comment).

Infield Fly

An infield fly is a fair fly (not including a line drive nor an attempted bunt) which can be caught by an infielder with ordinary effort, (rule does not preclude outfielders from being allowed to attempt to make the catch) and provided the hit is made before two are out and at a time when first and second bases or all bases are occupied. When it seems apparent that a batted ball will be an infield fly, the umpire immediately announces it for the benefit of the runners. If the ball is near a baseline, the umpire shall declare, "Infield fly, if fair" (2-19-1). The batter-runner is out when he hits an infield fly and the infield-fly rule is in effect (8-4-1j).

◪ Rationale

The purpose of the infield fly rule is to prevent the defense from allowing a ball to drop in order to turn a double or triple play that is not deserved.

Infield Fly: Caseplays

2.19.1 SITUATION: With one out, R2 is on second and R1 is on first when B4 hits an infield fly. Base runners believe there are two outs and start running as soon as the ball is hit. F4 fails to catch the infield fly and both runners cross home plate. **RULING:** B4 is out for hitting an infield fly, but the runs count since runners may advance at their own risk.

7.4.1 SITUATION E: The umpire calls, "Infield fly, if fair," but the ball curves to foul territory. **RULING:** The announcement is reversed. It is not an infield fly but an ordinary foul. The batter is not out unless foul fly is caught. If the fly is caught, each runner must retouch his base before attempting to advance (8-4-1j).

7.4.1 SITUATION F: With less than two outs and R2 on second and R1 on first, B4 hits a pop-up that comes down over foul territory. Is this an infield fly if (a) it touches the ground out of reach of all infielders and then takes a long hop into fair territory between home and first or (b) it is within reach of a fielder who does not touch it and ball bounces to fair territory? **RULING:** Not an infield fly in (a) if umpire thinks it is not within reach of any fielder, but it is a fair ball. In (b), it is an infield fly (2-19-1, 8-4-1j).

7.4.1 SITUATION G: With R2 on second and R1 on first and one out, B4 hits a high fly to second base which could have been caught by F4. Neither umpire declares "infield fly." F4 unintentionally drops the ball but picks it up and tags R1 who is off the base. **RULING:** The half-inning is over as R1's out is the third out. The infield fly out for the second out holds even though it was not declared. The situation determines the out, not the declaration. The umpires should always declare "Infield fly, if fair," to lessen any confusion.

10.2.3 SITUATION F: With R3 on third and no outs, B2 hits a high fly in the infield above the second baseman's head. The base umpire erroneously calls "Infield fly. The batter is out." F4 subsequently drops the ball. R1 scores from third and B2 ends up on second base. Does the play stand or is B2 out but the run allowed to score? **RULING:** The play would stand. Both teams have the responsibility to know when conditions exist for an infield fly. The batter-runner should attempt to reach base safely and then inform the umpire that his call was in error (7-4-1f).

10.2.3 SITUATION G: With R2 on second and R1 on first and no outs, B3 hits an infield fly, but the umpire fails to call "infield fly." Is the infield fly in effect or not? **RULING:** Even though the infield fly rule was not announced by the umpire, it is still in effect. Both teams have the responsibility to know when conditions exist for an infield fly.

Topic:
Ball Not Put Into Play

Base on Balls

A base on balls is an award of first base (often referred to as a "walk") if a batter receives four such balls. The batter must go immediately to first base before time-out is called (2-4-2). An intentional base on balls may be given by the defensive team by having its catcher or coach request the umpire to award the batter first base. This may be done before pitching to the batter or on any ball and strike count (2-4-3). The ball shall be declared dead before making the award (2-4-3, 5-1-3).

Did You Know ? When baseball was first invented, bases on balls were non-existent. To reach base, hitters had to hit the ball into play, even if it took 50 pitches.

Base on Balls: Caseplays

2.4.2 SITUATION: B1 receives ball four and he or a teammate or coach of Team A immediately requests time. **RULING:** The umpire shall ignore the request and order B1 to go to first base, after which a player or coach of Team A may request time.

5.1.1 SITUATION D: R1 is on first when B2 receives ball four. F2 (a) drops the ball or (b) ball four is caught and, while B2 is walking to first, it is thrown to F3 who drops it. In either case, R1 advances to third and B2 advances to second. Is the ball dead after the fourth ball? **RULING:** No. Those are legal advances.

Strikeout

A batter is out when a third strike is caught (7-4-1c) or a third strike is not caught with first base occupied and there are less than two outs. If there are two outs or if no runner occupies first base, the batter is not out unless the third strike is caught. He is entitled to try to reach first base before being tagged out or thrown out (7-4-1b).

The batter-runner is out when a third strike is caught by the catcher; or the third strike is not caught with first base occupied and there are less than two outs (8-4-1e).

The batter-runner is also out after a dropped third strike if the ball held by any fielder touches the batter before the batter touches first base; or if any fielder, while holding the ball in his grasp, touches first base or touches first base with the ball before the batter-runner touches first base (8-4-1f).

The batter-runner is out when, on a dropped third strike, he gives up by entering the bench or dugout area, or with two outs he does not attempt to reach first base before all infielders leave the diamond at the end of the half-inning (8-4-1i).

Strikeout: Caseplays

2.20.2 SITUATION: With two outs and R3 on third, B4 has a count of three balls and two strikes. The pitch hits the ground in front of home plate and bounces over it. B4 swings and misses. R3 crosses home plate, but B4 makes no effort to go to first. F2 catches the bounce and rolls the ball toward the pitcher's mound and all infielders leave the diamond. **RULING:** If the batter gives up and enters the dugout or other dead-ball area, the batter is out. The run would not count.

7.4.1 SITUATION A: With R1 on first, B2 has two strikes and swings at the next pitch. F2 drops the ball and fails to throw to F3 at first. There are (a) no outs or (b) two outs. **RULING:** In (a), B2 is out because first base was occupied. In (b), B2 is safe at first if he reaches first before the half-inning ends or before all infielders leave the diamond. He is out if he gives up by entering the bench or dugout area.

7.4.1 SITUATION B: With (a) one out or (b) two outs, and R3 on third and R2 on second, F2 drops the third strike delivered to B5. **RULING:** B5 is safe at first if, in either (a) or (b), he reaches base before the ball is held by the fielder touching the base, or before he is tagged, provided in (a), it is before the time of the next pitch to the following batter or before he enters his bench and, provided in (b), it is before the half-inning ends.

Topic:
Offensive Conferences

Each team, when on offense, may be granted not more than one charged conference per inning to permit the coach or any of that team's personnel to confer with base runners, the batter, the on-deck batter or other offensive team personnel. The umpire shall deny any subsequent offensive team requests for charged conferences (3-4-2).

An offensive charged conference is concluded when the coach or team representative initially starts to return to the coach's box or dugout/bench area (3-4-4).

Offensive Conferences: Caseplay

3.4.4 SITUATION: A coach requests an offensive charged conference with R1 who is on second base. The coach goes to second base for the conference with the runner and then starts to return to the coach's box. **RULING:** The offensive charged conference ends when the coach starts to return to his position.

Topic:
Batting Violations

Allowing Pitch to Hit Him

A batter shall not permit a pitched ball to touch him. The batter remains at bat (pitch is a ball or strike) unless pitch was a third strike or ball four (7-3-4).

Allowing Pitch to Hit Him: Caseplays

7.3.4 SITUATION C: B1 is at bat with a three-ball, no strike count. The batter rolls his elbow into the strike zone and a) the pitch hits B1 in the shoulder and would have been a ball; or b) the pitch hits the batter in the elbow and was in the strike zone. In both cases, the batter made no other movement. **RULING:** In a) B1 is awarded first base as it was ball four, and in b) B1 is charged with a strike.

7.3.4 SITUATION D: B1 is at bat with a two-ball, no strike count. The batter is fooled by the pitch and freezes in the box. The pitch hits B1 in the shoulder. The batter made no other movement. **RULING:** B1 is awarded first base.

Ball Illegally Batted

A batter shall not hit the ball fair or foul while either foot or knee is touching the ground completely outside the lines of the batter's box or touching home plate (7-3-2). The ball becomes dead immediately when it is illegally batted (5-1-1b).

The batter-runner is out when after hitting or bunting a ball, he intentionally contacts the ball with the bat a second time in fair or foul territory. The ball is dead and no runner(s) advance (8-4-1d). In the case of a foul ball, it must have a chance to become fair in the umpire's judgment (8-4-1d-1). If the bat and ball accidentally come in contact with each other a second time while the batter is holding the bat in the batter's box, it is a foul ball (8-4-1d-2).

⬚ Rationale

Only the umpire or defense can detect an illegal bat. If the offense could "appeal" for the penalty, it could possibly negate double plays and give the offense an unfair advantage.

Ball Illegally Batted: Caseplays

5.1.1 SITUATION F: With R1 on first, B2 steps out of batter's box and then hits a foul or a fair ball. **RULING:** B2 is out and R1 returns to first.

7.3.2 SITUATION A: When is a batter's foot considered to be inside the batter's box? **RULING:** The batter is considered to be in the batter's box when no part of either foot is touching the ground outside the boundary lines forming the batter's box. It is permissible for the feet to be touching the boundary lines that form the batter's box, since the lines are a part of the box. The batter may legally hit the ball with one foot in the box and the other foot in the air outside the box, and then contact the ground outside the box with the foot that was airborne.

7.3.2 SITUATION B: B1 assumes his batting stance (a) with his right foot on the back line but not outside the back line of the batter's box, (b) with his right foot partially on the back line and partially outside the back line of the batter's box, or (c) with his right foot completely outside the back line of the batter's box. **RULING:** The stance in (a) is proper. However, in (b) and (c), the umpire shall instruct the batter to assume his stance so neither foot is outside the lines of the batter's box.

7.3.2 SITUATION C: B1 strides forward when making contact with the pitched ball. His front foot (a) is in the air when contact is made and then lands completely outside the line of the batter's box, (b) is partially on the line of the batter's box, and partially on the ground outside the line of the batter's box, or (c) is on the ground entirely outside the line of the batter's box. **RULING:** In (a) and (b), this is legal, but in (c), the batter is out for making contact with the pitched ball while being out of the batter's box.

7.3.2 SITUATION D: B1 hits (a) a fair ball, (b) a foul ball, (c) a foul tip while either foot or knee is touching the ground completely outside the lines of the batter's box or touches home plate. **RULING:** Illegal in (a), (b) and (c). The batter is out for making contact with the pitched ball while being out of the batter's box or touching home plate.

*7.4.1 SITUATION D: With R2 on second and R1 on first, B3, using an illegal bat, hits a ground ball to F6 who steps on second base in time to force out R1, but then throws the ball into dead-ball territory. R2 advances to third base and then scores. B3 advances to second base.

Prior to the next pitch, the illegal bat is detected and brought to the attention of the umpire-in-chief. **RULING:** The umpire will give the defense the option of taking the result of the play or having the illegal bat penalty enforced, which would result in B3 being called out and R2 and R1 returning to the bases occupied at the time of the pitch. In addition, the penalties of 4-1-3b are applied to the head coach.

8.3.2 SITUATION F: With R1 on first base, B2 illegally hits a pitch that goes toward F6 and F4 obstructs R1 advancing to second base. **RULING:** The ball became dead at the time of B2's violation. B2 is out and R1 must return to first base.

8.4.1 SITUATION A: After bunting the ball, B1's bat, which is still in his hand, unintentionally strikes the ball a second time in fair territory while (a) he is still in the batter's box or (b) he is outside the batter's box. **RULING:** In (a), it is a foul ball. In (b), the ball is dead and the batter is out.

8.4.1 SITUATION B: B1 squares to bunt and hits the pitch. The batted ball bounces off the plate and hits B1's (a) leg or, (b) bat a second time while B1 is holding the bat in the batter's box (no foot is entirely outside of the batter's box). **RULING:** In (a), it is a foul ball. In (b), the ball is foul unless, in the umpire's judgment, the ball was contacted intentionally, in which case the ball would be dead and B1 declared out.

 COMMENT. The lines of the batter's box are within the box. When taking a stance in the box, both of the batter's feet must be completely in the batter's box (not touching the ground outside the batter's box). When making contact with the pitched ball, if the foot is touching the line of the batter's box, it is considered to be in the batter's box even if it is also touching the ground outside the line of the batter's box (7.3.2 Comment).

Batter's Box Rule

A batter shall not delay the game by failing to take his position promptly in the batter's box within 20 seconds. The batter must keep at least one foot in the batter's box throughout the time at bat (7-3-1).

A batter may leave the batter's box when he swings at a pitch, is forced out of the box by the pitch or attempts a "drag bunt." He may also leave the batter's box when the pitcher or catcher feints or attempts a play at any base, the pitcher leaves the dirt area of the pitching mound or takes a position more than five feet from the pitcher's plate after receiving the ball, a member of either team requests and is granted "Time," the catcher leaves the catcher's box to adjust his equipment or give defensive signals or the catcher does not catch the pitched ball (7-3-1 exception).

For failure of the batter to be ready within 20 seconds after the ball has been returned to the pitcher, the umpire shall call a strike. If the batter leaves the batter's box, delays the game, and none of the above exceptions apply, the plate umpire shall charge a strike to the batter. The pitcher need not pitch, and the ball remains live (7-3-1 penalty).

In Simple Terms

The batter must delay the game for the batter's box rule to apply. If there is no delay, there is no infraction to penalize.

Batter's Box Rule: Caseplays

5.2.1 SITUATION A: After F1 has started his delivery, B1 steps out of the batter's box without being granted "Time." **RULING:** If F1 delivers a legal pitch, the umpire shall call the pitch a strike regardless of the location. A second strike may be called, if, in the umpire's judgment, B1 caused unnecessary delay. The ball remains live. Whether time is granted to the batter shall be umpire judgment.

7.3.1 SITUATION A: B1, who is leading off the third inning, walks halfway to third base to get a sign from his coach who has not yet reached the coaching box. **RULING:** As soon as F1 has completed his warm-up throws, the 20-second count on the batter begins and he must be in the box ready for the pitch before the count ends. The umpire should caution B1 that he has "10 seconds" or "5 seconds" and, if he has not established himself in the box, after 20 seconds, a strike shall be called.

7.3.1 SITUATION B: With F1 on pitcher's plate ready to deliver, B1 in the batter's box holds up his hand while he digs a hole in the box to get better footing. **RULING:** The umpire will not permit the pitcher to pitch but will caution the batter as he nears the end of the 20-second count. If the batter's box is in poor condition because of rain during the game, or for some other good reason, the umpire will properly grant a time-out to the batter to make his adjustment.

7.3.1 SITUATION C: B1, who is leading off the inning, decides to try to upset F1 and delays entering the batter's box. F1, seeing B1 is not in the box, does not assume his pitching position on the pitcher's plate. Twenty seconds elapse. **RULING:** B1 is charged with a strike. While F1 did not deliver the pitch within 20 seconds, he cannot pitch until the batter is set in the batter's box and therefore is not penalized.

7.3.1 SITUATION D: B1 steps out of the batter's box (a) without requesting time, or (b) after he has requested time, or (c) fails to enter batter's box within 20 seconds. **RULING:** In (a), the umpire shall call a strike if he feels B1 delayed the game. In (b), if the umpire grants time, the 20-second count will begin again as soon as the ball is declared "live." If time is not granted by the umpire and B1 steps out of the batter's box, a strike shall be called on B1 if he delays the game. In (c), the umpire shall call a strike. The pitcher does not have to throw a pitch.

7.3.1 SITUATION E: With no runners on, B1 is properly in the batter's box and F1 is on the pitcher's plate. After 10 seconds F1 steps back off the plate to say something to F6. The 20-second count elapses. **RULING:** Since F1 was responsible for the delay, the umpire shall call a ball on B1. If F1 had returned to the pitcher's plate and delivered the ball within the 20-second count, there would have been no penalty.

 COMMENT: If F1 steps off the plate for good reason, such as to tie his shoe, wipe perspiration from his glasses, etc., he should request time, but if the reason is obvious, umpires should grant time regardless. The same would apply to batters.

7.3.1 SITUATION F: B1 has a count of three balls and one strike. In (a), F1 throws a pitch which B1 thinks is ball four and he starts running to first base prior to the umpire calling the pitch a strike or (b) B1 incorrectly thought the count was two balls and two strikes and heads to the dugout after the umpire called the pitch a strike. **RULING:** In both (a) and (b), as long as the umpire judges that B1 did not delay the game, he would be allowed to continue to bat with a count of three balls and two strikes. If the umpire felt that the game was delayed, he shall charge a strike to B1. Because of the additional strike which now has been called, the batter is declared out in both (a) and (b).

7.3.1 SITUATION G: B2 has a count of two balls and one strike (a) F1 delivers a pitch which gets past F2 and goes to the backstop. B2 steps out of the batter's box (b) B2 attempts a drag bunt, but does not swing at the pitch, and ends up out of the batter's box (c) F2, after receiving the pitch, attempts to pick R1 off third base. B2 steps out of the batter's box. **RULING:** In (a) only if the umpire judges that B2 delayed the game, shall he call a strike on B2 for violation of the batter's box rule. In (b), neither the pitcher nor the batter has violated the rule. In (c), neither the catcher nor the batter has violated the rule.

7.3.1 SITUATION H: B1 is at bat with a three ball, one strike count when F1 delivers a pitch. Thinking the pitch is a ball, B1 takes a couple of steps toward first base. Hearing the umpire call the pitch a strike, B1 (a) returns immediately to the batter's box, or (b) is disgusted with the call and takes his time returning to the batter's box. **RULING:** In (a), the umpire will not call an additional strike on B1 as he did not delay the game. The count is 3-2. In (b), since B1 delayed the game, the umpire shall declare an additional strike for violation of the batter's box rule. B1 is out.

7.3.1 SITUATION I: With no runners on base, B1 is properly in the batter's box and F1 is on the pitcher's plate. F1 steps back off the plate to say something to F5. Seeing this, B1 steps out of the box (a) without requesting "Time" or (b) after requesting and being granted "Time" by the umpire. **RULING:** In (a), the umpire shall call a strike on the batter if his action has delayed the game. In (b), neither the pitcher nor the batter has violated any rule.

7.3.1 SITUATION J: B1 does not swing at a pitch, which F2 catches then drops to the ground. There are less than two outs. **RULING:** B1 may not leave the batter's box and delay the game without penalty because F2 caught the pitch and then dropped it.

Batting Out of Order

Each player of the team at bat shall become the batter and shall take his position within a batter's box, on either side of home plate, in the order in which his name appears on the lineup card as delivered to the umpire prior to the game. This order shall be followed during the entire game except that an entering substitute shall take the replaced player's place in the batting order. A batter is in proper order if he follows the player whose name precedes his in the lineup, even though such preceding batter may have batted out of order. An improper batter is considered to be at bat as soon as he is in the batter's box and the ball is live. When the improper batter's infraction is first discovered by either team, time may be requested and the improper batter replaced by the proper batter with the improper batter's ball and strike count still in effect, provided the infraction is detected before the improper batter is put out or becomes a base runner (7-1-1).

After the first inning, the first batter in each inning shall be the player whose name follows that of the last batter who completed his time at bat in the preceding inning (7-1-2).

Fundamental #10

The proper batter is always the one called out for batting-out-of- order infractions.

Batting Out of Order: Penalty

For batting out of order, a batter shall be called out, on appeal, when he fails to bat in his proper turn and another batter completes a time at bat in his place. Only the defensive team may appeal batting out of order after the batter has completed his time at bat (7-1-2 penalty 1).

When an improper batter becomes a runner or is put out and the defensive team appeals to the umpire before the first legal or illegal pitch, or, play or attempted play, or prior to an intentional base on balls or before the infielders leave the diamond if a half-inning is ending, the umpire shall declare the proper batter out and return all runners to the base occupied at the time of the pitch (7-1-2 penalty 2).

When an improper batter becomes a runner or is put out and a legal pitch or illegal pitch has been delivered to the succeeding batter, or an intentional base on balls has occurred, or all infielders have left the diamond if a half inning is ending, and before an appeal is made, the improper batter becomes the proper batter and the results of his time at bat become legal (7-1-2 penalty 3).

When the proper batter is called out because he has failed to bat in turn, the next batter shall be the batter whose name follows that of the proper batter thus called out (7-1-2 penalty 4).

When an improper batter becomes a proper batter because no appeal is properly made as above, the next batter shall be the batter whose name follows that of such legalized improper batter. The instant an improper batter's actions are legalized, the batting order picks up with the name following that of the legalized improper batter. When several players bat out of order before discovery so that a player's time at bat occurs while he is a runner, such player remains on base, but he is not out as a batter (7-1-2 penalty 5).

▨ Rationale

The offense cannot appeal after the plate appearance has been completed because there could be an unfair advantage gained. If the plate appearance is still in progress, there is no extra advantage to be gained.

Batting Out of Order: Caseplays

3.3.1 SITUATION VV: The scorekeeper or a fan informs the umpire of a player batting out of order. **RULING:** The umpire shall remain silent, unless the defense brings the infraction to his attention.

7.1.1 SITUATION A: With R1 on first, B7 is the next batter in the batting order, but B8 erroneously takes his place. The error is discovered by opposing team personnel (a) after B8 has received two strikes, or (b) after B8 has received a base on balls or is hit by a pitch, or (c) after B8 has hit a foul that is caught or has made a safe hit to advance R1, or (d) after a pitch has been delivered to B9. **RULING:** In (a), there is no penalty. B7 takes the place of B8 at the plate with a two-strike, no-ball count. If R1 should have advanced through a steal or wild pitch while the incorrect batter was batting, it is a legal advance. In (b) and (c), B7, the proper batter, is declared out. B8 is removed from base and bats again with no balls or strikes. R1 must return to first. In (d), no correction is made and B7 and B8 do not bat again until their regular times. B9 is now the proper batter.

7.1.1 SITUATION B: B7 erroneously bats instead of B5. With a count of three balls, two strikes on B7, the batting infraction is detected by (a) B5, or (b) F6, or (c) the coach of the other team or (d) B7. **RULING:** When the improper batter's infraction is first discovered by either team, time may be requested and the improper batter replaced by the proper batter with the improper batter's ball-and-strike count still in effect, provided the infraction is detected before the improper batter is put out, or becomes a baserunner. In all cases B5 will take the place of B7 at the plate with a count of three balls, two strikes.

7.1.1 SITUATION C: The batting order is B1, B2, B3, B4. If B3 erroneously bats in place of B1 and the batting infraction is not detected by anyone before a pitch to the next batter, is B2 or B4 the next correct batter? **RULING:** B4, since he follows B3 in the batting order. Neither B1 nor B2 may legally bat until their turns come again as listed.

7.1.1 SITUATION D: With R3 on third and two outs, improper batter B5 appears at bat. During F1's windup, R3 breaks for home base and beats the pitch there, and is called safe by the umpire. The pitch is not strike three or ball four. The team in the field then realizes that B5 is an improper batter and calls it to the attention of the umpire. **RULING:** The proper batter shall take his place at the plate with B5's accumulated ball-and-strike count. The run scored by R3 counts. The activity of improper batter B5 did not assist nor advance R3. The advance was made on merit. Of course, if the pitch to improper batter B5 had been strike three and the catcher either caught the ball or threw out B5 before he reached first base, then R3's run would not count.

7.1.2 SITUATION A: B1 singles and is followed by (a) improper batter, B3, who has a two-ball, two-strike count, or (b) improper batter, B3, who also singles. In (a) and (b), the defense discovers the irregularity at that point. **RULING:** In (a), the proper batter, B2, takes the place of B3 at the plate and assumes his accumulated count. In (b), B2 is out and any advance or score is nullified. B3 then becomes the next batter.

7.1.2 SITUATION B: B5 is batting instead of the proper batter, B4. The count is (a) 2-2 or (b) 1-1 and two outs. R3 is on third. On the pitch, B5 swings and misses, but F2 cannot come up with the ball. In (a), B5 reaches first base safely and in (a) and (b) R3 scores. Batting out of order is then appealed by the defense. **RULING:** In (a), B4 is declared out and since the third out was made by the batter-runner, who technically did not reach first base, R3's run does not count. In (b), R3's run counts. B4 would simply replace B5 and assume B5's ball-and-strike count.

Disconcerting Pitcher
A batter shall not disconcert the pitcher by stepping from the box on one side of home plate to the box on the other side while the pitcher is in position ready to pitch (7-3-3).

Disconcerting Pitcher: Penalty
The ball becomes dead immediately and the batter is out (7-3-3 penalty).

Intentional Deflection
A batter is out when he intentionally deflects a foul ball which could become fair (7 4 1i).

Interference by Batter
The batter-runner is out when he intentionally interferes with the catcher's attempt to field the ball after a third strike (8-4-1a).

A batter shall not interfere with the catcher's fielding or throwing by leaning over home plate, stepping out of the batter's box, making any other movement, including follow-through interference, which hinders actions at home plate or the catcher's attempt to play on a runner, or failing to make a reasonable effort to vacate a congested area when there is a throw to home plate and there is time for the batter to move away (7-3-5). The batter shall not commit backswing interference. The ball shall be declared dead (7-3-7 penalty).

◪ Rationale
There are numerous infractions that involve a batter altering or disrupting the flow and execution of the game, including follow-through interference. That particular type of interference was not addressed in the rules before 2014.

Interference by Batter: Penalty

When there are two outs, the batter is out. When there are not two outs and the runner is advancing to home plate, if the runner is tagged out, the ball remains live and interference is ignored. Otherwise, the ball is dead and the runner is called out. When an attempt to put out a runner at any other base is unsuccessful, the batter is out and all runners must return to bases occupied at the time of the pitch. If the pitch is a third strike and in the umpire's judgment interference prevents a possible double play (additional outs), two may be ruled out (7-3-5 penalty).

It is a delayed dead ball when there is interference by a batter. When the batter interferes with the catcher attempting to play on a runner, if an out does not result at the end of the catcher's throw, the ball shall become dead immediately (5-1-2a).

The batter is out when any member of the offensive team or coach interferes with a fielder who is attempting to field a foul fly ball (7-4-1f). The ball becomes dead immediately (5-1-1e).

The batter is out when any member of the offensive team or coach other than the runner(s) interferes with a fielder who is attempting to field a foul fly ball (7-4-1f). The ball becomes dead immediately (5-1-1e).

Interference by Batter: Caseplays

2.21.1 SITUATION C: With two outs, B3 strikes out, but F2 drops the ball, which rebounds into B3's base path. As B3 begins running to first, B3 accidentally kicks ball. **RULING:** B3 is not guilty of interference and the ball remains live, unless in the umpire's judgment B3 intentionally kicked the ball.

5.1.1 SITUATION T: Prior to the pitch with R1 on first base, B2 makes contact with the catcher while taking a practice swing. **RULING:** The ball is immediately dead.

* 5.1.2 SITUATION A: What is meant by "delayed dead ball"? **RULING:** The term applies to situations in which an infraction is not to be ignored, yet the play not be immediately dead. The umpire declares the ball dead after appropriate play- ing action occurs for the purpose of making an award(s) or enforcing a penalty. These situations include interference by a batter, batter being obstructed, ball being touched with detached player equipment, runner being obstructed or a coach physically assisting a runner. "Delayed dead ball" also applies when a bat- ter commits batter interference or when a fielder touches the ball with an illegal glove/mitt. The infraction is not to be ignored, the penalty results in an out being declared or base awarded (8-1-1e, 8-3-1c, 8-3-2, 8-3-3).

7.3.5 SITUATION A: With R2 going to third, B2 steps across home plate to hinder F2 who is fielding the ball or throwing to third, or attempting to throw to third. **RULING:** If R2 is tagged out despite the hindrance, the interference is ignored, and with less than two outs, the ball remains live. If R2 is not tagged out, B2 is declared out, and when there are less than two outs, the ball becomes dead immediately and all runners must return to the bases occupied at time of the pitch.

7.3.5 SITUATION B: With one out and R1 on first base, B3 swings and misses making contact with F2 on his follow-through. This action interferes with F2's throw to second base in an effort to put out advancing R1. **RULING:** B3 is out and R1 is returned to first base.

7.3.5 SITUATION C: B1 is currently up to bat with a 3-2 count, swings and misses at the pitch and contacts the catcher on his follow-through. The result of contact knocks F2 to the ground causing him to drop the ball. B1 runs to first base and is safe. **RULING:** B1 is ruled out.

7.3.5 SITUATION D: With R1 on first base and R2 on second base, one out and two strikes on B4, R1 and R2 attempt a double steal. B4 swings and misses the pitch and interferes with F2's attempt to throw out either R1 or R2. **RULING:** If in the umpire's judgment F2 could have made a putout on the runner(s) but cannot determine where the play was going to be made because of the nature of the interference, the umpire will then call out the runner nearest home plate, which is R2.

7.3.5 SITUATION E: With less than two outs, R2 on second and B2 at the plate, R2 attempts to steal third. In the process, B2, who bats right-handed, after swinging or not swinging at the pitch (a) makes no attempt to get out of the way of F2 throwing to third or (b) is unable to make an attempt to get out of the way of F2 throwing to third. As a result, F2 cannot make a play on the runner. Is B2 out, and must R2 return to second? **RULING:** B2 is not guilty of interference in (a) or (b). B2 is entitled to his position in the batter's box and is not subject to being penalized for interference unless he moves or re-establishes his position after F2 has received the pitch, which then prevents F2 from attempting to play on a runner. Failing to move so F2 can make a throw is not batter interference.

7.3.5 SITUATION F: With R3 on third, one out and two strikes on B3, B3 swings at and misses the pitch. The ball bounces off F2's glove into the air, where it is hit by B3's follow-through. The ball rolls to the backstop.

B3 reaches first base safely and R3 scores. **RULING:** The ball is dead immediately. B3 is out for interference and R3 returns to third base. A batter is entitled to an uninterrupted opportunity to hit the ball, just as the catcher is entitled to an uninterrupted opportunity to field the ball. Once the batter swings, he is responsible for his follow-through.

7.3.5 SITUATION G: With no outs and F1 in the set position, R3, who is on third base, attempts to steal home. F1 legally steps backward off the pitcher's plate and throws home. B2 hits the ball. **RULING:** Typically, batter's interference is a delayed dead ball in order to give the defense an opportunity to make an out on the initial putout attempt. Since the batter hit the ball, the defense was not afforded an opportunity to make a play. Therefore, the ball is declared dead immediately. R3 is out because of B2's interference (5-1-2a, 7-3-5, 8-4-2l).

7.3.5 SITUATION H: With no one out and R3 on third and R1 on first, R1 attempts to steal second. B3 interferes with F2. F2's throw is in time to retire R1. On the play, R3 scores. **RULING:** Since F2 was able to retire R1, the interference is ignored and the ball remains live. Therefore, R3's run counts (7-3-5).

7.3.5 SITUATION I: With a runner on third base and one out, B3 receives ball four for a base on balls. B3 takes several steps toward first base and then realizes he is still holding onto the bat. With his dugout on the third base side, he stops and tosses the bat in front of home plate towards his bench. As he tosses the bat, F2 throws the ball to third in an attempt to put out R3. The ball contacts the bat in mid-air and is deflected into dead-ball territory. **RULING:** The ball is dead. Interference is declared on the batter. If R3 had been attempting to steal home, R3 would be declared out and B3 awarded first base on the base on balls. If R1 was attempting to return to third base on the play, B3 is declared out for the interference (7-3-5).

7.3.5 SITUATION J: With R1 on first base, B2 swings and misses the pitch for strike one. His follow-through hits the catcher while he is attempting to throw out advancing R1. **RULING:** B2 is out, and R1 is returned to first base.

7.3.5 SITUATION K: With less than two outs, R3 attempts to steal home. B2 swings and misses the pitch for strike two. On the follow-through, his bat releases and strikes F2 in the facemask. **RULING:** The ball is dead and R3 is declared out. With two outs, the batter is declared out.

7.3.7 SITUATION: Prior to the pitch R1 is on first base, R2 is on second base, R3 is on third base. B4 makes contact with the catcher while taking a practice swing. **RULING:** The ball is immediately dead. No runners advance.

8.4.1 SITUATION H: B1 swings and misses a pitch for strike three. As F2 is attempting to catch the pitch, B1 hits F2 with the bat on the follow-through, hindering F2's attempt to catch the ball. **RULING:** B1 is out for interference.

8.4.1 SITUATION I: B1 swings and misses a pitch for strike three. The ball ricochets from F2's mitt and rolls several feet down the first-base line in fair territory. As F2 goes for the ball, B1 accidentally kicks or steps on the ball. **RULING:** If, in the judgment of the umpire, B1 did not intentionally interfere, then the ball remains live and the play stands.

Throwing Equipment

A coach, player, substitute, attendant or other bench personnel shall not carelessly throw a bat (3-3-1c) or deliberately throw a bat or helmet (3-3-1l). If the umpire judges it to be a careless throw, he shall, at the end of playing action, issue a warning to the coach of the team involved and the next offender on that team shall be ejected (3-3-1c penalty). If deliberate, the offender is ejected from the game. Failure to comply shall result in game being forfeited (3-3-1m penalty).

If the bat breaks and is hit by the ball or hits a runner or a fielder, no interference shall be called. If a whole bat is thrown and interferes with a defensive player attempting a play, interference will be called. The batter is out and runners return. If, in the umpire's judgment, interference prevented a possible double play, two players may be ruled out (7-3-6).

Did You Know? When the warning rule for throwing equipment was first adopted, it required separate warnings for each person on a team that violated. The team warning was adopted in 1987.

Throwing Equipment: Caseplays

3.3.1 SITUATION CC: After hitting a line drive toward F5, B1 releases the bat, which strikes F2 or the umpire. The act was judged by the umpire to be (a) intentional or (b) unintentional. **RULING:** In (a) and (b), this is a delayed dead-ball situation. In (a), the offender will be ejected from the game. If his fair hit ball is a base hit, he will be replaced with a substitute runner. In (b), the umpire will warn the coach of that player's team that the next player on that team to violate the rule shall be ejected from the game.

3.3.1 SITUATION LL: With Team B at bat (a) B1 receives ball four and on his way to first base, B1 carelessly flips the bat toward his bench, almost hitting the on-deck batter, or (b) after hitting a ground ball to F5, B1 flips the bat behind him as he begins his advance to first base and the bat strikes F2, or (c) F1, while backing up home plate, picks up a bat and tosses it out of the way, but in doing so almost hits the plate umpire. **RULING:** In (a), (b) and (c), the umpire shall issue a team warning to the head coach of the player committing the infraction (3-3-1c).

7.3.6 SITUATION: In hitting a slow roller to F5, the (a) whole bat slips out of his hands and interferes with F5 or (b) his bat breaks and hits the ball or F5 as F5 attempts to field the ball. **RULING:** In (a), the ball is dead immediately. B1 is declared out for interference, because B1 is responsible for controlling his bat and not allowing it to interfere with a defensive player attempting a play. In (b), there is no penalty and the ball remains live.

Topic 5
Baserunning

PlayPic®

Key Terms

A runner is a player of the team at bat who has finished his time at bat and has not yet been put out. The term includes the batter-runner and also any runner who occupies a base (2-30-2). A retired runner is a player of the team at bat who has been put out, or who has scored and is still in live-ball area (2-30-3).

An awarded base is the right to advance without a play being made. When bases are awarded, it is the responsibility of the runner to legally touch those bases (2-2-1).

Offensive interference is an act (physical or verbal) by the team at bat which interferes with, obstructs, impedes, hinders or confuses any fielder attempting to make a play; or when a runner creates malicious contact with any fielder, with or without the ball, in or out of the baseline; or a coach physically assists a runner during playing action (2-21-1).

Overrunning or oversliding is the act of a runner who, after touching the base to which he is advancing, allows his momentum to carry him past the base so that he loses contact with it (2-25-1).

A run is the score made by a runner who legally advances to and touches home plate (2-30-1).

A legal slide can be either feet first or head first. If a runner slides feet first, at least one leg and buttock shall be on the ground. If a runner slides, he must slide within reach of the base with either a hand or a foot (2-32-1).

Topic:
Becoming a Runner

A batter becomes a runner with the right to attempt to score by advancing to first, second, third and home bases in the listed order when:

- He hits a fair ball. He becomes a batter-runner when entitled to run (8-1-1a).
- He is charged with a third strike. If third strike is caught, he is out an instant after he becomes a runner (8-1-1b).
- He is awarded an intentional base on balls, or a fourth ball is called by the umpire (8-1-1c).
- A pitched ball hits his person or clothing, provided he does not strike at the ball (8-1-1d). If he permits the pitched ball to touch him, or if the umpire calls the pitched ball a strike, the hitting of the batter is disregarded except that the ball is dead. It is a strike or ball depending on location of the pitch (8-1-1d-1). If a batter's loose garment, such as a shirt that is not worn properly, is touched by a pitched ball, the batter is not entitled to first base (8-1-1d-2).

- The catcher or any other defensive player obstructs him. The coach or captain of the team at bat, after being informed by the umpire-in-chief of the obstruction, shall indicate whether or not he elects to decline the obstruction penalty and accept the resulting play. Such election shall be made before the next pitch (legal or illegal), before the award of an intentional base on balls, or before the infielders leave the diamond. Obstruction of the batter is ignored if the batter-runner reaches first and all other runners advance at least one base (8-1-1e).

In Simple Terms

A batter's turn at bat ends when he becomes a runner.

Any runner attempting to advance (i.e., steal or squeeze) on a catcher's obstruction of the batter shall be awarded the base he is attempting. If a runner is not attempting to advance on the catcher's obstruction, he shall not be entitled to the next base, if not forced to advance because of the batter being awarded first base. If obstruction is enforced, all other runners on the play will return to base occupied at time of the pitch. The batter is awarded first base, if he did not reach base (8-1-1e-1). If obstruction is not enforced, all other runners advance at their own risk (8-1-1e-2).

Becoming a Runner: Caseplays

8.1.1 SITUATION A: With R1 on first base, B2 bunts to F3 who fields the ball on the first bounce near the foul line. B2 stops and reverses toward home to avoid being tagged out by F3, who then throws to F6 for a force-out on R1, and the relay throw fails to retire B2 at first base. **RULING:** As long as B2 did not touch or run beyond home nor leave the base path to avoid a tag, the action is legal.

8.1.1 SITUATION B: F2 drops the third strike. B1 starts toward the dugout and F2 does not throw to first. B1 then makes a quick dash to first. **RULING:** If F2 does not throw to first, he risks failure to put out B1. However, B1 should be declared out for failure to attempt to reach first within a reasonable time if he does not reach the base before the time of the next pitch, he reaches his bench or dugout area, or a half inning is ended because the infielders have left the diamond (8-4-1i).

8.1.1 SITUATION D: When may a batter be hit by a pitch and not be awarded first base? **RULING:** (a) When the pitch is a strike; (b) when the batter does not attempt to avoid being hit; (c) with no runners on base, the pitch is illegal and is not ball four or (d) when the batter attempts to hit the pitch.

8.1.1 SITUATION E: R2 is on second. F2 obstructs B2 but he hits and reaches first safely but R2, who was not moving on the pitch, is thrown out at home plate. **RULING:** Obstruction is ignored since R2 advanced one base and B2 reached first base safely. R2's advance past third was at his own risk and he is out (5-1-2b, 8-3-3d).

8.1.1 SITUATION F: R2 is on second base. After B2 takes his position in batter's box, F2 clearly reaches out over home plate (a) prior to; (b) after F1 has made a movement that has committed him to pitch; or (c) to receive the pitch. **RULING:** It is catcher obstruction in both (b) and (c), and B2 is awarded first base and R2 is awarded third base only if he was stealing on the pitch. F2 may not catch the pitch until it has passed home plate. In (a), there is no violation provided F2 and his equipment are removed from the area over home plate before pitcher has made a movement that committed him to pitch (8-3-1c).

8.1.1 SITUATION H: R2 is on second with one out. F2 obstructs B3, but he hits a ground ball to F4 who throws him out. F3 overthrows third in attempt to retire R2 who scores on overthrow. **RULING:** The coach of the offense may elect to take the result of the play, scoring R2, or he may accept the catcher's obstruction penalty, placing R2 on second and B3 on first.

8.1.1 SITUATION K: With the bases loaded and the infield-fly rule in effect, F2 obstructs the batter's swing which results in a high fly ball. Umpires invoke the infield-fly rule. The ball is caught. **RULING:** Because of the result of the batter being awarded first base, each runner will be awarded one base because of the force situation.

8.1.1 SITUATION L: With R3 on third base and trying to score on a steal or squeeze play, F2 obstructs the batter's swing. **RULING:** This is defensive obstruction and R3 is awarded home. The batter is awarded first base.

COMMENT: If the catcher, or any other defensive player, obstructs the batter before he has become a batter-runner, the batter is awarded first base. If on such obstruction a runner is trying to score by a steal or a squeeze from third base, the play will be a delayed dead ball which results in the runner on third scoring and the batter being awarded first base. Runners not attempting to steal or not forced to advance remain on the bases occupied at the time of the obstruction.

8.1.1 SITUATION M: With R2 on second base, B2 is obstructed by F2 but he hits to F6 who throws B2 out at first base. F3 throws to third base to retire R2 who overslides third base. R2 was not attempting to steal on the pitch. **RULING:** This is defensive obstruction. B2 is awarded first base. R2 is returned to second base.

8.1.1 SITUATION N: R3 is on third base and R2 on second base, with one out. F2 obstructs B4 who hits a ground ball to F4. R2 was attempting to steal third, even though third was occupied. B4 is thrown out at first on the play. **RULING:** B4 did not reach first safely, so the coach has the option of taking the play or the penalty. If he takes the penalty, B4 is awarded first. R2 is awarded third because he was attempting to steal on the pitch, and R3 is forced to advance to home.

8.1.1 SITUATION O: With two outs, R2 attempts to steal third. F2 obstructs B4 as B4 swings. F2 overthrows F5 at third trying to get R2. R2 attempts to score and is thrown out at the plate by F7. **RULING:** The coach of the team at bat, after being informed of F2's obstruction, elects to have the penalty for defensive obstruction enforced. Therefore, B4 is awarded first base and R2 is awarded third base (8-1-1e).

8.1.1 SITUATION R: B1 hits a fair ball in front of home plate. Both the batter-runner and catcher make contact while trying to complete their respective responsibilities. **RULING**: If either player attempts to alter the play, interference or obstruction shall be called depending on who violates the rule. If neither player attempts to alter the play, no call shall be made.

Topic:
Touching Bases

Acquiring Right to Base

A runner acquires the right to the proper unoccupied base if he touches it before he is out. He is then entitled to this base until he is put out, or until he legally touches the next base while it is unoccupied or until a following runner is forced to advance to the base he has occupied. A runner need not vacate his base to permit a fielder to catch a fly ball in the infield, but he may not interfere (8-2-8).

If two runners are on the same base, at the same time and both are tagged, the following runner is declared out. Exception: On a force play situation, the runner who was forced to advance shall be declared out when tagged (8-2-8a).

◪ Rationale

Only one runner has legal standing at a base. On a force play, the runner loses his right to the base and must attempt to advance. If the runner is not forced, he still has right to that bag, so the following runner would be called out.

Fly Ball Caught

If a fair or foul batted ball is caught, other than a foul tip, each base runner shall touch his base after the batted ball has touched a fielder (8-2-4).

Any runner is out when he does not retouch his base before a fielder tags him out or holds the ball while touching such base after a fly ball is caught. The umpire may also call him out at end of playing action upon proper and successful appeal (8-4-2i).

Overrunning First Base

A batter-runner who reaches first base safely and then overruns or overslides may immediately return without liability of being put out provided he does not attempt or feint an advance to second. (8-2-7).

8.2.7 SITUATION A: The leadoff hitter has a 3-2 count. There is a check-swing situation and the umpire calls ball four. The base umpire upholds the plate umpire's decision and B1 overruns first base. In (a), the defense tags the batter-runner returning to first base. In (b), the defense tags the batter-runner after the batter/runner attempts to go to second base before returning to first base. **RULING:** In (a), the batter-runner is safe. In (b), the batter-runner is out.

8.2.7 SITUATION B: The leadoff hitter has a 3-2 count. There is a check-swing situation and the plate umpire calls ball four. The base umpire reverses the call on appeal and calls strike three. B1 overruns first base. In (a), the defense tags the batter-runner returning to first base. In (b), the defense tags the batter-runner after the batter-runner attempts to go to second base before returning to first base. **RULING:** In (a), the batter/runner is safe. In (b), the batter/runner is out.

Runner Advancing

An advancing runner shall touch first, second, third and then home plate in order, including awarded bases (8-2-1).

When the ball becomes dead, any runner may advance when awarded a base(s) for an act which occurred before the ball became dead provided any base in (b) above is retouched and all bases are touched in their proper order (5-2-2c).

Did You Know?

Prior to 1981, a runner was not required to touch all bases on an award. A runner awarded third base while standing on first could cut across the diamond and did not have to touch second.

Runner Advancing: Caseplays

8.2.1 SITUATION A: With R1 on first, B2 hits safely to right field. An overthrow at first (a) goes into the stands or (b) hits the fence behind home plate and rebounds to the catcher. In going to third, R1 misses second base and has passed second or is approaching second when ball leaves the hand of F9. **RULING:** In (a), R1 will be awarded home if he is past second base or awarded third base if he has not reached second base when the throw leaves the hand of F9. R1 is responsible for touching all bases regardless of whether or not the bases are awarded. At the end of the play, upon a proper defensive appeal, the umpire will call R1 out for any base he did not touch. In (b) upon a proper defensive appeal, the umpire will call R1 out for any base he misses in advancing.

8.2.1 SITUATION B: With R2 on second base, R1 on first base and no outs, B3 doubles. Both runners cross home plate, but R2 fails to touch third and (a) R2 gets back to third before ball arrives at third or (b) after all play has ended, the defensive team properly appeals the missed base by R2 and the umpire calls him out for failing to touch third base. Does run by R1 count? **RULING:** In both (a) and (b), the run by R1 counts. In (a), if there is no defensive appeal, the play will stand. If the defense properly appeals, R2 will be called out as he cannot return to correct a missed base when a following runner has scored behind him.

8.2.1 SITUATION C: With R1 on first base, B2 hits safely to center field. (a) The ball goes over the fence in flight, (b) bounces over the fence or (c) is fielded by F8 after which his overthrow at first goes into the stands. Both runners advance, but R1 fails to touch second or B2 fails to touch first. **RULING:** In (a) and (b), each –runner is awarded bases when the ball goes out of play. In (a), R1 and B2 will be awarded home. In (b), R1 will be awarded third base and B2 second base. In (c), R1 and B2 will be awarded two bases from where each was located when the ball left the hand of F8. However, the runners must touch all awarded bases or risk being called out by the umpire upon a proper defensive appeal for not touching each base while advancing (8-3-3).

Runner Returning

A returning runner shall retouch the bases in reverse order. If the ball is dead because of an uncaught foul, it is not necessary for a returning runner to retouch intervening bases. The umpire will not make the ball live until the runner returns to the appropriate base (8-2-2).

Runner Returning: Caseplay

8.2.1 SITUATION E: With R1 on first, B2 hits a long foul fly down the right field line that F9 cannot catch. R1, who is almost at third, does not retouch second on his way back to first. **RULING:** R1 is not out. If the ball is dead because of being an uncaught foul, it is not necessary for a returning runner to retouch intervening bases.

Topic:
Scoring Runs

A runner scores one run each time he legally advances to and touches first, second, third and then home plate before there are three outs to end the inning (9-1-1).

A run is not scored if the runner advances to home plate during action in which the third out is made by the batter-runner before he touches first base; by another runner being forced out; by a preceding runner who is declared out upon appeal because he failed to touch one of the bases or left a base too soon on a caught fly ball; when a third out is declared during a play resulting from a valid defensive appeal, which results in a force out (this out takes precedence if enforcement of it would negate a score); or when there is more than one out declared by the umpire which terminates the half inning, the defensive team may select the out which is to its advantage (9-1-1a through e).

If a fielder illegally obstructs a runner and is responsible for failure of that runner to reach home plate, the umpire has authority to award home plate to that runner (9-1-1 note 1).

When the winning run is scored in the last half inning of a regulation game, or in the last half of an extra inning, as the result of a base on balls, hit batter or any other play with the bases loaded which forces the runner on third base to advance, the umpire shall not declare the game over until all runners have advanced to the next base (9-1-1 note 2).

Runs Scoring on Third Out

If a runner leaves a base too soon on a caught fly ball and returns in an attempt to retag, this is considered a time play and not a force out. If the appeal is the third out, all runs scored by runners in advance of the appealed runner and scored ahead of the legal appeal would count (8-2-6h).

An appeal may be made after the third out as long as it is made properly and the resulting appeal is an apparent fourth out (8-2-6i).

If a baserunning infraction is the third out, runs scored by the following runner(s) would not count. With two outs, if the base missed was the first to which the batter or runner was forced to advance, no runs would score. When a runner is legally returning after a fly ball has been caught, he can be put out by being tagged with the ball by a defensive player or merely by the defensive player with the ball touching the base occupied by the runner at the time of the pitch (8-2-6k).

Fundamental #11

A run can never score if the third out was made by the batter-runner failing to reach first base or any other runner before reaching the base to which he was forced.

Runs Scoring on Third Out: Caseplays

5.2.1 SITUATION D: With two outs and R3 on third base and R2 on second base, B5 hits a line drive that scores both R3 and R2. As B5 leaves the batter's box, his knee goes out and he collapses to the ground, and is unable to advance. The ball is relayed to first base. **RULING:** B5 will be declared out and both runs nullified, since the third out resulted because B5 did not reach first base safely.

8.4.2 SITUATION R: With R3 on third base, R1 on first and two outs, B5 hits a fair slow roller toward first base. B5 interferes with F3, who is trying to field the ball. However, R3 scores before the interference. Does the run score since R3 touched home plate before the interference? **RULING:** The run does not score if the runner advances during action in which the third out is made by the batter-runner before he touches first base (9-1-1a).

9.1.1 SITUATION A: R2 is on second and R1 on first with one out. B4 hits a long fly that appears to be uncatchable, but is caught by F8. R2 advances home but misses third base. R1 fails to retouch first base and advances to third base. **RULING:** Upon proper appeal, the umpire will rule both R2 and R1 out for failing to touch third base and retouching first base, respectively. The defensive team is allowed to select the out that is to its advantage. Defense selects R2's out and cancels his run (8-2 Penalty).

9.1.1 SITUATION B: With one out, R3 is on third and R2 is on second base when B4 hits a long fly ball that is caught by F8. R3 remains in contact with his base but R2 has nearly advanced to third. The throw to F4 arrives at second base ahead of R2's return. **RULING:** R2 is out for the third out. If R3 scored before R2 was retired, the run counts. The inning ended with a play in which the third out was not a force out. Hence, it was a timing play.

9.1.1 SITUATION C: With two outs and R1 on first, B4 hits the next pitch for an inside-the-park home run. In circling the bases, B4 misses second. **RULING:** When all action stops, upon appeal, the umpire will rule B4 out for failing to touch second base. The run scored by R1 will count. Had the infraction been the missing of first base and B4 ruled out, the run by R1 would be canceled (8-2-1).

9.1.1 SITUATION D: With two outs, R3 on third base and R1 on first base, B5 receives a fourth ball. An overthrow at third permits R3 to reach home. In advancing (a) R1 fails to touch second or (b) B5 goes to second base but fails to touch first base. **RULING:** Upon appeal, the umpire will rule R1 out for failing to touch second base in (a) and B5 out for failing to touch first base in (b). The run by R3 will not count in either case (8-2 Penalty).

9.1.1 SITUATION E: With R3, R2 and R1 on third, second and first, respectively, B5 hits a fly ball to F8 for the second out. All base runners tag up and try to advance one base. F8's throw to F5 retires R2 for the third out, but after R3 has scored. R1 did not tag up and was detected leaving first base early, and at the conclusion of all action, upon appeal, the umpire declares R1 out (fourth out). Does the run by R3 count? **RULING:** The only time a fourth (or fifth) out would take precedence is if it negates a score(s). In the above case the fourth out would not negate R3's run, because R1's out was not a force out.

9.1.1 SITUATION F: R3 is on third with two outs and two strikes on B4. As F1 winds up, R3 starts to steal home. B4 swings at the ball but misses. The catcher drops the ball. While he is looking for the ball, R3 crosses home plate, after which the catcher recovers the ball and throws B4 out at first. Does the run score? **RULING:** No. The batter-runner made the third out without reaching first base safely.

9.1.1 SITUATION G: With R3 on third base, R2 on second base and R1 on first base and one out, B5 hits safely to right field. R3 scores, R2 misses third base and scores and R1 is thrown out at third base. At the end of playing action, time is called, the defense makes a proper appeal and the umpire declares R2 out. How many runs score? **RULING:** No runs score since the putout of R2 at third base was a force out and also the third out of the inning (9-1-1d).

9.1.1 SITUATION H: With the bases loaded and one out, B5 hits a line drive to the right field fence. R3 and R2 score. R1 is thrown out at the plate. B5 goes to third but misses first. **RULING:** Upon appeal, B5's out for missing first was the third out. No runs scored.

 COMMENT: No runs can score if the third out is a force out or if the batter does not reach first (8-2-6k Penalty).

9.1.1 SITUATION J: With no outs and the bases loaded, B1 grounds into a 6-4-3 double play as R3 and R2 score. R2 misses third base and is declared out for the third out upon proper appeal. **RULING:** R2's out is not a force out for the third out, therefore, R3 scores.

9.1.1 SITUATION K: With the bases loaded and one out, B5 hits a home run out of the park. While advancing to second base, B5 passes R1 (force is removed) and B5 is declared out. R1 fails to touch second base, but touches third base on his way home. **RULING:** For missing a base or leaving a base too soon, the umpire will declare the runner out upon proper appeal. R3 and R2 score, because R1's out was not a force out for the third out (8-2 Penalty).

Topic:
Awarded Bases

Ball Dead
"Time" shall be called by the umpire and play is suspended when the umpire suspends play for the awarding of a base after an infraction (5-2-1f).

Determining Point of Award
If an award is the penalty for an infraction such as a balk, use of detached player equipment, or an illegal glove/mitt, the award is from the base occupied at the time of the infraction.

If any pitch (batted or unbatted) is followed by a dead ball before the pitcher is in position for the next pitch and before there is any throw by the fielding team, any award is from the base occupied at the time of the pitch.

When a runner, who is returning to touch a base after a batted ball has been caught is prevented from doing so because a thrown live ball has become dead, his award shall be from the base he occupied at the time of the pitch. In any situations other than those listed above, on a batted ball which is the first play by an infielder, all runners including the batter-runner are awarded two bases from their positions at the time of the pitch. For purposes of this rule, the act of fielding is not considered a play. If every runner, including the batter-runner, has advanced one base at the time of the first play, the award is two bases from the time of the throw. For any subsequent play by an infielder or for any throw by an outfielder, the award is two bases from the time of the throw (8-3-5).

Fundamental #12

Base awards on throws into dead ball territory are made from either the time of the pitch or throw. The location of a runner when the ball enters dead-ball territory does not matter.

Determining Point of Award: Caseplay

8.3.3 SITUATION D: There is an overthrow at first. Are bases always awarded and from which base is an award started? **RULING:** Bases are awarded only in case something happens to cause the ball to become dead, such as the ball going into the stands or dugout. If the ball does become dead, the number of bases awarded is indicated in 8-3-3 and the place for starting is indicated in 8-3-4. If a pitch or any pitcher's throw from pitching position becomes dead, it results in the award of only one base. If the pitcher fields a batted ball and his overthrow (first play following a pitch) becomes dead, he is considered the same as any other infielder and his overthrow results in the awarding of two bases measured from the time of the pitch (8-3-3c,d, 8-3-5).

 **Did You Know?** Fielding the ball and feinting a throw are not plays for the purpose of determining the first play by an infielder. Making a throw, attempting a tag or trying for an unassisted force out are plays.

Missed Base During Awards

An appeal must be honored even if the base missed was before or after an award (8-2-6g).

Missed Base During Awards: Caseplays

8.2.6 SITUATION C: R1 is on first when B2 hits a fly ball to F9 who overthrows first in an attempt to double up R1. The throw goes wild and into the dugout. R1 is awarded second and third (a) R1 fails to retouch first, or (b) R1 fails to touch second on his way to third. **RULING:** Upon proper defensive appeal, the umpire will declare R1 out in (a) and (b).

8.2.6 SITUATION D: B1 singles to right. At the time of F9's throw, B1 is past first base. The throw goes into the dugout. The umpire awards B1 third base. B1 cuts across infield to third. **RULING:** Upon proper defensive appeal, the umpire will declare B1 out for failure to touch second.

Topic:
Number of Bases Awarded

One-Base Awards

A batter-runner is awarded first base if he is a runner because he receives a base on balls (intentional or not), he is hit by a pitch (provided he does not strike at the ball) or the catcher or any other defensive player obstructs him (8-1-2a). A batter-runner is also awarded first base if his fair ball, other than an infield fly, becomes dead and provided a preceding runner or retired runner does not interfere in such a way as to prevent a potential double play (8-1-2b).

Unless awarded first base as above, a batter-runner is entitled to first base only if he reaches it before being tagged out or thrown out or called out for hitting an infield fly (8-1-2 note).

Each runner other than the batter-runner is awarded one base:

• When there is a balk or a pitch strikes a runner (8-3-1a).

• When he is forced from the base he occupies by a following runner who must advance because a batter receives a fourth ball, is hit by a pitched ball or hits a fair ball which becomes dead (8-3-1b).

• When he is attempting to steal or he is forced from the base he occupies by a batter-runner or runner who must advance because the catcher or any fielder obstructs the batter, such as stepping on or across home or pushing the batter to reach the pitch or touching the bat. Instances may occur when the infraction may be ignored (8-3-1c).

• When a pitch or any throw by the pitcher from his pitching position on his plate goes into a stand or bench or over or through or lodges in a fence or backstop or touches a spectator or lodges in an umpire's or catcher's equipment.

• With less than two outs, when the batter hits a fair or foul ball (fly or line drive) which is caught by a fielder, who then leaves the field of play by stepping with both feet or by falling into a bench, dugout, stand, bleacher or over any boundary or barrier such as a fence, rope, chalk line or pre-game determined imaginary boundary line (8-3-3d).

• If, in the umpire's judgment, the runner was attempting to advance at the time the ball becomes lodged in an offensive player's uniform or equipment. If the lodged ball occurs during play when the batter-runner was attempting to reach first base, the batter-runner will be awarded first base. Preceding runners will be awarded bases needed to complete the award (8-3-3f).

One-Base Awards: Caseplays

5.2.1 SITUATION B: The third strike by B1 is missed by F2. The ball lodges between his body and protector. While F2 hunts for the ball, B1 continues to second. **RULING:** The umpire shall call "Time" and give the dead-ball signal as soon as it is clear that the ball is trapped behind F2's chest protector. B1 is entitled to first base only since he was en route there when the ball became dead. Had there been other base runners, they would have been awarded one base as well.

8.1.1 SITUATION C: With the count of ball three on B2 and (a) R2 on second or (b) none on base, the next pitch is ball four and goes into the stands. **RULING:** In both (a) and (b), B2 is entitled to first base only and in (a), R2 is awarded third base (8-3-3d).

8.3.1 SITUATION A: With R3, R2 and R1 on third, second and first bases, respectively, and (a) two outs or (b) one out, R3 attempts to steal home. With a 1-2 count, the pitch hits R3 while the ball is in the strike zone. **RULING:** In both (a) and (b), ball becomes dead immediately and batter is out because of third strike. In (a), no run is scored since batter became third out. In (b), all base runners are awarded one base from where they were at time of pitch and R3 scores (5-1-1a, 6-1-4, 8-1-1 note 1, 9-1-1a).

8.3.1 SITUATION B: R3 is on third and R2 is on second. R3 breaks from third in an attempted suicide squeeze play. As B3 attempts to bunt, F2 touches tip of bat or steps across home plate, catches the ball and tags R3. R2 remains on second. **RULING:** Catcher obstruction. The umpire awards B3 first base and R3 home. Since R2 was not attempting to steal or was forced, he remains on second.

8.3.1 SITUATION C: R2 is on second when F2 tips the bat of B2 who swings and misses the pitch. **RULING:** The umpire awards B2 first base. Since he was not attempting to steal nor forced, R2 remains on second.

8.3.3 SITUATION A: Batter hits toward F6. The throw from F6 lodges in batter-runner's shirt prior to batter-runner touching first base. **RULING:** Ball is dead immediately. Batter-runner is awarded first base. All other runners move up if forced to advance because of the award to batter-runner.

8.3.3 SITUATION B: The batter hits a single to right. The batter-runner is caught in a rundown between first and second. During the rundown, the ball becomes lodged in the batter-runner's shirt while he is a) headed toward first or b) headed toward second. **RULING:** The ball is dead immediately in both cases, (a) batter-runner is placed on first; in (b) batter-runner is awarded second. In either case, all other runners move up, if forced to advance because of the award to batter-runner.

8.3.3 SITUATION K: F1 throws a pitch that strikes F2 on a shinguard and rolls away. The ball (a) has stopped moving and F2, attempting to pick it up, kicks it into dead-ball territory, or (b) is rolling and deflects off F2's glove into dead-ball territory, or (c) F2 intentionally kicks the ball into dead-ball territory. **RULING:** In (a), F2 applied the force that caused the ball to go into dead-ball territory, so the kick (throw) results in all runners being awarded two bases from the base occupied at the time of the kick (throw). The pitch is considered to be over. In (b), the force on the pitch caused the ball to go into dead-ball territory, so the award to all runners is one base from the base occupied at the time of the pitch. In (c), if the umpire judges the pitch would have gone into dead-ball territory without the kick, one base is awarded from the time of the pitch. If the kick is judged to have caused the ball to go into dead-ball territory, two bases are awarded from the time of the throw/kick.

8.3.5 SITUATION A: With runners on bases, the ball becomes dead in a dugout resulting from a (a) throw by F1 while in contact with the plate, (b) a pitch that caroms off shinguard of F2 or (c) F5 falling into the dugout following the catch of a batted fly ball. What are the awards and for what bases? **RULING:** Award one base in each. Awards are from bases occupied at the time of throw in (a) and at the time of the pitch in (b) and (c).

8.3.5 SITUATION E: R3, R2 and R1 are on third, second and first bases, respectively. There are two outs and a count of three balls, two strikes on B6. As F1 starts pumping, runners begin to advance. F1 pumps three times and umpire signals dead ball. The violation occurs after R2 and R1 each have advanced one base. F1 delivers following his violation and B6 swings and misses a third strike. **RULING:** Balk. Each runner is awarded one base from where he was at the time of the pitch when F1 started his pumping motion. Count remains three balls, two strikes on B6.

Two-Base Awards

Each runner is awarded two bases if a fair batted or thrown ball becomes dead because of bouncing over or passing through a fence, or lodges in a defensive player's or umpire's equipment or uniform.

Each runner is awarded two bases if a live thrown ball, including a pitch, is touched by an illegal glove or mitt, or by detached player equipment which is thrown, tossed, kicked or held by a fielder.

Each runner is awarded two bases if a live ball goes into a stand for spectators, dugout or player's bench or over or through or lodges in a fence and it is not thrown by a pitcher from his plate (8-3-3c).

When two runners are between the same bases on an overthrow into dead ball territory, the lead runner receives two bases and the following runner is awarded one, since both runners cannot share the same awarded base. Runners between second and third would score, because the award does not result in both runners occupying the same base (8-3-3c note).

Two-Base Awards: Caseplays

5.1.1 SITUATION Q: With a runner on first base, on a bounding ball F6 lays out and catches the ball in his glove. After several attempts to remove the ball from his glove, he is finally successful after the batter-runner acquires first base. **RULING:** There is no base awarded; the play stands. The ball was temporarily stuck, not lodged, in F6's glove.

8.3.3 SITUATION C: R2 is on second and R1 is on first when B3 hits ground ball to F6. F6 fields the ball, steps on second for a force on R1 advancing from first, and then throws wildly to F3. F3 tosses his glove into the air, intentionally hitting the ball. **RULING:** R1 is out. Both R2 and B3 are awarded two bases from their positions on base when the detached mitt or glove of F3 touched the thrown ball. In this situation or any other situation where a detached glove or mitt touches a ball, prior to the ball becoming dead because of going into a dead-ball area, the rule that applies to detached player equipment prevails. If the detached glove or mitt touches the ball after the ball has become dead because of going into a dead-ball area, the ruling governing detached player equipment has no bearing.

8.3.3 SITUATION E: With runners on first and third bases, the pitcher assumes his position on the pitcher's plate in the set position with the ball in both hands in front of his body. R3 makes a break towards the plate. F1 steps clearly backward off the pitcher's plate. F1 then runs several steps towards home plate and throws the ball to the catcher while R3 continues to advance. The throw bounces away from F2 and into the stands. How far should R1, who is on first, be allowed to advance? **RULING:** When the pitcher legally stepped clearly backward off the pitcher's plate, he became an infielder and his throw into the stands resulted in all base runners being awarded two bases from where they were at the time the throw left the fielder's hand. R1 would be awarded third base in this situation.

8.3.3 SITUATION H: B1 hits a long fly ball to left field. F7 goes back to the fence, leaps, but is not able to touch the fly ball. The ball then rebounds off the fence, strikes the fielder's glove and ricochets over the fence in fair territory. Is this a home run or ground-rule double? **RULING:** This would be considered a ground-rule double. To be a home run, the ball must clear the fence in flight. Action secondary to the hit (ball ricocheting off the fence and then off the fielder's glove) caused the ball to go into dead-ball area. Therefore, the hit shall be ruled a ground-rule double.

8.3.3 SITUATION I: R3 is on third and R1 is on first with one out. B4 hits a fly ball that is caught in right-center field. Both runners tag to advance. R3 legally tags and scores after the catch. R1 stays on first as the batter-runner rounds first and makes a break toward second. F8 throws wildly to F4 who deflects the ball into dead ball territory. **RULING:** Legal. B4 was out with the catch. Each runner would be awarded two bases from the time the ball left the hand of F8. Therefore, R3 scores and R1 is on third.

8.3.3 SITUATION J: B1 singles to right field, (a) the ball rolls to a stop and F9, attempting to pick it up, kicks the ball into dead-ball territory or (b) the bouncing ball strikes F9 on the leg and deflects into dead-ball territory. **RULING:** In (a), F9 applied the impetus that caused the ball to go into dead-ball territory, which is the same as if he had thrown it there. The award to any runner is two bases from the base occupied at the time of the kick (throw). In (b), the force on the batted ball caused the ball to go into dead-ball territory, so the award to any runner is two bases from the base occupied at the time of the pitch.

8.3.3 SITUATION K: F1 throws a pitch that strikes F2 on a shinguard and rolls away. The ball (a) has stopped moving and F2, attempting to pick it up, kicks it into dead-ball territory, or (b) F2 intentionally kicks the ball into dead-ball territory. **RULING:** In (a), F2 applied the force that caused the ball to go into dead-ball territory, so the kick (throw) results in all runners being awarded two bases from the base occupied at the time of the kick (throw). The pitch is considered to be over. In (b), if the umpire judges the pitch would have gone into dead-ball territory without the kick, one base is awarded from the time of the pitch. If the kick is judged to have caused the ball to go into dead-ball territory, two bases are awarded from the time of the kick (throw).

8.3.3 SITUATION L: With two outs and R2 on second, B4 strikes out, but the pitch gets by F2 and is rolling toward the backstop. F2 chases the ball down and stops it with his mask. **RULING:** This is a delayed dead-ball situation. R2 is awarded two bases from the time of the infraction at the end of playing action.

8.3.5 SITUATION A: With runners on bases, the ball becomes dead in a dugout resulting from a (a) throw by F9 on a base hit or (b) throw by F1 not preceded by a pitch while not in contact with the plate. What are the awards and for what bases? **RULING:** Award two bases in each case from the time of the throw.

8.3.5 SITUATION B: On hit-and-run single, R1 has reached and passed second before the ball batted by B2 bounces over or through the fence in right field. **RULING:** The award of two bases is from first for R1 and from home plate for B2.

8.3.5 SITUATION C: With two outs and R1 on first, the third strike is dropped and rolls along first base line enabling B4 to reach first and R1 second while F2 is trying to scoop up the ball. F2 then overthrows third attempting to put out R1 and ball goes into the stands. **RULING:** Since all runners have advanced one base before F2's overthrow, awards are measured from the bases occupied at the time of the throw. Both R1 and B4 are awarded two bases from the base each occupied when the ball left the hand of F2 on the overthrow.

8.3.5 SITUATION D: With R1 on first base and one out, B3 hits a looper to right field. R1 goes halfway to second and B3 rounds first base. F9 traps the ball. However, believing he has caught the ball, F9 throws to first with intentions of doubling off R1. His throw is wild and goes into dead-ball territory. What bases are awarded? **RULING:** In this instance, there were two runners between first and second bases when the ball left F9's hand. The runners will be placed on second and third, because no runner can be awarded more than two bases in this situation. This means, technically, B3 is awarded only one base.

8.3.5 SITUATION F: With R2 on second and R1 on first base, B3 hits a fly ball in shallow right field area between F3, F4 and F9. All three players converge on the ball as it falls safely but is fielded on the bounce by F4. R2 is beyond third, R1 beyond second and B3 is beyond first when F4 throws to home base (or third base). Ball bounces into stand. **RULING:** Though F4's throw was the first play by an infielder following a pitch, award each runner (including batter-runner) two bases from the base he occupied when the ball left the hand of F4, since all runners already have advanced one base. If B3 had not reached first base, award all runners two bases from their location at the time of the pitch.

8.3.5 SITUATION G: B1 hits a hard line drive to F5, who knocks the ball down. F5 recovers and overthrows first base and the ball goes into dead-ball territory. At the time of the throw, B1 had not yet touched first. **RULING:** B1 is awarded second.

8.3.5 SITUATION H: R1 is at first when B2 hits to F6, who feints a throw to second and then throws the ball into the dugout. At the time of the throw, R1 has touched second but B2 has not touched first. **RULING:** Because the feint by F6 is not considered a play, R1 is awarded third base and B2 is awarded second base. The award is based on the positions of R1 and B2 at the time of the pitch.

8.3.5 SITUATION I: R1 is at first when B2 hits to F6, who throws to second for one out. F4's relay to first goes into dead-ball territory. At the time of the throw, B2 has (a) not touched first or (b) touched first. **RULING:** Because F4's throw was the second play by an infielder, the award is from the time of the throw. Therefore, in (a), B2 is awarded second base. In (b), B2 is awarded third base.

8.3.5 SITUATION J: R2 is at second when B2 hits to F6, who tries to tag R2 but misses. F6 then overthrows first into dead-ball area. R2 remains at second, but B2 has touched first at the time of the throw. **RULING:** Because it was the second play by an infielder, R2 is awarded home, and B2 is awarded third.

8.3.5 SITUATION K: R1 is at first when B2 hits to F6, who runs toward second for the force out. Realizing he cannot beat R1 to the base, he throws to first and the ball goes into dead-ball territory. At the time of the throw, R1 had touched second, but B2 had not touched first. **RULING:** F6's attempt to put out R1 at second is considered a play. The overthrow by F6 is considered a second play. Because it was the second play by an infielder, R1 is awarded home and B2 is awarded second.

8.3.5 SITUATION L: B1 hits a slow roller to F5 who makes no play. The batter-runner feints an attempt to go to second and F5's subsequent throw goes into dead-ball territory. **RULING:** B1 is awarded third.

Though F5's throw was the first play by an infielder, all runners (in this case, only the batter-runner) have already advanced a base. Therefore, the awards are measured from the time of the throw.

Three-Base Awards

Each runner is awarded three bases if a batted ball (that is not a prevented home run) is touched by an illegal glove or mitt, or by detached player equipment which is thrown, tossed, kicked or held by a fielder, provided the ball when touched is on or over fair ground, or is a fair ball while on or over foul ground, or is over foul ground in a situation such that it might become a fair ball (8-3-3b).

Three-Base Awards: Caseplay

8.3.3 SITUATION F: B1 hits a fair line drive over the head of F5, who jumps high attempting to field ball. As he jumps upward, his glove accidentally dislodges from his hand and touches ball. If the umpire decides the detached glove was not thrown or tossed at contacted ball, there is no penalty. If the umpire should decide the act was deliberate, he shall advance B1 to third.

Four-Base Awards

Each runner is awarded four bases (home) if a fair ball goes over a fence in flight or hits a foul pole above the fence, or is prevented from going over by being touched by a spectator, or is touched by an illegal glove/mitt or detached player equipment which is thrown, tossed, kicked or held by a fielder (8-3-3a)

Advancing Beyond Awarded Base

Illegal use of detached player equipment or an illegal glove/ mitt does not cause ball to immediately become dead. If each runner advances to or beyond the base which he would reach as a result of the award, the infraction is ignored. Any runner who advances beyond the base he would be awarded does so at his own risk and may be put out (8-3-4).

Obstruction Awards

When a runner is obstructed while advancing or returning to a base, the umpire shall award the obstructed runner and each other runner affected by the obstruction the bases they would have reached, in his opinion, had there been no obstruction. If the runner achieves the base he was attempting to acquire, then the obstruction is ignored. The obstructed runner is awarded a minimum of one base beyond his position on base when the obstruction occurred. If any preceding runner is forced to advance by the awarding of a base or bases to an obstructed runner, the umpire shall award this preceding runner the necessary base or bases. Malicious contact supersedes obstruction. When obstruction occurs, the umpire points and calls "obstruction." If an award is to be made, the ball becomes dead when time is taken to make the award (8-3-2).

Fundamental #13

Obstruction requires the award of at least one base.

Obstruction Awards: Caseplays

8.3.2 SITUATION A: R2 and R1 are on second and first, respectively, when B3 beats out an infield hit. R1 advances to and past third toward home. In a rundown, F5 obstructs R2. However, R2 gets back to third safely and finds R1 there. F5 tags R1 with the ball. **RULING:** Umpire shall call "Obstruction!" when the infraction by F5 occurs. At the conclusion of playing action, he declares the ball dead, then awards home to R2 and allows R1 to remain at third. When a runner is obstructed, the obstructed runner is awarded a minimum of one base beyond his position on base when the obstruction occurred.

8.3.2 SITUATION B: While (a) B1 is moving toward second base on a hit to right-center field, F6, who does not have the ball in his possession, fakes a tag on B1 or (b) B1 is returning to first base and F3, who does not have the ball, fakes a tag on B1. **RULING:** In both cases it is ruled obstruction, and B1 is awarded second base or if, in the umpire's judgment, the runner could have advanced farther had obstruction not occurred, the umpire could award additional bases.

8.3.2 SITUATION C: F2 is in the path between third base and home plate while waiting to receive a thrown ball. R3 advances from third and runs into the catcher, after which R3 is tagged out. **RULING:** Obstruction. F2 cannot be in the base path without the ball in his possession, nor can he be in the base path waiting for a ball to arrive without giving the runner some access to home plate.

8.3.2 SITUATION D: With one out, R2 on second and R1 on first, B4 hits ground ball directly to F1 who throws to F5 for force on R2 at third. F5 then throws to F3 in time to put out B4. F6 holds R2, preventing him from advancing to third. **RULING:** The umpire will signal obstruction when it occurs, and then call time after runners have advanced as far as possible, which in this situation would probably be second for R1. R2 will then be awarded third. Because of the obstruction of F6, the out at first stands. B5 will come to bat with two outs and R2 is on third and R1 is on second base.

8.3.2 SITUATION E: R1, who is on first base, attempts to steal second base (a) F2 does not make throw or (b) F2 throws the ball into center field. In both cases F6 fakes a tag on R1. **RULING:** In (a), R1 is awarded second base on the obstruction call. In (b), the umpire shall call a delayed dead ball and award bases that in his or her judgment the runner would have obtained had the obstruction not occurred. The umpire shall issue a warning to the defensive coach for F6 faking a tag.

8.3.2 SITUATION G: F1 attempts to pick off R1 at first base. As F3 is about to receive the throw, he drops his knee and (a) blocks the entire base prior to possessing the ball or (b) blocks part of the base prior to possessing the ball or (c) blocks the entire base while being in possession of the ball. **RULING:** Obstruction in (a); legal in (b) and (c).

8.3.2 SITUATION H: With no outs, R2 is obstructed rounding third. R1 had advanced beyond second. B3 then interferes with F3. **RULING:** The umpire shall deal with obstruction and then interference, since this is the order in which the infractions occurred. If R2 was obstructed after he rounded third, he would be awarded home. If he was obstructed before reaching third, the umpire may award him home if, in the umpire's judgment, R2 could have scored had he not been obstructed. The umpire then shall enforce the interference penalty, which would place R1 at second base and declare B3 out (8-4-2g).

8.3.2 SITUATION I: R3 is attempting to score from third and F8 throws the ball to F2. F2 is four or five feet down the line between home and third, but is not actually able to catch the ball in order to make the tag. R3, rather than running into F2, slides behind F2 into foul territory and then touches home plate with his hand. After R3 slides, F2 catches the ball and attempts to tag R3 but misses. The coach of the offensive team coaching at third base claims that obstruction should have been called even though there was no contact. **RULING:** Obstruction. Contact does not have to occur for obstruction to be ruled. F2 cannot be in the baseline without the ball if it is not in motion and a probable play is not going to occur, nor can he be in the baseline without giving the runner access to home plate.

8.3.2 SITUATION J: F1 feints a throw to first base. Someone in the defensive team's dugout throws a ball against the fence alongside first base, making R1 think an overthrow took place. **RULING:** The umpire shall call obstruction and award R1 second base. He or she shall also eject the offender from the game and issue a warning to the coach (2-22-1, 8-3-2, 3-3-1g(4)).

8.3.3 SITUATION P: With R1 at first, B2 hits a sharp line drive down the line into the right-field corner. As he rounds second base, F6 reaches out and neckties R1, bringing him to the ground. **RULING:** F6 is guilty of not only of obstruction, but of malicious contact. The play becomes dead immediately, and F6 is ejected. R1 will be awarded at least third base and B2 at least first base. If in the umpire's judgment both R1 and B2 could have attained additional bases had the malicious contact not occurred, those additional bases will be awarded.

Spectator Interference

Spectator interference is an act by a spectator which impedes the progress of the game (2-21-3).

The umpire shall award bases or impose penalties that, in his judgment, will nullify the act of spectator interference with any thrown or batted ball. The ball shall become dead at the moment of the interference. It is not spectator interference if a spectator physically hinders a fielder who is reaching into a dead ball area to make a play on a batted or thrown ball (8-3-3e).

 Did You Know ?

Prior to 1995, fielders were protected even when reaching into the stands to make a play. Spectators could be called for interference even in dead-ball territory.

Spectator Interference: Caseplays

8.3.3 SITUATION G: R1 is on first when B2 hits a fair ball (a) down the right-field line that rolls into foul territory or (b) to the left-center field gap. In both cases, a spectator picks up the ball in live-ball territory and tosses it to the fielder. **RULING:** In both (a) and (b), ball is dead immediately at the moment of interference and the umpire shall award R1 and B2 the bases they would have reached, in his or her opinion, had there been no spectator interference.

8.3.3 SITUATION M: F3 reaches into the stands to make a catch on a foul fly ball. A spectator touches the ball or glove of F3 and prevents the catch. **RULING:** Interference is not called. Fielders are not covered by the spectator interference rule when the fielder reaches into a dead-ball area.

8.3.3 SITUATION N: F9 reaches into the designated media area and a photographer prevents F9 from catching the ball. **RULING:** Since the media area is a dead-ball area and the photographer is considered a spectator, under this rule no interference has occurred.

Interference by Umpire: Catcher's Throw

When a plate umpire hinders, impedes or prevents a catcher's throw attempting to prevent a stolen base or retire a runner on a pickoff play, if an out is not made at the end of the catcher's initial throw, the ball shall be dead and all runners shall return to the bases occupied at the time of the interference (8-4-6).

8.3.6 SITUATION: R1 is on first base and attempts to steal second base. On the catcher's throw, contact with the plate umpire hinders his attempt to retire R1. **RULING:** If R1 is not retired at the end of the catcher's initial throw, the ball is dead and he shall return to first base.

Touched in Proper Order

Each runner shall touch his base after the ball becomes dead. All awarded bases must be touched in their proper order. The runner returns to the base he had reached or passed when the ball became dead. In the event of interference, a runner returns to the base he had legally reached at the time of the interference. If the interference does not cause the batter to be out and any other runner cannot return to the base last legally occupied at the time of the interference, he is advanced to the next base (8-2-9). The runner returns to the base occupied at the time of the pitch if his advance was during an uncaught foul (8-2-9 exception).

Topic:
Baserunning Violations

Baserunner Deliberately Knocking Ball

A runner is out when he deliberately knocks the ball from a fielder's hand (8-4-2r).

Baserunner Abandons Effort to Run

A runner is out when after at least touching first base, he leaves the baseline, obviously abandoning his effort to touch the next base. Any runner, after reaching first base, who leaves the baseline heading for the dugout or his defensive position believing that there is no further play, shall be declared out if the umpire judges the act of the runner to be considered abandoning his efforts to run the bases (8-4-2p).

Baserunner Abandons Effort to Run: Caseplays

8.4.2 SITUATION C: (a) B1 reaches first base safely but thinks he is out and abandons his effort to return to first base and heads for the team bench, or (b) R2, running to third base, thinks he is out because of a possible force play at third base and leaves the field for the team bench when the coach tells him to return. **RULING:** The umpire will rule an out in both (a) and (b), because in each play the runner abandoned his effort to reach the entitled base. Upon reaching base a runner abandons his effort when he leaves the baseline (8-4-2p).

8.4.2 SITUATION V: With the bases loaded, B4 hits a ball that is trapped by F8. R2 at second thinks the ball is caught and begins to return to second base. R1 attempts to advance to second. F8's throw reaches F4 at second before R2 and R1 arrive at the base. The umpire signals an out. However, both runners think they are out and begin leaving the field. **RULING:** R1 is out because of being forced. However, once the force was removed, R2 would have to be tagged out if he left the base. When R2 began leaving the field, he should be considered as having abandoned his effort to return or advance, and shall be declared out (8-4-2j).

Baserunner Leaves Baseline

Any runner is out when he runs more than three feet away from a direct line between bases to avoid being tagged or to hinder a fielder while the runner is advancing or returning to a base (8-4-2a). This is not an infraction if a fielder attempting to field a batted ball is in the runner's proper path and if the runner runs behind the fielder to avoid interfering with him (8-4-2a-1). When a play is being made on a runner or batter-runner, he establishes his baseline as directly between his position and the base toward which he is moving (8-4-2a-2).

Batter-Runner Runs Outside Running Lane

The batter-runner is out when he runs outside the three-foot running lane (last half of the distance from home plate to first base), while the ball is being fielded or thrown to first base (8-4-1g). This infraction is ignored if it is to avoid a fielder who is attempting to field the batted ball or if the act does not interfere with a fielder or a throw (8-4-1g-1). The batter-runner is considered outside the running lane lines if either foot is outside either line (8-4-1g-2).

Batter-Runner Runs Outside Running Lane: Caseplays

8.4.1 SITUATION C: With R3 on third base, B2 hits a fair ground ball to F3 who fields ball beyond first base. He throws to F2 attempting to retire R3. The throw hits B2 who is running on the foul line. **RULING:** B2 has not interfered, since he was running in the prescribed base path, the same as if he were advancing toward any other base. Since no play is made on B2 at first base, 8-4-1g does not apply. Had B2 intentionally made contact with the throw, the ball would be dead. B2 would be out and the umpire could call R3 out for B2's interference. Otherwise, R3 returns to third base on the interference call.

8.4.2 SITUATION Q: With the bases loaded, B4 hits a ground ball to F3 who is left-handed. The ball is just inside the foul line. F3 throws to F2, but hits B4 who is on his way to first base. B4 is in fair territory, but has not reached the 45-foot running lane. **RULING:** There is no violation, unless the batter-runner intentionally interfered with F3's throw (8-4-2a).

Coach Physically Assisting a Runner

No coach shall physically assist a runner during playing action. The runner shall be called out immediately (3-2-2, 8-4-2s).

In Simple Terms

To be considered a "physical assist," the coach must have helped (or attempted to help) a runner gain an advantage. The act of touching a runner does not necessarily constitute physical assistance.

Coach Physically Assisting a Runner: Caseplays

3.2.2 SITUATION A: B1 hits a home run out of the park and, while rounding third, trips over the base. The third-base coach helps B1 to his feet. **RULING:** The ball is dead and, since B1 is awarded four bases for the home run, he is allowed to score with this type of assistance by the third-base coach.

3.2.2 SITUATION B: With R3 on third base and one out, B3 hits a fly ball that (a) F8 is about to catch, (b) is going over the fence for a home run or (c) bounces off the fence into play, as R3's coach at third physically assists R3 at third base. **RULING:** R3 is called out immediately because of his coach's physical assistance. In all cases the ball shall remain live and any subsequent outs or advances by runners shall be allowed. In (a), F8's catch would be the third out of the inning. In (b), if there had been two outs instead of one out at the time of the pitch, the physical assistance by the coach would have been the third out. As a result, B3's home run would not have counted.

Failing to Legally Avoid Fielder

Any runner is out when he does not legally attempt to avoid a fielder in the immediate act of making a play on him (8-4-2c). The ball remains live unless interference is called (8-4-2c penalty).

◪ Rationale

For the safety of both players involved, the fielder must be lying on the ground for jumping, hurdling or leaping to be legal. Since 1994, diving has been illegal no matter the position of the fielder because of the potential injury to the runner.

Failing to Legally Avoid Fielder: Caseplays

8.4.2 SITUATION A: On a play at the plate, F2, who is on his knees, is about to receive the throw. R3 decides to hurdle F2 or jump over him feet-first. **RULING:** The runner is out. A runner is entitled to slide legally or legally attempt to get around a fielder who has the ball waiting to make the tag. Going over the top of the fielder who is not lying on the ground by hurdling, jumping over or diving over the fielder is dangerous and, therefore, illegal. A runner may jump or hurdle a fielder who is lying on the ground, but diving over a fielder always is illegal.

8.2.1 SITUATION D: R3 is on third with no outs. R3 attempts to score on a fly ball to F8. F8's throw to F2 is near perfect. R3 sees that the play is going to be close. As F2 stretches for the ball to tag R3, R3 attempts to hurdle F2's outstretched arms as the ball bounces in front of the plate and skips into dead-ball territory. As R3 is in the air, F2's glove catches R3's foot and both lose their balance and tumble to the ground (a) R3 gets up and proceeds to the dugout or (b) R3 crawls back and touches the plate. **RULING:** Hurdling the outstretched arms of a fielder is legal. Hurdling or jumping over a fielder who is not lying on the ground is illegal. In (a), the umpire shall call R3 out for missing the plate upon a proper defensive appeal. In (b), R3's run would count.

8.4.2 SITUATION S: F4 is in the baseline without the ball (a) on both knees or (b) bending over. R1 hurdles, jumps, leaps or dives over F4. **RULING:** In (a) and (b), obstruction is ignored. If the runner hurdles, jumps or dives over the fielder, he shall be declared out. These illegal acts supersede obstruction.

8.4.2 SITUATION U: R1 is advancing toward second base on a ground ball by B2 and is obstructed by F4. R1, in an attempt to avoid F4, dives over the top of F4. **RULING:** R1 is declared out immediately, and unless he makes contact or alters the play of F4, the ball remains live. The act of obstruction is superseded by the act of diving over a fielder.

Illegal Slide

A slide is illegal if:
• The runner uses a rolling, cross-body or pop-up slide into the fielder (2-32-2a).
• The runner's raised leg is higher than the fielder's knee when the fielder is in a standing position (2-32-2b).
• Except at home plate, the runner goes beyond the base and then makes contact with or alters the play of the fielder. At home plate, it is permissible for the slider's momentum to carry him through the plate in a straight line (baseline extended). (2-32-2c)
•The runner slashes or kicks the fielder with either leg (2-32-2d).
• The runner tries to injure the fielder, or the runner (2-32-2e)
• The runner, on a force play, does not slide on the ground and in a direct line between the two bases (2-32-2f).

A runner may slide or run in a direction away from the fielder to avoid making contact or altering the play of the fielder (2-32-1).

Any runner is out when he does not legally slide and causes illegal contact and/or illegally alters the actions of a fielder in the immediate act of making a play, or on a force play, does not slide in a direct line between the bases (8-4-2b).

A runner may slide in a direction away from the fielder to avoid making contact or altering the play of the fielder (8-4-2b-1).

Runners are never required to slide, but if a runner elects to slide, the slide must be legal. Jumping, hurdling, and leaping are all legal attempts to avoid a fielder as long as the fielder is lying on the ground. Diving over a fielder is illegal (8-4-2b-2).

Illegal Slide: Penalty

The runner is out. Interference is called and the ball is dead immediately. On a force-play slide with less than two outs, the runner is declared out, as well as the batter-runner. Runners shall return to the bases occupied at the time of the pitch. With two outs, the runner is declared out (8-4-2b penalty).

Illegal Slide: Caseplays

2.32.1 SITUATION: With R1 at first base, a ground ball is hit to F6, who throws to F4 covering second. R1 slides late at second, stays in the baseline, but R1 makes contact with F4 who is in front of the base, causing him to overthrow first base. **RULING:** Providing the slide is legal and the contact is not malicious, there is no violation.

2.32.2 SITUATION A: With R1 on first base, B2 hits a ground ball to F4, who makes a throw to F6 in an effort to turn a double play. R1 (a) slides directly into second base, (b) does not slide directly to the base, but slides or runs away from F6. **RULING:** In (a) and (b), the actions are legal.

2.32.2 SITUATION B: R3 is on third base and R1 is on first base with no outs. A ground ball is hit to F6, who throws to F4 at second base. R1 slides out of the base path in an attempt to prevent F4 from turning the double play. **RULING:** Since R1 did not slide directly into second base, R1 is declared out, as well as the batter-runner. R3 returns to third base, the base occupied at the time of the pitch.

2.32.2 SITUATION C: Bases loaded. A ground ball to F1 is thrown to F2. R3 slides directly into and past home plate. F2 on his throw to another base is contacted by R3 in the baseline extended. **RULING:** Because R3 slid directly into home plate in the baseline extended and the contact was not malicious this is not a violation of Rule 8-4-2(b).

2.32.2 SITUATION D: Bases loaded. A ground ball to F1 is thrown to F2. R3 slides on the ground not in a direct line to the plate, reaching out with his hand to touch the plate. His contact hinders F2's attempted throw to another base. **RULING:** This is force-play, slide-rule interference. The ball is immediately dead. R3 is out as well as the batter-runner.

2.32.2 SITUATION E: R2 is on second base with one out. B3 hits a single and R2 scores. After catching the throw, F2 tries to throw to second base. R2's slide was (a) not in a straight line through the plate, or (b) in a straight line into, over and through the plate in the baseline extended. In both cases his contact hinders F2's throw. **RULING:** In (a), the ball is immediately dead ball, R2's run counts and B3 is called out on the interference. In (b), R2's slide is legal.

5.1.1 SITUATION O: With R1 at first base, a ground ball is hit to F6, who throws to F4 covering second. R1 slides late at second, stays in the baseline, but R1 makes contact with F4 in front of the base, causing him to overthrow first base. **RULING:** Providing the slide is legal and the contact is not malicious, there is no violation (2-32-2f).

8.4.2 SITUATION O: R1 is on first base. B2 hits a one-hopper to F5 who throws to F4 at second base for the force out of R1. R1 slides illegally into second base. **RULING:** R1 is out, as well as B2, because of R1's interference (illegal slide on force play). The ball is dead immediately and runners return to their bases occupied at the time of the pitch and no runs can score.

8.4.2 SITUATION P: R3 is on third and R1 is on first with no outs. B3 hits a ground ball to F4 who throws to F6 to force R1. R1 slides illegally, contacts F6 and interference is called by the umpire. **RULING:** R1 is out. B3 is out, and R3 is returned to third.

8.4.2 SITUATION W: The bases are loaded with (a), less than two outs, or (b), two outs. B5 hits a ground ball to F4, who throws to F2 for the force out at home. The throw pulls F2 off home plate several steps toward the first-base side. R3, seeing F2 ready to make a play on B5 at first base, touches home plate and mali- ciously crashes into F2. **RULING:** (a) Since this is a force-play situation, R3 and B5 are declared out and no one scores. R3 will be ejected from the game. In (b), R3 will be declared out and ejected for the contact, and no run will score.

 In 1992, a slide was considered legal when the runner could touch the base with either a hand or foot. The rule was adjusted in 1998 to create a force-play slide rule and require that if the runner slides, it must be directly into the bag.

Inciting Balk

A coach, player, substitute, attendant or other bench personnel shall not call "Time" or use any command or commit any act for the purpose of causing a balk (3-3-1n).

Inciting Balk: Penalty

It is a when this occurs (5-1-2d). The umpire shall eject the offender from the game. Failure to comply shall result in the game being forfeited (3-3-1o Penalty).

Intentionally Removing Helmet

When an umpire observes anyone who is required to wear a batting helmet deliberately remove his batting helmet while in live-ball territory and the ball is live (non-adult ball/bat shaggers required to wear batting helmet in live-ball area even if ball is dead), the umpire shall issue a warning to the coach of the involved team, unless the ball becomes dead without being touched by a fielder or, after being touched, goes directly to dead-ball area. A subsequent violation of the rule shall result in ejection. A violation by a non-adult bat/ball shagger shall result in a warning to the coach of the team and the individual. A subsequent violation may result in the individual not being allowed on the field (1-5-1 penalty).

It is a delayed-dead ball when anyone who is required to wear a batting helmet deliberately removes his helmet while the ball is in live-ball territory and the ball is live (5-1-2e).

Did You Know ? There are no outs awarded for this violation, only warnings and ejections, and those penalties come at the end of playing action.

Intentionally Removing Helmet: Caseplays

1.5.1 SITUATION A: In (a) B1, upon reaching first base, adjusts his helmet by lifting it, but not above the temples, and replaces it; or (b) B1 doubles and upon reaching second, he removes his helmet, tossing it above his head in celebration; or (c) the bat boy, without a helmet, leaves the dugout to retrieve a ball between home plate and the backstop. RULING: In (a), there is no violation because the helmet was not considered to have been removed. In (b), because the helmet was deliberately removed, the player is to be penalized as provided. In (c), bat boys and shaggers shall wear helmets when in live-ball area, even if the ball is dead. After being warned, any subsequent violation could result in that individual not being allowed on the field.

1.5.1 SITUATION B: In (a) after hitting a home run, B4 removes his helmet upon touching second base or (b) R3 scores and removes his helmet on the way to the dugout while R2 advances to third, or (c) R1 is called out sliding into second and as he leaves the field and play continues, he removes his helmet. **RULING:** In (a), there is no penalty. In (b) and (c), the player who removes his helmet shall be ejected if a team warning already had been issued.

1.5.1 SITUATION D: B1 receives a walk (not intentional). On his way to first base he removes his helmet to give it to the on-deck batter. **RULING:** This is a delayed dead-ball situation. At the end of playing action, B1 and his coach are warned that subsequent violators shall be ejected. B1 is not declared out. If a team warning previously had been given to that team, B1 would be ejected and replaced by a legal substitute.

Interference by Runner/Retired Runner

A runner is out when he intentionally interferes with a throw or a thrown ball; or he hinders a fielder on his initial attempt to field a batted ball (8-4-2g).

A fielder is not protected, except from intentional contact, if he misplays the ball and has to move from his original location (8-4-2g).

Any runner is also out when he is contacted by a fair batted ball before it touches an infielder, or after it passes any infielder, except the pitcher, and the umpire is convinced that another infielder has a play. If a runner is touching his base when he is hit by an infield fly, he is not out, but the batter is out by the infield fly rule. If a runner is hit by an infield fly when he is not touching his base, both he and the batter are out. The ball is dead (8-4-2k).

Any runner is also out when he attempts to advance to home base when the batter interferes with a play at home base, with less than two outs. If there are two outs, the batter is out because of his interference and since he is the third out, the runner cannot score. But if there are not two outs, the runner is out and the batter is not penalized (8-4-2l).

If, in the judgment of the umpire, a runner including the batter-runner interferes in any way and prevents a double play anywhere, two shall be declared out (the runner who interfered and the other runner involved). If a retired runner interferes, and in the judgment of the umpire, another runner could have been put out, the umpire shall declare that runner out. If the umpire is uncertain who would have been played on, the runner closest to home shall be called out (8-4-2g).

The batter-runner is out when any runner or retired runner interferes in a way which obviously hinders an obvious double play (8-4-1h).

⬦ Rationale

Where runners were placed following an interference call was ruled upon differently before a rule change in 1993 that made it clear that runners must return to the base occupied at the time of interference.

Interference by Runner/Retired Runner: Caseplays

2.21.1 SITUATION A: With R2 on second base, B2 hits a grounder to F6. Just as F6 starts to throw to first base, R2 on his way to third base, yells at F6, which startles F6, causing him to throw the ball over F3's head into dead-ball territory. **RULING:** R2 is called out immediately for verbal interference, and if in the judgment of the umpire the interference prevented a possible double play, B2 also would be called out.

2.21.1 SITUATION B: R3 is on third and R2 on second. B4 hits down the left-field line. R3 scores, but R2 maliciously runs over F5 after R3 touches home plate. **RULING:** Interference because of malicious contact. The ball is dead immediately. R3's run counts because he scored before the interference. R2 is called out and ejected because of malicious contact. The batter-runner shall be returned to the base he last legally touched before interference occurred.

5.1.1 SITUATION G: B1 hits a ground ball to left field. F7 throws the ball to the infield where it hits an umpire or baserunner. Is the ball dead? **RULING:** Not unless it is ruled interference on the base runner. Such ruling would be made if the runner deliberately allowed the ball to hit him.

5.1.1 SITUATION J: With a fielder in position to make a play, R1 is on first and R2 is (a) between second and third or (b) touching second. R2 is hit by ball batted by B3. **RULING:** The ball becomes dead immediately in (a) and (b). In (a), R2 is out. He is also out in (b), unless it is declared an infield fly. In (a) and (b), unless B3 is out because it is an infield fly, he is entitled to first base. R1 is awarded second base.

5.1.1 SITUATION N: With R3 at third and F5 playing deep, B2 hits a ball that caroms off the base into foul territory where it touches R3. **RULING:** A runner who is hit by a batted fair ball in foul territory is not out and the ball remains live.

8.2.6 SITUATION A: With R2 on second base and R1 on first base, B3 hits toward third base. R2 interferes by touching the batted ball or by illegally hindering F5 in his fielding or throwing. R1 reaches second base before the interference. **RULING:** R2 is out. B3 may also be out if the interference prevented a double play involving him at first. Since R1 reached second base before the interference, he is entitled to that base.

8.2.6 SITUATION B: With the bases full and one out, B5 hits a ground ball to F6. The batted ball hits R2 without first passing an infielder other than the pitcher. May two runners be called out and does the run score? **RULING:** The ball is dead immediately, because of R2's interference. The run does not score since each runner shall return to the base he occupied at the time of the interference. R2 is out. A second runner cannot be called out unless, in the umpire's opinion, the interference prevented a double play (8-4-1h, 8-4-2g).

8.4.2 SITUATION B: With R3 on third and R1 on first and a count of one-and-one, B3 hits a foul fly ball near the third-base line with one out. R3 interferes with F5 in his attempt to catch the ball. **RULING:** The ball is dead immediately. R3 is declared out because of his interference with F5. B4 remains at bat with a count of one-and-two.

Fundamental #14

To call interference with a thrown ball, the act must be intentional.

8.4.1 SITUATION D: With R3 on third and R2 on second base, B3 hits a sharp ground ball toward F6 who is pushed by R2. **RULING:** Interference causes the ball to become dead and R2 is out. If, in the umpire's opinion, F6 could have tagged R2 with the ball and then thrown out R3 at home, the umpire shall declare R3 out also. If it is apparent F6 was about to tag R2 and also would retire B3 at first for a double play, then umpire would declare both R2 and B3 out. If the umpire rules that even if F6 fielded ball cleanly he could not have retired any runner, then only R2 is out. When interference occurs, runners shall return to the bases occupied at the time of the interference, unless they had scored prior to the time of interference or were put out. There was no force play in effect. (8-4-1h, 8-4-2g).

8.4.1 SITUATION E: With bases loaded, B4 hits a one-hopper to F5, who throws to the plate. The throw is off line and hits B4's bat that had been tossed away from the plate by the umpire. Is this interference? **RULING:** No. The bat in this situation is considered part of the playing field. Therefore, the ball remains live.

8.4.2 SITUATION D: All bases are occupied with no outs when B4 hits a ground ball to F4 and R1 collides with him as he is fielding the ball. **RULING:** The ball became dead when interference occurred. R1 is declared out. If the umpire rules that F4 could have executed a double play, then the umpire shall declare two outs (the runner who interfered, and the other runner or batter-runner involved). If the umpire rules that only one runner could have been put out, then only R1 is out. No runs may score and all other runners shall return to bases occupied at the time of interference.

8.4.2 SITUATION E: With all bases occupied and no outs, B4 bunts, which results in a fly ball in the infield (not an infield fly). As R3 advances toward home, he contacts F5, causing him to drop the fly ball. How should the umpire rule? **RULING:** The ball is dead immediately. R3 is out for interference and B4 is out, since the interference prevented a double play involving R1 and B4.

8.4.2 SITUATION K: With R3 on third, R1 on first and no one out, R1 attempts to steal second base. The pitch to the batter is strike three. As F2 attempts to throw out R3, the batter interferes. The ball goes into the outfield and R3 scores. **RULING:** The batter is out because of strike three. R3 returns to third base because that is the base he occupied at the time of the interference. If the umpires judge R1 would have been out on the steal had the interference not occurred, R1 will be declared out. If the umpires judge he would not have been out had the interference not occurred, R1 will be returned to first base.

8.4.2 SITUATION F: In the opinion of the umpire, R1, when leading off first base, moves up to the front of the baseline, thus effectively screening F3 from the ball on F1's attempted pickoff. **RULING:** R1 shall be called out for interference.

 COMMENT: If this is not ruled to be interference, the runner gains an advantage not intended by the rule. This maneuver taught by some coaches shall be penalized.

8.4.2 SITUATION G: R3, R2 and R1 are on third, second and first bases, respectively, when B4 hits an infield fly ball. The umpire calls B4 out. R1, thinking the ball will not be caught, advances past R2 just beyond second. The fly ball hits R2 while he is off second base. **RULING:** Ball becomes dead when it hits R2. The play results in three outs. B4 is out by the infield-fly rule. R1 is out for passing an unobstructed preceding runner, and R2 is out for being hit by a batted fair ball (8-4-1j).

8.4.2 SITUATION H: With R2 on second, R1 on first and one out, B4 hits a ground ball or an infield fly. F4, standing behind second base, is in position to field the ball. The ball strikes R1 who is (a) near second or (b) standing on second. **RULING:** In both (a) and (b), the ball is dead immediately. If the hit is an infield fly, B4 shall be declared out (8-4-1j). In (a), R2 is out on either type of hit. In (b), R2 would be out on the ground ball, but not on an infield fly. A runner need not vacate his base to permit a fielder to make a catch, but he shall give the fielder a reasonable opportunity to make the play (7-4-1f, 5-1-1f).

8.4.2 SITUATION I: R1 is advancing to second when the ball batted by B2 (a) is dropped by F4 and is deflected toward R1 or (b) passes several feet to the left of F4 who is playing in front of the baseline. In either case, the ball then touches R1. **RULING:** In (a), the touching is ignored because the ball touched a defensive player first. In (b), touching is ignored unless R1 purposely allows the ball to touch him or, in the opinion of the umpire, another player who was in an infielder's position when the pitch was made had a play on the ball.

Fundamental #15

A base is not a sanctuary except on an infield fly.

8.4.2 SITUATION J: With R2 on second, B2 hits toward second. The batted ball hits R2 while he is standing on second or while he is on his way to third. F4 and F6 (a) are playing deep behind the baseline or (b) F6 is playing in front of the baseline. **RULING:** In (a), the ball is dead immediately. R2 is out and B2 is awarded first base. In (b), the touching is ignored unless it is ruled intentional, and the ball remains live because no other fielder had a chance to make a play on the batted ball (5-1-1f).

8.4.2 SITUATION Q: R1 is on third and R2 is on first with no outs. B3 hits a ground ball to F4 who throws to F6 to force R2. R2 slides illegally, contacts F6 and interference is called by the umpire. **RULING:** R2 is out. B3 is out, and R1 is returned to third.

8.4.2 SITUATION R: With R3 on third base, R1 on first and two outs, B5 hits a fair slow roller toward first base. B5 interferes with F3, who is trying to field the ball. However, R3 scores before the interference. Does the run score since R3 touched home plate before the interference? **RULING:** The run does not score if the runner advances during action in which the third out is made by the batter-runner before he touches first base (9-1-1a).

8.4.2 SITUATION T: With two outs and R2 on second base, B4 hits a pop fly to F6. While moving underneath the ball, F6 enters R2's basepath. As R2 starts to go around F6, the wind blows the ball beyond F6. F6 backs up suddenly into the runner and, as a result, drops the ball. **RULING:** R2 is guilty of interference. F6 is entitled to an unhindered opportunity to field the ball.

8.4.2 SITUATION X: Team A has runners at second and third bases. R3 has taken his lead in foul territory. B3 hits a foul fly between third base and home. F5 goes to field the ball in foul territory. He makes contact with R3 who is attempting to return to third base. **RULING:** (a) R3 would be declared out. If there were two outs, this ends the inning; (b) If less than two outs, R3 is declared out and a strike is added to the batter's count, unless the batter already has two strikes, in which case the pitch is counted as a foul ball.

COMMENT: The umpire has authority to declare two runners out when a runner or retired runner illegally interferes and prevents a double play. In such circumstances, the runner who interferes is out and the other runner involved is also out. Also, when the batter-runner interferes, the umpire may declare two outs. The batter-runner is declared out and so is the runner who has advanced the nearest to home plate (8.4.2 Comment).

Malicious Contact

A coach, player, substitute, attendant or other bench personnel shall not initiate malicious contact on offense or defense (3-3-1m, 8-4-2e). The ball is immediately dead, if on offense, the player is ejected and declared out, unless he has already scored. Malicious contact always supersedes obstruction (8-4-2e-1).

Malicious Contact: Caseplays

3.3.1 SITUATION DD: R3 is advancing to home and initiates malicious contact with F2, who is standing out of the baseline. F2 does not have the ball, and there is no play at the plate. **RULING:** This is considered to be interference, and the ball is dead immediately. R3 is declared out, and because the act is malicious, R3 is also ejected from the game. Any other runners must return to the bases they last touched at the time of the interference. If the declaring of a dead-ball prevented the defense from completing an obvious double play, the umpire shall award the additional out.

3.3.1 SITUATION EE: Upon rounding second, R1 maliciously runs into F6 who is (a) in the baseline or (b) not in the baseline. **RULING:** In (a), the malicious contact supersedes the obstruction. In (a) and (b), R1 is out and is also to be ejected because of the unsportsmanlike act.

3.3.1 SITUATION FF: With two outs and the bases loaded, B6 hits a home run out of the park. R1 maliciously runs over (a) F4 before touching second base or (b) F5 before touching third. **RULING:** In both (a) and (b), R1 is declared out and ejected. In (a), the third out is a force, so no runs score. In (b), the third out was not a force play, so runners who have touched the plate prior to the infraction would score. Please note that in awarded situations it is not the base that is awarded, but rather the right to advance and legally touch a base with no play being made.

3.3.1 SITUATION GG: While sliding into second base feet first, R1 maliciously slashes out with his right leg and trips F6 who is in the act of making the pivot in an attempt to complete a double play. Consequently,

F6's throw is wild and goes out of play. **RULING:** The ball is dead immediately. R1 is out and ejected for malicious contact. B2 shall be called out by the umpire because this was a force play slide situation and R1 did not execute a legal slide (8-4-2b).

3.3.1 SITUATION HH: R1 slides safely into second base and, in doing a pop-up slide, maliciously crashes into the second baseman, who was standing by the base without the ball. **RULING:** The ball is dead immediately, and R1 is called out and ejected from the game for malicious contact.

3.3.1 SITUATION II: With no outs, and R2 on second base, B2 hits the ball in the gap, R2 touches and rounds third and heads for home, and initiates malicious contact with F2 (a) before touching the plate, or (b) after scoring. **RULING:** In (a) the ball is dead, the runner is out and ejected for malicious contact. In (b) the run counts, the ball is dead and the runner is ejected for malicious contact. In either case the batter-runner must return to the last legally acquired base at the time of the malicious contact.

Missed Base or Leaving Early

For missing a base, a runner may return by retouching the bases in reverse order (8-2-2). Any runner who misses a base while advancing may not return to touch it after a following runner has scored (8-2-3). If a runner who misses any base (including home plate) or leaves a base too early, desires to return to touch the base, he must do so immediately (8-2-5).

When the ball becomes dead, a runner may return to a base he left too soon on a caught fly ball or that was not touched during a live ball. A runner who is on or beyond a succeeding base when the ball became dead, or advances and touches a succeeding base after the ball became dead, may not return and shall be called out upon proper and successful appeal (5-2-2b, 8-2-5). A runner may also not return to touch a missed base or one left too soon on a caught fly ball if he has left the field of play or a following runner has scored (8-2-6d).

If a runner correctly touches a base that was missed (either in advancing or returning), the last time he was by the base, that last touch corrects any previous baserunning infraction (8-4-2g EXCEPTION).

Missed Base or Leaving Early: Caseplays

8.2.6 SITUATION E: With two outs and runners on second and third, B5 hits a line drive over F3's head. F9 makes a spectacular play and makes a wild throw to F3 allowing both runners to score and B5 to advance to second base. However, B5 misses first base. F3 (a) retrieves the ball and kicks the bag in disgust. He then returns the ball to F1 who subsequently delivers a pitch (b) at the end of playing action, touches first base indicating a live appeal, or (c) calls time and appeals B5 missing first. **RULING:** In (a), both runs score and B5 is safe on second base because the action of F3 is not an intentional or valid appeal; (b) and (c), no runs score and that half of the inning is over.

8.2.6 SITUATION F: With R1 at first, B2 hits a double into right center, sending R1 to third. However, R1 misses second base. F6 is standing on second when he catches the throw from the outfield. He then throws the ball to the pitcher. **RULING:** Although R1 missed second, no call will be made by the umpire because F6 did not make an intentional appeal of the missed base.

8.2.6 SITUATION G: With R1 at first, B2 hits a triple to left. However, both R1 and B2 miss second. The ball is then returned to the infield, where F4 stands on second and appeals that B2 missed the base. **RULING:** The umpire will uphold the appeal on B2 and call him out. However, the umpire will not make a call on R1 unless properly appealed by the defense.

8.2.6 SITUATION H: R1 is stealing on the pitch and a fly ball is hit to right field. R1 misses second base by (a) a few inches or (b) a greater distance because he cuts across the infield missing second base as he advanced toward third base. F9 catches the fly ball and R1 now retouches second base as he retreats to first base. F9's throw is errant and R1 reaches first base ahead of the throw. The defense now appeals that R1 should be out as he did not initially touch second base. **RULING:** In (a), R1 is not declared out as he touched second base on his return to first and as a result corrected his mistake by touching second on his last time by the base. In (b), R1 is out on the appeal because a runner who misses a base by such a great distance in order to gain an advantage would still be vulnerable to appeal under the principle of last time by.

8.4.2 SITUATION N: R3 is on third with one out when B3 hits safely. R3, while watching the ball, misses home plate. F2 calls for the ball, steps on home to retire R3 and throws to third to get B3 sliding in. **RULING:** Legal. Runner may be declared out for missing base during playing action upon proper appeal.

Offense Creating Confusion

No member of a team may be near a base for which a runner is trying so that a fielder may be confused; nor be on or near the baseline in such a way as to draw a throw; nor shall the base coach or members of the team at bat fail to vacate any area needed by a fielder in his attempt to put out a batter or runner. If a thrown live ball unintentionally touches a base coach in foul territory, or a pitched or thrown ball touches an umpire, the ball is live and in play. If the coach is judged by the umpire to have interfered intentionally with the thrown ball, or interferes in fair territory, the interference penalty is invoked (3-2-3).

A runner is also out when he runs bases in reverse to confuse opponents to make a travesty of the game (8-4-2n).

Offense Creating Confusion: Caseplay
3.2.3 SITUATION: The third-base coach is accidentally hit by a thrown ball when standing in (a) the coach's box, (b) foul territory or (c) fair territory. **RULING:** There is no penalty in (a) and (b), and the ball remains live. In (c), it is automatic interference.

Passing a Runner
A runner is out when he passes an unobstructed preceding runner before such runner is out, including awarded bases (8-4-2m).

Passing a Runner: Caseplays
8.4.2 SITUATION G: R3, R2 and R1 are on third, second and first bases, respectively, when B4 hits an infield fly ball. The umpire calls B4 out. R1, thinking the ball will not be caught, advances past R2 just beyond second. The fly ball hits R2 while he is off second base. **RULING:** Ball becomes dead when it hits R2. The play results in three outs. B4 is out by the infield-fly rule. R1 is out for passing an unobstructed preceding runner, and R2 is out for being hit by a batted fair ball (8-4-1j).

8.4.2 SITUATION L: With two outs, R2 on second base and R1 on first base, B5 singles. B5 passes R1 between first and second base (a) just before R2 touches the plate or (b) just after R2 touches the plate. **RULING:** In (a), the run does not count, while in (b), it does count. A runner is called out at the moment he passes a preceding runner, but the ball remains live. Acts such as attempts of a runner to profit by running too far from the baseline to avoid a tag, or outside the three-foot lane while advancing to first, or running the bases in reverse, or other-wise making a travesty of the game may not be appealed. The umpire calls the runner out without waiting for the defensive player to call attention to the act.

8.4.2 SITUATION M: The bases are loaded with one out. B5 hits a home run over the fence. However, he passes R1 after rounding first. R1 misses second base while advancing to home. **RULING:** B5 is out at the point he passes R1. Upon proper defensive appeal, R1 is called out at the end of playing action by the umpire. Two runs score. B5, being declared out for passing R1, removed the force situation on R1 at second base.

9.1.1 SITUATION L: With the bases loaded and one out, B5 hits a home run out of the park. While advancing to second base, B5 passes R3 (force is removed) and B5 is declared out. R3 fails to touch second base, but touches third base on his way home. **RULING:** For missing a base or leaving a base too soon, the umpire will declare the runner out upon proper appeal. R1 and R2 score, because R3's out was not a force out for the third out (8-2 Penalty).

Running Start

A runner is out when he positions himself behind a base to get a running start (8-4-2o).

Topic 6
Game Administration

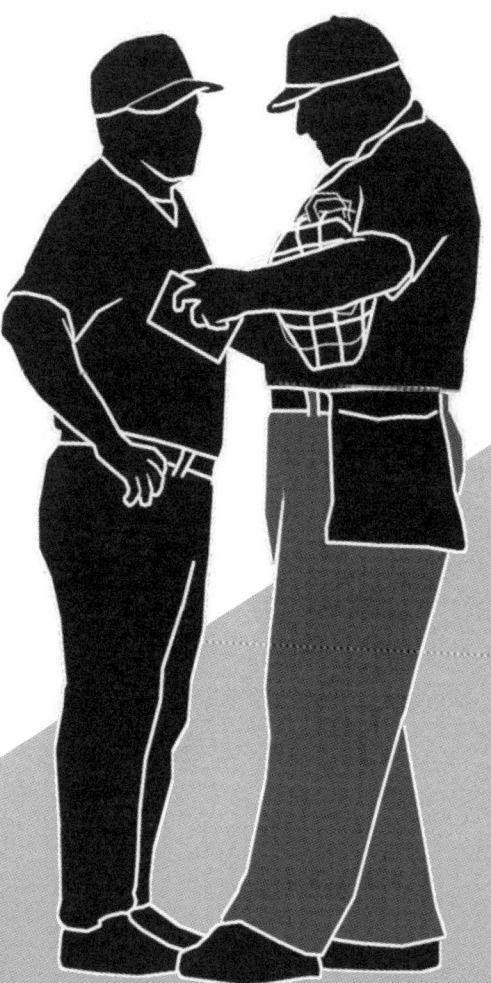

PlayPic®

Key Terms

An inning is that portion of a game which includes a turn at bat for each team (2-20-1).

A regulation interscholastic game is seven innings (turns at bat) for each team unless shortened as in 4-2-2 (home team not needing final at-bat or 10-run rule) and 4-2-3 (weather or darkness), or unless extra innings are necessary to break a tie score (2-17-1).

A called game is one which is ended by order of the umpire (2-17-2). If a game is called before completion of the required number of innings or other conditions, the umpire shall declare the contest "no game," unless play is terminated by a state-adopted game-ending procedure (4-3-1).

A suspended game is a called game to be completed at a later time (2-17-3). A forfeited game is one awarded to the opponent of the offending team (2-15).

A penalty is the action taken by the umpire against a player, coach or team for a rule infraction. Penalties include restricting the coach to the dugout, ejecting offending player or coach, declaring a batter or runner out, awarding a base to a batter or runner, awarding a ball to the batter (for an illegal pitch when there is no runner or for delay by the pitcher, charging the batter with a strike (for delay), forfeiting a game or removing non-players from the bench or field (2-27-1). An extra inning is one which extends the game in an attempt to break the tie score (2-20-3).

Topic:
Substitutions

A substitute is a player who is eligible to replace another player already in the lineup (2-36-1). An unreported substitute is a player who, by rule, can be in the game but has entered without reporting (2-36-2).

⬛ Rationale

The rule allowing unreported substitutes to remain in the game came about from confusion that was created by an unreported substitute who happened to be batting out of order. This change, in 1994, removed the penalty for not reporting.

Substitutions: Caseplay

3.1.1 SITUATION A: B1 has a count of one ball and two strikes when the captain or coach decides to put in pinch hitter S1. **RULING:** The coach should ask the umpire to call time to make a substitution. When S1 enters, he is charged with one ball and two strikes. If S1 strikes out, the strikeout and time at bat are charged against B1, since he had more than half of the allotted number of strikes. In any other case, the time at bat is charged to S1 (9-3-6).

Changing Positions

A player may change to a different fielding position at any time except that a pitcher, after being listed as such on the official lineup card handed to the umpire, cannot change until certain conditions are met. Changes should be reported to the umpire-in-chief and scorekeeper (1-1-5). The player listed as pitcher on the lineup card shall pitch until the first opposing batter has been put out or has advanced to first base (3-1-1). If the starting pitcher does not face one batter, he may play another position, but not return to pitch (3-1-1 penalty). If a pitcher is replaced while his team is on defense, the substitute pitcher shall pitch to the batter then at bat, or any substitute for that batter, until such batter is put out or reaches first base, or until a third out has been made (3-1-2).

Illegal Substitute

An illegal substitute is player who enters or re-enters the game without eligibility to do so (2-36-3a); a player who re-enters the game in the wrong position in the batting order (2-36-3b); a player who enters the game on defense while the player for whom he is batting is on defense (2-36-3c); when the player for whom the DH is batting enters the game as a batter or runner in a different position in the batting order (2-36-3d); or a player who violates the courtesy runner rule (2-36-3a through e).

Illegal Substitute: Penalty

An illegal substitute shall be restricted to the dugout for the remainder of the game (3-1-1). On offense, a batter or batter/runner is out when he enters the game as an illegal substitute and is discovered (7-4-1h, 8-4-1k).

For discovery of an illegal player on offense by an umpire or either team, that player shall be called out and restricted to the bench/dugout for the duration of the game. An illegal player discovered on defense shall be restricted to the bench/dugout for the duration of the game. If a restricted player re-enters the game on offense, he shall be called out immediately and ejected upon discovery by an umpire or either team. If he is a defensive player, he shall be ejected upon discovery by an umpire or either team.

The penalty for illegal substitution shall supersede the penalty for batting out of order.

If the player should score a run, advance or cause a play to be made that allows another runner(s) to advance, discovery must be made by an umpire or either team before the first pitch to the next batter of either team. This would invalidate the action of the illegal offensive player. Any out(s) made on the play stands and all other runners return to the base(s) occupied at the time of the pitch.

In a game-ending situation, discovery must be made before all infielders leave the diamond (i.e., all infielders cross the foul lines).

An illegal player on defense shall be replaced immediately upon discovery by the umpire or either team. If an illegal player on defense is involved in a play, and the infraction is discovered by an umpire or either team prior to the first pitch to the next batter of either team, the team on offense has the option to let the play stand or to allow the batter to bat again.

Any player for whom an illegal player substitutes may re-enter only if he is eligible to do so under the re-entry rule (3-1-1 penalty).

Illegal Substitute: Caseplays

3.1.1 SITUATION C: S1, who was not a starter and has already been in and out of the game once, appears at bat in place of B2. This is discovered while S1 is at bat by (a) the offensive team; (b) the defensive team; or (c) an umpire. **RULING:** In each case S1 is an illegal substitute and is restricted to the dugout for the duration of the game. He shall also be called out. The penalty for an ineligible substitute supersedes the penalty for batting out of order. The out is credited to F2.

3.1.1 SITUATION G: With two outs and an illegal substitute at second base, B4 hits a home run out of the park. Before the next pitch, the illegal substitute is discovered. **RULING:** The illegal substitute is called out and restricted to the bench. No runs score, since the out on the runner at second base was the third out. The home run is nullified. B4 leads off the next inning.

3.1.1 SITUATION I: S1, who is an illegal substitute, scores, but B4 is thrown out for the third out attempting to advance to second base on a base hit. As both teams change positions, and before a pitch to the next batter can be made, the umpire is informed by the opposing team's coach that S1 is an illegal substitute. **RULING:** Even though both teams changed positions, a pitch had not been thrown to the next batter. Therefore, the previous play is nullified. S1 is called out, his run does not count, and B4 shall lead off the next inning (2-36-3, 3-1-1, 8-4-1k).

3.1.1 SITUATION J: S1 comes in for F7 in the second inning, but is not discovered. In the seventh inning, S1 comes in for F8 and is batting when the opposing team contends that S1 was a substitute earlier in the game.

RULING: Unless the umpire has knowledge that S1 had in fact been in the game earlier, S1 cannot be treated as an illegal substitute.

3.1.1 SITUATION L: With one out and R3 on third, S1, an illegal substitute, bats and hits an inside-the-park home run, scoring R3 and himself. The illegal substitute is detected by the opposing team (a) before the next pitch or (b) after the next pitch. **RULING:** In both (a) and (b), the illegal substitute is declared out and restricted to the bench. In (a), R1 shall return to third base. In (b), the run counts.

3.1.1 SITUATION M: With the bases loaded and two outs, an illegal substitute (a) hits a home run or (b) while at bat, F1 throws a wild pitch, which allows R3 to score. The illegal substitute is detected before the next pitch. **RULING:** In (a), the illegal substitute is restricted to the bench and no runs score because the illegal substitute was the third out. In (b), the run counts and the illegal substitute is declared out and restricted to the bench. The inning is over.

3.1.1 SITUATION O: S1, who is an illegal substitute, is discovered playing second base and who was previously restricted to the dugout. **RULING:** S1 is ejected upon discovery by an umpire or either team.

3.1.1 SITUATION P: With runners on second and third bases, respectively, S1, who is an illegal substitute, and was previously restricted to the dugout, bats and advances to second base. **RULING:** S1 is called out and ejected. All other runners are returned to bases occupied at the time of the pitch.

3.1.1 SITUATION Q: With R1 on first base, B2 doubles and, (a) before the next pitch R1 is discovered to be an illegal player, (b) after the next pitch R1 is discovered to be an illegal player. **RULING:** In both (a) and (b), R1 is out and restricted to the dugout for the remainder of the game.

3.1.1 SITUATION R: In the first inning, C1 is a courtesy runner for the pitcher. In the second inning, C1 is a courtesy runner for the catcher. **RULING:** Upon discovery, C1 is called out and restricted to the dugout for the remainder of the game.

3.3.1 SITUATION VV: The scorekeeper or a fan informs the umpire of an illegal substitute. **RULING:** The umpire shall call the illegal substitute out and restrict him to the bench, because once the umpire is aware of the infraction, he shall enforce the penalty.

Injuries

Any player who exhibits signs, symptoms or behaviors consistent with a concussion (such as loss of consciousness, headache, dizziness, confusion or balance problems) shall be immediately removed from the game and shall not return to play until cleared by an appropriate health-care professional (3-1-5). One of the umpire-in-chief's duties is to prohibit any player who exhibits signs, symptoms or behaviors consistent with a concussion (such as loss of consciousness, headache, dizziness, confusion or balance problems) from returning to play until cleared by an appropriate health-care professional (10-2-3k).

A player or coach who is bleeding or who has an open wound shall be prohibited from participating further in the game until appropriate treatment has been administered. If medical care or treatment can be administered in a reasonable amount of time, the individual would not have to leave the game. The length of time that is considered reasonable is umpire judgment. The re-entry rule applies to starters. If there is any amount of blood on the uniform, it shall be changed or cleaned before that individual participates again (3-1-6).

Injuries: Caseplays

3.1.5 SITUATION A: In the second inning, F8 runs into a fence chasing a fly ball and later exhibits signs of a concussion. The coach and the player's father agree that F8 is okay to continue in the game. **RULING:** Any player who exhibits signs, symptoms or behaviors consistent with a concussion shall be immediately removed from the game and shall not return to play until cleared by an appropriate health-care professional.

3.1.5 SITUATION B: In the first inning, Jones is hit on the helmet with a pitch. In the fourth inning, Jones is hit again on the helmet by a pitch. In the sixth inning, Jones exhibits some balance problems. **RULING:** Jones shall be removed from the game and shall not return until cleared by an appropriate health-care professional.

3.1.6 SITUATION A: R1, upon sliding into second base, (a) suffers an open wound on his elbow, or (b) is bleeding from the nose, or (c) twists his ankle involving no external bleeding or open wound. **RULING:** In both (a) and (b), R1 must receive appropriate treatment before participating further in the game. In (a), (b) and (c), if the umpire believes that an undue delay would result or if the bleeding or injury requires extensive treatment, the player must leave the game. The re-entry rule applies.

3.1.6 SITUATION B: R1, after sliding into second base, has an excessive amount of blood on his uniform jersey. The umpire rules that R1 must change his jersey (a) R1 changes his jersey with a teammate who is not presently in the game (b) The coach of Team A replaces R1's uniform jersey with a white tee shirt and writes a number eight inches high on the back of the tee shirt using a permanent marker (c) The JV team has returned from its game and the coach of Team A requests R1 to wear a JV shirt, which is a different color. **RULING:** Legal in (a). The umpire shall change R1's uniform number on the lineup card and scorebook. In (b) and (c), it is umpire judgment whether or not the change should be allowed. Every effort should be made to allow the player to participate.

5.2.1 SITUATION C: B1 (a) hits a home run over the fence or (b) receives a base on balls or, (c) is struck by a pitched ball. In each instance, B1 is unable to reach his awarded base because of an injury sustained during the play. **RULING:** In (a), (b) and (c), because bases are awarded, a pinch runner may replace the injured player and continue to the awarded bases. In (b), since the ball is live, the umpire has to call "Time." He will then permit a substitute to run for the injured player according to 10-2-3g.

No Eligible Substitutes

A game shall be forfeited to the offended team by the umpire when a team is unable to provide at least nine players to start the game or cannot provide eight players to finish the game (4-4-1f). If a team drops to eight players, an out will be called each time that spot in the batting order comes to bat. If the offensive player must be substituted for after reaching base, the most recent batter not on base is allowed to run for that player. Also, a team playing with fewer than nine players may return to nine players (4-4-1f notes, 7-4-1g).

Rationale

This 2007 rule change allows a team to return to nine players if they had dropped to eight during the game for any reason, as long as they have eligibility in the game. An injured player may return once he is able to continue (if he has re-entry privileges available) or a player that has arrived late may be entered into the game.

No Eligible Substitutes: Caseplays

4.4.1 SITUATION A: F8 must leave the game in the sixth inning (a) due to an ankle injury, (b) for band practice or (c) because he was ejected for unsportsmanlike behavior. There are no eligible substitutes available. **RULING:** In (a), (b) and (c), the game will be continued with an automatic out being called whenever it is F8's turn at bat. The team may play with eight and if an eligible substitute shows up later, they may return to playing with nine players.

Did You Know?

When the rule allowing a team to finish a game with eight players was adopted in 1985, it provided that if the team dropped to eight players because of an ejection, the game would still be forfeited. If a player left the game because of injury or illness, the team would be able to finish with eight players. The rule was changed in 1989 when it was reported that coaches were holding back a player in case of ejection instead of giving him an opportunity to play.

4.4.1 SITUATION B: B1 is injured (a) before reaching first on ball four, (b) sliding safely into second base or (c) while running to third base. Team A has no eligible substitutes available. **RULING:** Team A can continue playing with eight players. The most recent batter not on base may serve as a courtesy runner for the injured B1 in (a) and (b) but not in (c) if he is tagged, provided he is not awarded a base. An out will be called out whenever that batter's turn is reached in the batting order. Depending on the circumstances, time is normally not called when a player is injured.

4.4.1 SITUATION C: Because of an injury in the fourth inning and with no substitutes available, Team A is forced to play with eight players. In the sixth inning, (a) several junior varsity players, or (b) a couple of varsity players who were involved with exams arrive at the game. The coach of Team A would like to return to a nine player line-up by replacing the injured player. Is this legal? **RULING:** Yes in (a) and (b). Even though these players were not at the game or listed on the lineup card when it started, they would not be prohibited from playing.

 COMMENT: Team A is not required to return to a nine player line-up. The players in (a) and (b) may be used as substitutes for any of the remaining players.

4.4.1 SITUATION D: While sliding into second base, R1 cuts his knee or twists his ankle. The injured or bleeding player is given a reasonable amount of time to treat the wound or recover from the injury. However, the injured player is unable to continue in a reasonable time and is replaced by a legal substitute. If there are no available substitutes and the team is forced to play with eight players, is the injured player allowed to return if he is a starter? **RULING:** Yes. The injured or bleeding player may re-enter if he was a starter.

Re-entry

Any of the starting players may be withdrawn and re-entered once, including a player who was the designated hitter, provided such player occupies the same batting position whenever he is in the lineup. A substitute who is withdrawn may not re-enter (3-1-3). A starting pitcher who is replaced in the top of the first inning while his team is at bat shall be governed by the rules covering pitching substitutions (3-1-3 note).

In Simple Terms

All players, including the DH, listed on the starting lineup can leave the game and return one time. Subs may never re-enter after leaving the game.

Re-entry: Caseplays

3.1.3 SITUATION A: A starting player re-enters the game a second time (third time in the game) either as (a) F1, or (b) F8 or (c) batter. **RULING:** In (a) and (b), the fielder shall be restricted to the bench immediately when discovered. In (c), the illegal substitute is out and restricted to the bench.

3.1.3 SITUATION B: Jones is a starting player in center field and batting second in the batting order. In the third inning he is withdrawn and Smith replaces him. Subsequently the coach desires to re-enter Jones as catcher and have him bat in eighth position. **RULING:** Illegal. Jones may re-enter only to replace Smith. If Smith had been replaced earlier by Gregory, when Jones re-entered he would have to replace Gregory. Jones, Smith and Gregory are all required to occupy the second place in the batting order. However, they may play various positions. Neither Jones, Smith nor Gregory may be transferred to any other position in the batting order nor may they replace any other players already in the lineup, and only Jones could re-enter (once) because of being a starting player. When a substitute is withdrawn from the game, he may not be re-entered.

 COMMENT: Rule 3-1-3 permits any of the starting players to be withdrawn from the game and re-entered once, provided such player occupies the same batting position whenever he is in the lineup. Additionally, 3-1-3 Note indicates that a substitute or a player who replaces the pitcher whose team is not at bat shall pitch to the first opponent to bat against him until that batter has advanced to first base, or has been put out, or until there is a third out. This is an excellent rule because it provides more players an opportunity to participate (3.1.3 Comment).

Umpiring Procedure

The umpire-in-chief shall record any reported substitutions on the lineup card and then announce immediately any change(s) to the opposing team. Projected substitutions are not allowed (3-1-1, 10-2-3d).

"Time" shall be called by the umpire and play is suspended when a player or coach requests it and it is granted by the umpire for a substitution (5-2-1e).

 **Did You Know?** A "liberalized" re-entry plan first appeared in the 1947 rulebook as being in use in some areas. Before being made an official rule, it was allowed by mutual consent of coaches.

Umpiring Procedure: Caseplays

3.1.1 SITUATION E: The coach of Team A tells the umpire that Jones will hit for Smith, who is the next batter, and replace Lee in left field the next time on defense. **RULING:** The umpire-in-chief shall accept the substitution of Jones hitting for Smith. However, no substitution shall be reported to the umpire-in-chief until such time as the substitution actually is made. Therefore, the umpire will tell the coach of Team A to wait until his team is going on defense before reporting any defensive substitution.

Fundamental #16

Defensive substitutions can only be made when a team is on defense.

3.1.1 SITUATION N: Smith is the catcher and Jones is the left fielder as their team leaves the field to come to bat. Their coach tells PU that Smith will go to left field and Jones will go in as catcher when the team returns to defense. The coach is really wishing to make the change so that the slower Jones can have a courtesy runner if he gets on base in the half-inning. **RULING:** The umpire shall not allow a projected substitution. Therefore, a courtesy runner would only be allowed to run for the player who was the catcher on defense before coming to bat (Courtesy Runner Rules).

Unreported Substitutions

Should there be no announcement of substitutions, a substitute has entered the game when the ball is live and a runner takes the place of a runner he has replaced; a pitcher takes his place on the pitcher's plate; a fielder reaches the position usually occupied by the fielder he has replaced; or a batter takes his place in the batter's box (3-1-1a through d).

Unreported Substitutions: Caseplays

3.1.1 SITUATION B: S1, who is an unreported eligible substitute, steps into the batter's box in place of B1, and after the first pitch to S1 (a) member of team at bat discovers that S1 has not been properly reported to umpire-in-chief; or (b) member of defensive team discovers that S1 has not been properly reported to umpire-in-chief; or (c) umpire discovers that S1 has not been properly reported to umpire-in-chief. **RULING:** In (a), (b) and (c), S1 was officially in the game once he entered the batter's box and the ball was live. Therefore, he assumes the count. There is no penalty.

3.1.1 SITUATION D: S1 enters the game for starter F3. S1 or his coach fails to report to the umpire-in-chief. While S1 is playing, the (a) team at bat; or (b) the defensive team; or (c) an umpire discovers the infraction. Has F3 been out of the game? **RULING:** Yes. F3 may re-enter according to Rule 3-1-3.

3.1.1 SITUATION F: S1 replaces B5 in the third inning. In the seventh inning with two outs, R2 on second and R1 on first, B5 re-enters without reporting. B5 hits to F4 who misplays the ball, and all runners are safe after advancing. The defensive team's coach approaches the plate umpire to question if B5 had been reported. **RULING:** S1 is out of the game; B5 is a legal substitute even though he did not report.

3.1.1 SITUATION H: S1, an unreported substitute, is batting for B2 instead of B3. While at bat, S1's coach realizes S1 is not batting for the correct player. **RULING:** Since S1 became a legal substitute upon entering the batter's box when the ball became live, S1 is officially at bat and B2 is considered out of the game. The next batter is B3 (2-36-2, 3-1-1).

3.1.1 SITUATION J: S1 comes in for F7 in the second inning, but is not discovered. In the seventh inning, S1 comes in for F8 and is batting when the opposing team contends that S1 was a substitute earlier in the game. **RULING:** Unless the umpire has knowledge that S1 had in fact been in the game earlier, S1 cannot be treated as an illegal substitute.

Warming Up

Whenever team members are loosening up in an area which is not protected by a fence or other structure, another member of the team with a glove must be positioned between them and the batter to protect them from a batted or thrown ball within the confines of the playing field. No one is to interfere with a live ball (3-3-4).

Did You Know?	In 1977, substitutes that did not report to the umpire-in-chief were disqualified for the game as illegal substitutes. In addition, the player they replaced was considered out of the game, so an additional player would have to be inserted into the lineup. The current rule was adopted in 1994.

Warming Up: Caseplay

3.3.4 SITUATION: Player(s) are loosening up beyond first base and in foul territory, the area is unprotected (a) a player with a glove is positioned between the player(s) loosening up and the batter to serve as a protector. (b) No player is available to assume a position between the player(s) loosening up and the batter to serve as a protector. (c) a player without a glove is positioned between the player(s) loosening up and the batter to serve as a protector. **RULING:** In (a), legal. In (b), illegal, if no player is available to assume a position between the player(s) loosening up and the batter, the player(s) must loosen up outside the confines of the field. In (c) illegal, the player serving as the protector to the player(s) loosening up must have a glove.

 COMMENT: It is not mandatory, but recommended that the protector wear a helmet.

Topic:
Coaches

Coaching Box Requirements

One player or coach may occupy each coach's box while his team is at bat. A coach who is not in the uniform of the team shall be restricted to the bench/dugout. However, a coach may leave the bench/dugout to attend to a player who becomes ill or injured. He may address base runners or the batter. Coaches may wear prostheses and use mobility devices. Any member of the team at bat, who has not been ejected for unsportsmanlike conduct, may occupy a coach's box (3-2-1).

It is mandatory for players/students in the coaches boxes to wear a batting helmet that has a non-glare (not mirror-like) surface and meets the NOCSAE standard at the time of manufacture (1-5-1).

◰ Rationale

The 2008 rule change took out the restriction that a coach must be in the box for a certain length of time. The baseball rules committee determined the rule was not needed.

Coaching Box Requirements: Caseplays

3.2.1 SITUATION A: The first-base coach occupies the coaching box in a wheelchair. **RULING:** This is legal.

3.2.1 SITUATION B: The visiting team's head coach occupies the third-base coaching box with a walker. **RULING:** This is legal.

3.2.1 SITUATION C: The home team's head coach was in a car accident and as a result has his leg in a cast and must use a cane. **RULING:** As long as the cast is padded with at least one-half inch of closed-cell, slow-recovery rubber, he may occupy the coaching box. The use of a cane is legal.

3.2.1 SITUATION D: During the game, the coach from Team A goes onto the field to have a defensive conference. The coach is not wearing the team uniform. **RULING:** Illegal. Coaches are required to be in team uniform. If the coach is not properly attired, then he cannot leave the bench/dugout unless attending to a player.

3.2.1 SITUATION E: (a) The home team's assistant coach appears in the first base coaches' box wearing team-colored wind pants and jacket (b) The assistant coach appears in the first base coaches' box wearing team pants and a batting practice top. **RULING:** (a) Illegal. In (b), while occupying a coach's box, he shall be in the uniform of his team. However, state associations may allow for reasonable accommodations that are consistent with the team uniform.

3.2.1 SITUATION F: The home team's head coach appears in the game not in the team uniform but in business casual dress (a) The head coach calls time-out and calls the infield over to the dugout; (b) the head coach calls time and walks out to the mound to confer with the pitcher; (c) the head coach calls time-out to attend to an injured player. **RULING:** (a) No penalty, coaches who have been restricted to the dugout are permitted to conduct charged conferences from their team bench/dugout. That conference shall end when the players involved start to return to their positions on the field (b) Illegal. Only persons in uniform shall appear outside of the bench/dugout (c) Legal. A coach not in uniform may leave the bench/dugout, when requested by the umpire, to attend to a player who becomes ill or injured.

3.2.1 SITUATION G: Team D's coach is not able to be in the coaching box due to the fact that Team C's facility does not have lines drawn on the field. He wants the umpire-in-chief to declare a forfeit of the game. **RULING:** The umpire-in-chief does not honor Team D's forfeiture request, advises Team C's coach that the lines need to be put down, allows the game to begin and monitors the positioning of the coaches during the contest.

7.4.1 SITUATION H: B1 batting, he hits a high foul pop up just beyond first base. F3 starts toward the ball, B1's coach tries to get out of F3's way but hinders his attempt to catch the ball. **RULING:** The ball is dead and B1 is out due to his coach's interference with F3. Though unintentional, the inference still stands.

Forbidden Equipment

Use of any object in the coach's box other than a stopwatch, rule book (hard copy), scorebook (3-3-1h), and use of amplifiers or bullhorns for coaching purposes during the course of the game (3-3-1k) are forbidden.

◰ Rationale

Technology has improved to the level that mobile devices can accurately video different aspects of the game and provide an unfair advantage to a coach by replaying the footage in the dugout/bench during the contest. Too many items in the coach's box could possibly draw the attention of the coach away from the game and the oversight of the students under his charge. Restriction of certain items creates a positive and focused environment for the players and officials.

Forbidden Equipment: Caseplays

3.3.1 SITUATION O: An individual occupying a coach's box has (a) stopwatch, (b) rule book (hard copy) or (c) scorebook (hard copy). **RULING:** Legal in (a), (b) and (c).

3.3.1 SITUATION P: An individual occupying a coach's box has (a) miniature radar gun or (b) any electronic device, including but not limited to a cell phone, smartphone, tablet, netbook or notebook computer. **RULING:** Illegal in (a) and (b). The umpire may either restrict the coach to the bench/dugout or eject him from the game.

3.3.1 SITUATION OO: The umpire observes the assistant coach in uniform videotaping the game from the (a) dugout or (b) stands. **RULING:** Legal in (a); illegal in (b).

3.3.1 SITUATION PP: The third-base coach is in the coach's box using a video camera to tape the pitcher's move to first base. **RULING:** This is not legal. The third-base coach shall be restricted to the dugout bench for the remainder of the game or ejected.

Leaving the Dugout
A coach, player, substitute, attendant or other bench personnel shall not leave the dugout during a live ball for an unauthorized purpose (3-3-1a). A coach, player, substitute or other bench personnel shall not be outside the designated dugout (bench) or bullpen area if not a batter, runner, on-deck, batter, in the coach's box or one of the nine players on defense (3-3-1i).

Leaving the Dugout: Penalty
At the end of playing action, the umpire shall issue a warning to the coach of the team involved and the next offender on that team shall be ejected (3-3-1 penalty).

Leaving the Dugout: Caseplays
3.3.1 SITUATION A: Score tied and R3 at third. B2 hits single to right. R3 scores and several players leave dugout to congratulate R3. **RULING:** At the end of playing action, the umpire will issue a warning to the coach of Team A and eject the next offender. If a warning has already been issued all players leaving the bench/dugout area will be ejected.

3.3.1 SITUATION B: B1 hits a single and the batboy runs out to retrieve the bat. Should the bat boy be ejected? **RULING:** No the intent is to limit offensive players from flooding the plate area and possibly interfering with play around home plate.

3.3.1 SITUATION C: As the go ahead run scores on a gapper to left center field, several players come out of the dugout/bench to congratulate the runner and to celebrate the run. Following cessation of play, the opposing coach argues that they should all, or at least some of them be ejected. **RULING:** The umpire-in-chief will treat this incident as a single incident. He will warn the team's coach that a subsequent violation of the rule by a member of the team will result in an ejection and will record this warning on the lineup card.

3.3.1 SITUATION D: The home team, having previously been given a warning for players approaching home to congratulate a teammate while the ball was still live and in play, Smith and Black rush out to "high-five" Jones who just scored on a sacrifice fly. **RULING:** Following the end of playing action, the umpire-in-chief will inform the home team coach that Smith and Black are ejected for leaving the dugout during a live ball. He should remind the coach of the previous incident and warning which has led to these ejections because of the repeated offense.

3.3.1 SITUATION E: The runner scores on the batter's double, while the ball is still live, players from the offensive team dugout come out to congratulate the runner. **RULING:** At the end of playing action, the umpire shall issue a warning to the coach of the team involved and the next offender on that team shall be ejected.

3.3.1 SITUATION F: During live playing action Team A sends two players out to the bullpen down the left field line to warm up. **RULING:** Legal, warming up a pitcher is an authorized reason for players to be outside their dugouts while play is live.

3.3.1 SITUATION AAA: A player from Team A (who has been previously warned) hits a 3-run home run out of the field of play and wins the game by one run. The teammates of Team A rush out of the dugout and excitedly cheer for their teammate. The coach from Team B wants the players' violation of the rule to be the second violation and have the game forfeited to Team B because Team A failed to comply with the previous warning. **RULING:** Incorrect interpretation. By rule, no one should be out of the dugout/bench area or bullpen if not a batter, runner, on-deck batter, in the coach's box or one of the nine players on defense during a live ball. The home run is an exciting element in the game of baseball. Since the ball is dead, the teammates of the batter are permitted to be out of the dugout to celebrate. However, precautions should be taken not to interfere with the umpire's ability to see the batter touch all the bases. In fact, the players should be behind the umpire until the runner scores.

3.3.1 SITUATION BBB: Between innings, the non-playing players of Team A run in foul territory toward the outfield fence to stay loose. The coach of Team B protests that this is not legal and is delaying the contest. **RULING:** The coach of Team B is incorrect. It is legal provided this activity does not delay the start of the next half-inning.

Topic:
Umpire's Decisions

Lights
The umpire-in-chief's shall order the lights turned on whenever he believes darkness could make further play hazardous. Whenever possible, lights should be turned on at the beginning of an inning (10-2-3n).

Lights: Caseplay
10.2.3 SITUATION L: With R1 on first and one out, B3 hits a ground ball to F6. F6 flips the ball to F4 who steps on the base to force R1 out. As F4 throws the ball to F3, the lights go out. **RULING:** R1 is out at second base. The umpire uses his best judgment in ruling on the play at first base.

Penalizing Infractions
The umpire-in-chief shall penalize for rule infractions, such as balk, interference, baserunning infractions, delay, unwarranted disputing of decision or unsportsmanlike conduct (10-2-3f).

Rectifying Decisions
The umpire-in-chief shall rectify any situation in which an umpire's decision that was reversed has placed either team at a disadvantage (10-2-3l).

Rectifying Decisions: Caseplays
10.2.3 SITUATION E: With R1 on first and a three-ball, two-strike count on B2, R1 attempts to steal second on the next pitch, which is ball four. The base umpire, R1 and F4 do not realize it was ball four and R1 is called out on the play. R1 then quickly heads for the bench and is tagged out during the confusion. **RULING:** The umpire shall put R1 back on second base because it was his decision that caused R1 to leave the bag.

10.2.3 SITUATION H: With a count of three balls and two strikes on B2 and R1 on first base, the batter takes what appears to be a half swing. The plate umpire calls ball four and R1, upon hearing ball four, then trots to second base. The catcher throws the ball to F4 who tags R1 before he reaches base. The catcher asks the plate umpire to check with the base umpire to see if B2 did, in fact, attempt to hit the pitch. The base umpire indicates that the batter did swing at the ball. **RULING:** The plate umpire will declare the batter out and return R1 to first base. The umpire-in-chief can rectify any situation in which an umpire's decision that was reversed has placed a base runner in jeopardy.

In Simple Terms

The umpire-in-chief may correct mistakes, as long as he acts within the rules in doing so.

10.2.3 SITUATION I: With a count of three balls and two strikes on B1 and no runners on base, the pitch is made and the batter takes what appears to be a half swing. The plate umpire calls ball four as the ball gets away from F2. B1 trots to first base and F2 throws the ball to F3, who tags B1 prior to his reaching the base. F2 asks the plate umpire to check with the base umpire to see if it was a strike. The base umpire indicates that B1 did swing at the ball. **RULING:** If, in the judgment of the umpire-in-chief, B1 would have reached first base before the throw if it had not been called ball four, the plate umpire can award B1 first base. The umpire-in-chief can rectify any situation in which an umpire's decision has placed a batter-runner in jeopardy. Advances and outs made by runners following a reversed call stand, if the call that was changed clearly did not place them in jeopardy.

10.2.3 SITUATION M: With R3 on third base and R1 on first base, B3 hits a ground ball to F4. F4 moves forward to field the ball and R1 collides with him. The umpire mistakenly calls obstruction and R3 scores. The umpire then realizes that he should have called interference. **RULING:** By reversing his decision, the umpire shall call R1 out and return R3 to third base.

10.2.3 SITUATION N: With two outs and runners on first and second bases, B5 hits a ground ball to F3 who backhands the ball and shovels a throw to F1. The base umpire calls B5 out, but B5 asks the base umpire to check with the plate umpire because B5 thought F1 pulled his foot. During the discussion, R2 from second scores. The plate umpire indicates that F1 did in fact pull his foot. The base umpire then calls the batter-runner safe. The coach of the defensive team tells the umpire that because the call was reversed, a run scored. Therefore, R2 should have to return to third base. **RULING:** The umpire shall return R2 to third, R1 to second, and B5 to first base in accordance with Rule 10-2-3l.

 COMMENT: If proper umpire mechanics were used, this situation would not have occurred.

Suspension of Play

"Time" is the command of the umpire to suspend play. The ball becomes dead when it is given (2-38-1, 5-1-1a).

The ball becomes immediately dead when the umpire handles a live ball or calls "time" for inspecting the ball or for any other reason or gives the "Do Not Pitch Signal" or inadvertently announces "Foul" on a ball that touches the ground (5-1-1h).

"Time" shall be called by the umpire and play is suspended when an umpire or player is incapacitated, except that if injury occurs during a live ball, time shall not be called until no further advance or putout is possible. If there is a medical emergency or if, in the umpire's judgment, further play could jeopardize the injured player's safety, "Time" shall be called (5-2-1d).

Suspension of Play: Caseplays

5.1.4 SITUATION A: The umpire decides the ball is not suitable for play and gives F2 a new ball. Is the ball live? **RULING:** When the umpire calls "Time" for inspection of a ball, it remains dead until held by F1 while on the pitcher's plate, B1 and F2 are in their respective boxes and the umpire calls "Play." He then should give the proper signal.

5.2.1 SITUATION C: B1 (a) hits a home run over the fence or (b) receives a base on balls or, (c) is struck by a pitched ball. In each instance, B1 is unable to reach his awarded base because of an injury sustained during the play. **RULING:** In (a), (b) and (c), because bases are awarded, a pinch runner may replace the injured player and continue to the awarded bases. In (b), since the ball is live, the umpire has to call "Time." He will then permit a substitute to run for the injured player according to 10-2-3g.

Topic:
Conduct

Tobacco Use

A coach, player, substitute, attendant or other bench personnel shall not use tobacco or tobacco-like products within the confines of the field. The umpire shall eject the offender from the game. Failure to comply shall result in game being forfeited (3-3-1o).

Umpires shall not use tobacco or tobacco-like products on or in the vicinity of the playing field (10-1-8).

▨ Rationale

In 1996, the committee said that "Because umpires are considered role models, they are prohibited from using tobacco or tobacco-like products on or in the vicinity of the playing field."

Tobacco Use: Caseplays

3.3.1 SITUATION RR: The umpire discovers Team A's coach (a) using tobacco while on the bench, (b) using tobacco while outside the confines of the field or (c) with a tin of smokeless tobacco in his hip pocket. **RULING:** In (a), the umpire shall eject the coach. In (b), there is no penalty since the coach is outside the confines of the field. In (c), the umpire shall ask the coach to rid himself of tobacco or tobacco-like products.

3.3.1 SITUATION SS: While on the bench, two players appear to the umpire to be using tobacco. The umpire discovers that the substance is not tobacco, but a tobacco-like product. **RULING:** Both players are in violation of the rule and shall be ejected. Even though the players were not using tobacco, they gave the appearance of using a tobacco product, which is not acceptable.

3.3.1 SITUATION TT: B1 hits a home run over the fence. Before he touches home plate, the umpire notices that B1 has smokeless tobacco in his mouth. **RULING:** At the end of playing action, B1 shall be ejected. The run counts.

10.1.8 SITUATION A: On the way to the parking lot after the game, the umpire is seen using tobacco or a tobacco-like product by a coach or someone from the home team's management. **RULING:** An umpire who uses tobacco or tobacco-like products in the vicinity of the playing field is in violation of the rule. The state association should be notified of the infraction.

10.1.8 SITUATION B: Before the game, an umpire is observed by one of the coaches using tobacco or a tobacco-like product near the bleachers. **RULING:** The coach should report the infraction to the state association. Umpires are prohibited from using tobacco or tobacco-like products in the vicinity of the playing field.

Unsportsmanlike Acts

A coach, player, substitute, attendant or other bench personnel shall not commit any unsportsmanlike act to include, but not limited to use of words or actions to incite or attempt to incite spectators demonstrations; use of profanity, intimidation tactics, remarks reflecting unfavorably upon any other person, or taunting or baiting. The NFHS disapproves of any form of taunting that is intended or designed to embarrass, ridicule or demean others under circumstances including race, religion, gender or national origin; use of any language intended to intimidate; behavior in any manner not in accordance with the spirit of fair play; be in live ball territory (excluding team's bullpen area) during the opponent's infield practice prior to the start of the game; or any member of the coaching staff who was not the head coach (or designee) in 3-2-4 leaves the vicinity of the dugout or coaching box to dispute a judgment call by an umpire (3-3-1f 1 through 6).

A coach, player, substitute, attendant or other bench personnel shall not commit any unsportsmanlike act to include, but not limited to confronting or directing unsportsmanlike conduct to the umpires after the game has concluded and until the umpires have departed the game site (3-3-1f (7)). For violations, the state association shall determine appropriate action.

A coach, player, substitute, attendant or other bench personnel shall not enter the area behind the catcher while the opposing pitcher and catcher are in their positions (3-3-1g); charge an umpire (3-3-1j) or leave their positions or bench area during a fight or physical confrontation (3-3-1p).

The umpire-in-chief shall keep a written record of team and coach warnings (10-2-3j).

In Simple Terms

The head coach is the only person permitted to leave his position for the purposes of discussing a call with an umpire.

Unsportsmanlike Acts: Penalties

For coaches who violate (3-3-1) f (1-5), g, h, i, j, and k, the umpire shall warn the offender unless the offense is judged to be major, in which case an ejection shall occur. A warning may be verbal or written. If written, the offender shall be restricted to the bench/dugout for the remainder of the game. If a coach has previously received a verbal warning, he shall receive a written warning (10-2-3j) and be restricted to the bench/dugout for the remainder of the game. If a coach has previously received a written warning, he shall be ejected for any subsequent offense. Any offense judged to be major in nature shall result in an immediate ejection. For coaches who violate f (1-5), g, h, i, j or k, the umpire may: (1) issue a ver- bal warning to the offender, (2) issue a written warning to the offender (any offender receiving a written warning shall be restricted to the bench/dugout for the remainder of the game), or (3) eject the offender for a major offense. For violation of f(6) both the head coach and offending coach shall receive a writ- ten warning and be restricted to the dugout for the remainder of the game unless the offense is so severe the umpire may eject the offender and restrict or eject the head coach. A coach may leave the bench/dugout to attend to a player who becomes ill or injured.

Leaving their position or bench area for the purpose of fighting or physical confrontations shale result in the offender being ejected from the game. Failure to comply shall result in game being forfeited. A coach who attempts to prevent a fight or restore order is not in violation of the rule (3-3-1 penalty).

A coach who is ejected shall leave the vicinity of the playing area immediately and is prohibited from further contact, direct or indirect, with the team during the remainder of the game. He may return when requested to attend to an ill or injured player (3-3-2).

The umpire-in-chief's duties include ejecting player or coach or clear the bench or send a coach from the field or restrict a coach or player (illegal substitution) to the bench/dugout if it becomes necessary (10-2-3c). A field umpire shall have concurrent jurisdiction with the umpire-in-chief in ejecting any coach or player for flagrant, unsportsmanlike conduct or infraction as prescribed by the rules (10-3-1).

Rationale

The rules committee, in 1989, instituted the rule that allows an umpire to restrict a coach to the dugout. Depending on state association rules, if a coach was ejected and another school faculty member was not available to take over, the game would be forfeited. The committee felt that every attempt should be made to keep the game from being forfeited. Even with this rule, the umpire still has the authority to eject a coach at any time if the umpire feels the coach's actions warrant such a penalty.

Unsportsmanlike Acts: Caseplays

3.3.1 SITUATION G: F1 is removed by his coach during the game. Following the last out of the game, (a) F1 makes an unsportsmanlike comment to PU near home plate regarding his strike zone; (b) F1 berates the umpires as they leave the field heading to their vehicles. **RULING:** In (a), the umpires have jurisdiction until both of them leave the confines of the field, F1 is ejected and a written report is sent to the state association; (b) while no longer having jurisdiction, the umpires shall send a written report to the state association, which will determine the appropriate response (10-1-2).

3.3.1 SITUATION H: Team A is taking infield practice and Team B has lined up along the first base foul line making unsportsmanlike comments to Team A members. **RULING:** The umpire warns Team B to return to its dugout or its bullpen or he will enforce the unsportsmanlike penalty (3-3-1f Penalty).

3.3.1 SITUATION I: Team B players have positioned themselves along the third base line. The umpire has previously issued a warning to Team B's coach. Jones makes disconcerting comments about Team A's player, Smith, during infield practice. Smith throws a ball at Jones and a fight ensues. **RULING:** Team B's coach is restricted to the bench for the duration of the game. Jones is ejected from the game. Smith is ejected from the game and any player who participated in the fight is ejected from the game.

3.3.1 SITUATION J: As Team A takes infield prior to the game, several members of Team B yell insulting remarks to various players of Team A and make fun of their uniforms. **RULING:** The umpire should warn the coach of Team B immediately that if any of his players make further remarks or try to antagonize Team A in any way, the offender(s) shall be ejected from the game and directed away from live-ball territory.

3.3.1 SITUATION K: With R3 at third, teammates in the third-base dugout, start yelling, "Squeeze, Squeeze," on each pitch as the pitcher starts his motion. The umpire requests that players refrain from continuing. The coach replies that there is no rule prohibiting such action. **RULING:** After a warning, the coach may be restricted to the dugout, or if warranted, ejected for failure to comply with an order from an umpire.

3.3.1 SITUATION L: The umpire-in-chief requests that the third-base coach remain within the confines of the coaches' box. However, the coach argues that he can be outside the box since he is outside the line farthest from home plate. **RULING:** After a warning, the coach may be restricted to the dugout, or if warranted, ejected for failure to comply with an order from an umpire.

3.3.1 SITUATION M: In the top of the second inning, the plate umpire judges a pitch to be a "ball." The defensive team's head coach, who had not previously received a verbal or written warning, yells at the umpire from the dugout in protest of the umpire's call. **RULING:** If the umpire judges the coach's yelling to be rudimentary in nature, he should verbally warn the head coach that any further arguing may result in the coach's restriction to the dugout or ejection from the game. If the umpire judges the coach's actions to be more ill-mannered, he may issue a written warning and restrict the coach to dugout. If the umpire judges the coach's action to be "innappropriate," the coach should be ejected.

3.3.1 SITUATION N: The defensive team's head coach, who had previously received a verbal warning, yells at the umpire from the dugout in protest of anoth- er call. **RULING:** If the umpire judges the coach's yelling to be rudimentary in nature, he should issue a written warning to the coach and restrict the coach to the dugout for the remainder of the game. The umpire should notate on his lineup card the coach's name, the point in the game of the warning (inning, number of outs and location of runners) and the reason for the warning. If the umpire judges the coach's yelling to be "inappropriate," the head coach should be ejected.

3.3.1 SITUATION Q: The defensive team's head coach, who had previously received a verbal warning and a subsequent written warning (and restriction to the dugout) now yells at the umpire from the dugout in protest of another call. **RULING:** The coach shall be ejected.

3.3.1 SITUATION R: The defensive team's head coach comes out of the dugout to argue a call. During the argument, the coach (a) swears at the umpire, (b) makes contact with the umpire, (c) turns to the crowd and incites the spectators. **RULING:** In (a) (b) and (c), if the umpire judges the coach's actions to be "inap- propriate," the coach shall be ejected even though he had not received a previous verbal or written warning.

3.3.1 SITUATION S: If an umpire judges a coach's unsportsmanlike conduct to be more than "rudimentary" in nature, but not "severe" enough to warrant an ejection, may the umpire issue a written warning and restrict the coach to the dugout? **RULING:** Yes, in such a situation an umpire may issue a written warning and restrict to the dugout a coach who had not previously been verbally warned.

3.3.1 SITUATION T: R3 is on third base with one out. B1 hits a pop fly to F7 and the ball is caught for an out. The assistant coach is in the dugout recording the play. The head coach brings the recording to the field to challenge that R3 left the base early and insists on reviewing the play. **RULING:** The umpire informs the coach to return to the dugout. If the coach continues to argue, the umpire shall restrict and, if deemed unsportsmanlike, may eject the coach.

3.3.1 SITUATION U: The coach is using a radar gun in the dugout to record the pitches of the opposing player. **RULING:** Legal. Coaches may use radar guns in the dugout, but not on the field.

3.3.1 SITUATION V: With a base runner on first and following an attempted steal, the assistant coach for Team A who is coaching first, leaves the coaching box and charges onto the field to talk to the base umpire in a two-person crew arguing that the runner was safe on the steal attempt. **RULING:** The assistant coach who was coaching first, and the head coach receive a written warning and are both restricted to the dugout for the remainder of the game. If the conduct of the either coach were of such gravity to violate rule 3-3-1f in other parts, the coach(es) could be ejected.

3.3.1 SITUATION W: With a base runner on first and following an attempted steal, the assistant coach for Team A who is coaching first, steps toward the base umpire but remains in the vicinity of the coaching box and asks for clarification from the umpire about the play. The coach commits no other 3-3-1f violation. **RULING:** There is no penalty against the assistant coach for this act.

3.3.1 SITUATION X: The batter/runner is called out on a close play at first base. The assistant coach for that team (which is in the third base dugout) leaves the vicinity of the dugout to voice his displeasure with the call by the first base umpire. **RULING:** The assistant coach who left the dugout, and the Head coach are now restricted to the dugout for the remainder of the game. If the conduct of the either coach were of such gravity to violate rule 3-3-1f in other parts, the coach(es) could be ejected.

3.3.1 SITUATION Y: Team A has three adult coaches. In the first inning, an assistant violates 3-3-1f(6) resulting in the restriction of the assistant coach and the head coach to the dugout. In the third inning, Assistant Coach B, leaves the dugout protesting the call on a check swing. **RULING:** The head coach remains restricted to the dugout even though two different assistant coaches have now been penalized in accordance with this rule.

COMMENT: Each act must be judged on its own merit and multiple violations do not automatically call for ejection of the head coach.

3.3.1 SITUATION Z: Team A has three adult coaches. One assistant coach leaves the dugout to object to a call at the plate. During the discussion, PU informs the assistant coach that he and the head coach will now receive a written warning and be restricted to the dugout for the remainder of the game. The second assistant now enters the discussion directing profanity toward the umpire or otherwise violating 3-3-1f(6). **RULING:** The second assistant coach is ejected from the contest. The first assistant coach and the head coach are restricted if no other violations occurred by these individuals.

 COMMENT: Each act must be judged on its own merit and it is possible that differing penalties are imposed on different people.

3.3.1 SITUATION AA: At the end of a half inning, the first-base coach leaves the coaching box to return to the third base dugout. In passing the umpire(s), the assistant coach asks for clarification on a play or stops for a quick discussion about a ruling. The coach commits no other 3-3-1f violation. **RULING:** There is no penalty against the assistant coach for this act as leaving the vicinity of the coaching box is required to go to the dugout between innings.

3.3.1 SITUATION BB: Team A has one of its players in uniform in the bleachers behind home plate or in the bleachers along the third-base line. **RULING:** All players, attendants and bench personnel shall remain in the dugout (bench) or bullpen at all times, unless they are a batter, runner, on-deck batter, an occupant of a coach's box or one of the nine players on defense. The umpire shall eject the offender from the game, unless the offense is judged to be of a minor nature, in which case the umpire may warn the offender and then eject him if he repeats the offense. Failure to comply shall result in the game being forfeited.

3.3.1 SITUATION MM: B1, the team's top hitter, goes to the plate representing the winning run. B1 works the count to 3-1. The opposing team decides to put B1 on and has the pitcher deliver an intentional ball. Upon receiving ball four, B1 angrily utters profanity. **RULING:** The umpire shall give the dead-ball signal and eject B1 at the end of playing action. A substitute is allowed to replace B1 at first base.

3.3.1 SITUATION QQ: Players from Team A begin taunting a player from Team B. **RULING:** If, in the judgment of the umpire, the infraction is of a minor nature, then the umpire shall issue a team warning to the coach of the involved players. Otherwise, the umpire shall eject the players, which also shall serve as a team warning.

3.3.1 SITUATION WW: R1 slides hard into F4. R1 and F4 begin pushing each other. F6 and the on-deck batter run to second base to break up the fight. **RULING:** All are ejected. Once F6 and the on-deck batter left their positions and advanced toward the fight, they were in violation of the rule.

3.3.1 SITUATION XX: R1 and F6 begin shoving each other. Their respective coaches rush to the field to control their players. **RULING:** R1 and F6 are ejected, but the coaches are not, because they are allowed on the field to break up the fight or to help restore order.

3.3.1 SITUATION YY: As a fight breaks out, Team A's coach rushed on to the field to control his player. As he begins to leave the field, a player from the other team advises the coach to have his team show better sportsmanship. The coach advances toward the player and says something to that player. **RULING:** The coach shall be ejected.

3.3.1. SITUATION ZZ: During the third inning, a fight breaks out between the batter and the pitcher near home plate, and (a) a non-participating player leaves the dugout/bench to retrieve a bat near the two combatants; (b) several players leave the dugout/bench to restore order; (c) F8 leaves his position to observe the confrontation. **RULING:** In (a), (b) and (c), the umpire shall eject all players who left the dugout/bench and/or their position during a fight.

3.3.2 SITUATION A: The coach has been ejected for unsportsmanlike conduct. Later in the game, his pitcher complains of a sore arm. The coach returns from the parking lot. **RULING:** This is not allowed. The coach must be requested by the umpire before he can return.

3.3.2 SITUATION B: After being ejected, Team A's coach (a) returns to the field to break up a fight; (b) returns to the field on his own to attend to an injured player; (c) returns on his own to check on a sick player; or (d) returns after being requested by the umpire to attend to an injured player. **RULING:** Illegal in (a), (b) and (c). A coach must first be requested by an umpire before he can return to attend to an ill or injured player. It is legal in (d).

3.3.2 SITUATION C: F4 is injured by R1's slide into second base. His coach, who is also the team trainer, was ejected earlier in the game. He is sitting in the parking lot away from the game. **RULING:** If the umpire believes that the injured player needs to be attended, he may request the ejected coach to return to the field. The coach cannot return unless requested by the umpire.

10.2.3 SITUATION J: During an extra-inning game, numerous team warnings were issued for various rules violations. B1, upon hitting the ball, carelessly throws his bat. The umpire proceeds to eject him at the end of playing action. The ejected player's coach claims a team warning should have been issued. The umpire said that he had already issued one. The coach asks to see the umpire's record of team warnings. The umpire said he did not record team warnings. **RULING:** The umpire is in violation of the rule but the ejection stands. The coach may wish to inform the state association or appropriate officials' association of the umpire's failure to record warnings.

Topic:
Conferences

A charged conference is a meeting which involves the coach or his non-playing representative and a player or players of the team (2-10-1). "Time" shall be called by the umpire and play is suspended when a player or coach's request for "Time" is granted by the umpire for a substitution, conference with the pitcher or for similar cause (5-2-1e).

The umpire-in-chief's duties include keeping a written record of defensive and offensive team charged conferences for each team and notify the respective coach each time a conference is charged to his team (10-2-3j).

In Simple Terms
A conference occurs when a coach meets with a member of his team and delays the game.

Defensive Conferences

Each team, when on defense, may be granted not more than three charged conferences during a seven-inning game, without penalty, to permit coaches or their non-playing representatives to confer with a defensive player or players. In an extra inning game, each team shall be permitted one charged conference each inning while on defense without penalty. The number of charged conferences permitted is not cumulative. A request for time for this purpose shall be made by a coach, player, substitute or an attendant. Time granted for an obviously incapacitated player shall not constitute a charged conference. Prior to accumulating three charged conferences in seven innings or less, a conference is not charged if the pitcher is removed as pitcher (3-4-1). After three charged conferences in a seven-inning game, or for any charged conference in excess of one in each extra inning, the pitcher shall be removed as pitcher for duration of the game (3-4-1 penalty).

A defensive charged conference is concluded when the coach or non-playing representative crosses the foul line if the conference was in fair territory. If the conference was in foul territory, the conference concludes when the coach or non-playing representative initially starts to return to the dugout/bench area (3-4-3).

Fundamental #17

Unused charged conferences do not carry over to extra innings.

Defensive Conferences: Caseplays

3.4.1 SITUATION A: The coach of the defensive team moves to the pitcher's mound in the eighth inning (a) after having used his three allowable defensive charged conferences in the first seven innings or (b) not having used any of his three allowable defensive charged conferences in the first seven innings. **RULING:** There is no penalty in either (a) or (b). A team is permitted three defensive charged conferences in a seven-inning game, and if a game goes into extra innings, that team is permitted only one charged defensive conference in each of the extra innings. Unused defensive charged conferences in the first seven innings are not accumulative.

3.4.1 SITUATION C: The coach of the defensive team has used his three charged conferences. In the seventh inning the coach (a) stops play to confer with his infielders about a bunt situation or (b) goes to the mound to check his pitcher who has just been hit by a batted ball. **RULING:** In (a), F1 must be removed as pitcher for the remainder of the game. In (b), this is not a charged conference.

3.4.1 SITUATION D: In the third inning the coach of the defensive team, who has yet to have a charged conference, goes to the mound to talk to his pitcher. He (a) changes pitchers or (b) does not change pitchers. The next inning he receives time to visit with his catcher. How many charged conferences has the coach accumulated? **RULING:** The meeting with the catcher is one charged conference. In (a), there is no charged conference, so the coach still has two charged conferences remaining. In (b), he has accumulated two charged conferences: one for the visit with the catcher and one for the pitcher who was not removed. Therefore, the coach would have one charged conference remaining.

3.4.1 SITUATION E: Team A has had two charged conferences. The coach of Team A is granted time to visit with his pitcher. At the same time his assistant coach goes out to talk to the first baseman. The opposing team's coach claims that another conference also should be assessed and that the pitcher would have to be removed, since it would be that team's fourth. **RULING:** As long as the assistant coach does not delay the game when play is to resume, there is no penalty. If he does delay, his team is subject to an additional charged conference being called, which then would require the pitcher to be removed as pitcher for the rest of the game.

3.4.1 SITUATION F: In the top of the fifth inning (a) the defensive team's head coach asks for "Time" to check on his center fielder who appeared to be ill. At the same time (b) the assistant coach goes to the pitcher's mound to visit with the pitcher. Has a charged conference occurred? **RULING:** A conference is not charged when "Time" is called for an obviously incapacitated player. In (a), if the umpire judged the player the coach went to check on was ill and unable to continue, then no conference would be called. In (b), since "Time" is out, the assistant coach is permitted on the field to talk to any defensive player. When play is to resume, if he is not off the field, he shall be charged a conference for delay. Note: If the umpire believes that a player is faking an injury so that a coach can talk to the pitcher or another defensive player without being charged a conference, the umpire may prohibit additional conferences from taking place at that time.

3.4.1 SITUATION G: Team A has had three charged conferences by the fifth inning. With the game tied in the sixth inning, the coach of Team A informs the umpire that (a) F6 and F1 are going to trade positions or (b) that S1 is replacing F1. Can the pitcher who is being replaced return to pitch later in the game, or is this considered a charged conference? **RULING:** In (a) and (b), the pitcher being replaced may return to pitch as long as all conditions of 3-1-2 Note are met. The umpire shall permit the coach to switch players or substitute, provided the coach does not take advantage of the situation by having a conversation with any of the players. A violation shall result in a charged conference being assessed, which would be more than allowed, resulting in the pitcher not being able to return to pitch (3-1-2 Note).

3.4.1 SITUATION H: Between innings the coach of Team A walks from the third base coach's box to the pitcher's mound and proceeds to visit with F1. **RULING:** F1 has one minute in which to complete his warmup throws. At that point, the coach should leave the field. The umpire should not allow play to begin until the coach is off the field. The umpire may assess the coach a charged conference if he delays leaving the field (6-2-2c Exception).

3.4.1 SITUATION I: The coach of the defensive team, just after the ball is returned to F1, yells from the dugout: (a) giving instructions to F4 and F6; or (b) to have F6 and F9 switch positions. **RULING:** Situations (a) and (b) do not warrant a charged conference being called (3-4-1, 3-4-3).

3.4.3 SITUATION: A coach goes to the pitcher's mound for a defensive charged conference. He (a) starts to return to his dugout but does not cross the foul line and returns to the pitcher's mound to continue the charged conference or (b) starts to return to his dugout, crosses the foul line, and then returns to the pitcher's mound. **RULING:** In (a) the coach is not charged for a second conference unless the umpire has told him previously his time was up. In (b), the coach is charged with a second conference as he ended the initial charged conference when he crossed the foul line unless he removes the pitcher after returning to the mound.

 **Did You Know?** In 1984, the rule concerning conferences was clarified to specify that a meeting between a catcher and pitcher was not a charged conference. A charged conference must involve a coach or his non-playing representative.

Offensive Conferences

Each team, when on offense, may be granted not more than one charged conference per inning to permit the coach or any of that team's personnel to confer with base runners, the batter, the on-deck batter or other offensive team personnel. The umpire shall deny any subsequent offensive team requests for charged conferences (3-4-2).

An offensive charged conference is concluded when the coach or team representative initially starts to return to the coach's box or dugout/bench area (3-4-4).

Offensive Conferences: Caseplay

3.4.4 SITUATION: A coach requests an offensive charged conference with R2 who is on second base. The coach goes to second base for the conference with the runner and then starts to return to the coach's box. **RULING:** The offensive charged conference ends when the coach starts to return to his position.

Length of Conferences

The coach shall be given a reasonable amount of time for the charged conference as determined by the umpire-in-chief (3-4-3, 3-4-4 notes).

Opposing Side Can Meet

When either team has a charged conference, the other team may also have a conference, which is not charged, provided the conference concludes when the opposing team's charged conference concludes, so that the game is not further delayed (3-4-5).

Opposing Side Can Meet: Caseplay

3.4.1 SITUATION B: The coach of the team at bat requests and is granted time so he may have a conference with either the batter or runner(s). Thereafter, if the defensive team's coach goes to the mound to talk to his pitcher, should the defensive team be charged with a conference also? **RULING:** No. When either team is granted time for a conference the other coach or representative may do likewise without being charged with a conference, unless the opposing coach or his representative delays the game by not being ready to play when the other team's charged conference is completed.

Restricted Coaches

If a coach who has been restricted to the dugout/bench area is involved in a charged conference, that conference shall end when the players involved initially start to return to their positions on the field (3-4-3, 3-4-4 notes).

Topic:
Game Stoppages

"Time" shall be called by the umpire and play is suspended when the umpire considers the weather or ground conditions unfit for play (5-2-1b). After 30 minutes, he may declare the game ended (5-2-1b note).

Game Stoppages: Caseplay

10.2.3 SITUATION A: After several innings have been played, it starts to rain and play is suspended by the umpire. If rain continues for 30 minutes, must the game be called? **RULING:** The umpire may call the game when he is convinced that conditions of the field will be such as to make continued play impossible. It is customary for the umpire to wait 30 minutes before making such an announcement. If, at the end of 30 minutes, there is still doubt as to whether or not the game may be resumed, such an announcement should be withheld until he is quite certain that no further play will be possible within a reasonable amount of time.

In Simple Terms
Participant safety is of fundamental importance. Chances should not be taken when weather is an issue.

Lightning

When thunder is heard or lightning is seen, the leading edge of the thunderstorm is close enough to strike your location with lightning. Suspend play and take shelter immediately. Suspend play for at least 30 minutes and vacate the outdoor activity to a previously designated safer location immediately. Once play has been suspended, wait at least 30 minutes after the last thunder is heard or flash of lightning is witnessed prior to resuming play. Any subsequent thunder or lightning after the beginning of the 30-minute count will reset the clock and another 30-minute count should begin.

When lighting-detection devices or mobile phone apps are available, this technology could be used to assist in making a decision to suspend play if a lightning strike is noted to be within 10 miles of the event location. However, you should never depend on the reliability of these devices and, thus, hearing thunder or seeing lightning should always take precedence over information from a mobile app or lightning-detection device.

Note: At night, under certain atmospheric conditions, lightning flashes may be seen from distant storms. In these cases, it may be safe to continue an event. If no thunder can be heard and the flashes are low on the horizon, the storm may not pose a threat. Independently verified lightning detection information would help eliminate any uncertainty (NFHS Guidelines on Handling Contests During Lightning Disturbances).

Topic:
Game Ends

Called Game

A called game is one which is ended by order of the umpires (2-17-2). The umpire-in-chief shall call the game if conditions become unfit for play (10-2-3e).

If a game is called before completion of the number of innings required to become a regulation game, the umpire shall declare the contest "no game," unless play is terminated by a state-adopted game-ending procedure (4-3-1). By state association adoption, a regulation called game where a winner cannot be determined shall be counted as a half-game won and a half-game lost for each team.

A called game that is to be completed at a later time is a suspended game (2-17-3).

Rationale

In 1996, specific rules concerning what game-ending procedures state could adopt were eliminated in favor of the current rule. There were too many possible adoptions, contributing to misunderstanding and misapplication of the rules. The committee decided state associations should be able to determine the game-ending procedures that best suit their individual philosophies and needs.

Called Game: Caseplays

4.3.1 SITUATION A: At the end of the fourth inning or during the top of the fifth inning, (a) the score is tied or (b) either team is ahead when rain halts play. **RULING:** Because the game has not gone the required number of innings to be regulation, the game shall be called "no game," unless the state association has adopted a game-ending procedure covering this situation. In (a) and (b), if 4 1/2 innings had been completed and the home team was leading, the game would be regulation.

4.3.1 SITUATION B: At the end of the fifth, sixth or seventh inning, (a) one team is ahead or (b) the score is tied when rain halts play. **RULING:** Since the required number of innings have been played to be a regulation game, a winner can be determined in (a). In (b), the game is tied, unless the state association has adopted a game-ending procedure covering the situation.

4.3.1 SITUATION C: At the end of five innings the score is tied. In the top of the sixth inning, the visiting team scores to go ahead when rain halts play. **RULING:** If a state association has adopted a game-ending procedure in which the game is suspended, it will be continued from the point of suspension with the lineup and batting order of each team the same as the lineup and batting order at the moment of suspension, subject to the rules of the game.

4.3.1 SITUATION D: In the top or bottom of the (a) second inning or (b) the sixth inning, the lights fail or the automatic sprinkler is activated and the game is halted. **RULING:** If there is the possibility that an individual purposely attempted to influence the outcome of a game by shutting off the lights or turning on the sprinklers, the state association may choose to suspend the game or adopt another game-ending procedure to cover this situation.

Forfeited Game

A forfeited game is one awarded to the opponent of the offending team (2-15-1). A game shall be forfeited to the offended team by the umpire when:

• A team is late in appearing or in beginning play after the umpire calls "Play." State associations are authorized to specify the time frame and/or circumstance before a forfeit will be declared for a late arrival by one of the teams.

• A team refuses to continue play after the game has started.

• A team delays more than a reasonable amount of time in resuming play, or in obeying the umpire's order to remove a player for violation of the rules.

• A team persists in tactics designed to delay or shorten the game.

• A team willfully and persistently violates any of the rules after being warned by the umpire.

• A team is unable to provide at least nine players to start the game or cannot provide eight players to finish the game.

• A team, on its home field, fails to comply with the umpire's order to put the field in condition for play (4-4-1).

The score of a forfeited game is 7-0 except if the game is forfeited after the number of innings required for a regulation game and the offending team is behind. Then the score remains as recorded. If the offending team is leading, the score shall be 7-0 (4-4-2).

The umpire-in-chief's duties include forfeiting the game for prescribed infractions by spectators, coaches, players or attendants (10-2-3h).

▟ Rationale

Prior to 1998, a team had only 15 minutes after the scheduled starting time to arrive or face forfeiture. The committee felt that was too restrictive since certain circumstances that might result in a game being delayed longer would not warrant a forfeit being declared.

Forfeited Game: Caseplays

4.4.1 SITUATION E: The opposing coaches submit their lineups to the umpire-in-chief. However, not all of the players of the visiting team are at the field. The coach lists the players not at the game as the eighth and ninth hitters to give them time to arrive. **RULING:** This is not allowable. At the time the lineups are exchanged, all starters must be at the field. Therefore, the coach of the visiting team must replace the players not at the game. If the coach does not have enough players to start the game, the game is forfeited (1-1-1).

4.4.1 SITUATION F: After waiting past the scheduled starting time for the visiting team to arrive, the coach of the home team asks the umpire-in-chief for a forfeit. **RULING:** State associations are authorized to determine circumstances and/or the time frame before a forfeit shall be declared for a late arrival by one of the teams.

Protest Procedure

It is optional on the part of a state association as to whether protests are permitted. When allowed, protests are permitted regarding rules one through nine only. When protests are submitted to organizations which do allow the filing, such protest must be submitted using a prescribed procedure (4-5-1).

When a game is played under the auspices of an organization which permits protests to be filed, the umpire-in-chief shall report the protest to the organization along with all related conditions at the time of the protested play, provided the protest is brought to the attention of an umpire by the offended team at the time of the play and before the next pitch after such play, or before the umpires leave the field if the play in question is the last play of the game. The umpire-in-chief shall then inform the coach of the opposing team and the official scorekeeper (10-2-3i). If there is a question about a rule that was possibly misapplied, the team's coach or captain shall inform the umpire at time of the play and before a pitch to the next batter of either team, or before the umpires leave the field if the play in question was the last play of the game (10-2-3i note).

Protest Procedure: Caseplay

4.5.1 SITUATION: The base umpire is out of position and calls R1 safe at third base while at the same time plate umpire calls R1 out. After consultation, it is decided that the base umpire's decision will stand. The coach of the team in the field protests the game. **RULING:** There is no protest allowed, since the play in question did not involve the misapplication of playing rules 1 through 9.

Regulation Game

A regulation interscholastic game is seven innings (turns at bat) for each team unless shortened as in 4-2-2 (Home team not needing final at-bat or 10-run rule) and 4-2-3 (weather or darkness), or unless extra innings are necessary to break a tie score (2-17-1), or unless shortened because the home team needs none of its half of the seventh or only a fraction of it or because of weather, or darkness (4-2-1). During each turn at bat, the offense attempts to score runs by having its batters become base runners who advance to and touch first base, second base, third base and home plate. The team in the field attempts to end each turn at bat of the opponent by causing three of its batters or base runners to be out (1-1-1).

The game ends when the team behind in score has completed its turn at bat in the seventh inning, or any inning thereafter if extra innings are necessary. If the home team scores a go-ahead run in the bottom of the seventh inning, or in any extra inning, the game is terminated at that point. Any game that is tied at the end of 4 1/2 or at least five full innings when the game is called shall be a tie game, unless the state association has adopted a specific game ending procedure. By state association adoption, the game shall end when the visiting team is behind 10 or more runs after 4 1/2 innings, or after the fifth inning, if either team is 10 runs behind and both teams have had an equal number of times at bat (4-2-2).

If weather or darkness interferes with play so that the game is called (ended) by the umpire, it is a regulation game if five full innings have been played, or if the home team has scored an equal or greater number of runs in four or four and a fraction turns at bat than the visiting team has scored in five turns at bat; or if play has gone beyond five full innings. If the game is called when the teams have not had an equal number of completed turns at bat, the score shall be the same as it was at the end of the last completed inning; except that if the home team in its half of the incomplete inning, scores a run (or runs) which equals or exceeds the opponent's score, the final score shall be as recorded when the game is called (4-2-3).

A state association may adopt game-ending procedures that determine how games are ended, including suspended games. However, if a state does not adopt game ending procedures, by mutual agreement of the opposing coaches and the umpire-in-chief, any remaining play may be shortened or the game terminated. If a state association has adopted game-ending procedures, only those game-ending procedures may be used, should the opposing coaches wish to terminate a game (4-2-4).

Rationale

For four years, starting in 1999, the 10-run rule was mandatory. The rule was changed to mandatory based on a survey of member associations. It reverted to an option for states in 2002 because the states wanted more flexibility in accepting or not accepting the rule.

Regulation Game: Caseplays

4.2.2 SITUATION A: A state association chooses not to use the 10-run mercy rule. RULING: This is permissible. The use of the 10-run mercy rule is by state association adoption.

4.2.2 SITUATION B: A state association wants to use a mercy rule, but wants to use: (a) a 15-run rule; or (b) an eight-run rule. **RULING:** Neither run rule is permissible. If a state association adopts a mercy rule, it must only be a 10-run rule.

4.2.2 SITUATION C: A state association establishes a run rule at (a) eight runs or (b) 12 runs. **RULING:** Illegal in (a) and (b). A 10-run rule is the only differential allowed.

4.2.2 SITUATION D: Team B is the visiting team and is leading by 10 runs (a) going into the bottom of the fifth or (b) after five complete innings. **RULING:** In (a), Team A must be permitted to bat in the bottom of the fifth. In (b), the game is terminated since Team B is 10 runs ahead after the fifth inning and each team has had an equal number of turns at bat.

4.2.2 SITUATION E: At the end of the (a) third inning or the (b) fifth inning, the home team is behind by 10 runs. **RULING:** In (a), the 10-run rule is not in effect because only three innings have been played. In (b), the game is over.

4.2.3 SITUATION A: In an interscholastic contest, seven innings is considered a full game. Rain or darkness causes a game to be called at the end of 3 1/2 innings with the home team leading 3 to 0. Is this considered a regulation game? **RULING:** No. In games that are seven innings in length, the regulations concerning a called game are that at least 4 1/2 innings are required for the game to be completed.

4.2.3 SITUATION B: At the end of the fourth inning, the score is H1, V2. There is no score in first half of the fifth, but in the last half H scores (a) one run or (b) two runs. In either case, game is called for rain when only one or two are out. **RULING:** In either case, it is a regulation game.

In (a), it is a tie game but all records count. If state associations treat regulation tie games as suspended games, the game will be continued from the point of interruption. In (b), H is the winner.

4.2.3 SITUATION C: At the end of the fourth inning, the score is H4-V5. In the fifth inning, V does not score and H has scored one run when the game is called because of rain. Does the score revert to that at the end of the last completed inning? **RULING:** No. It is a regulation tied game.

4.2.3 SITUATION D: A state association has not adopted special game-ending procedures. In the top of the fourth inning, rain, darkness or an automatic sprinkler system causes the game to end. The home team is leading at the time. **RULING:** A regulation game must go at least 4 1/2 innings to be regulation. Therefore, this game is declared "no game." Had the state association adopted a suspended game rule, the game would have continued from the point of interruption (4-2-4).

4.2.4 SITUATION A: The score is 19-1 in favor of the home team after three innings. The coach of the visiting team asks the coach of the home team and the umpire-in-chief to end the game because his team is so far behind. RULING: If the state association has adopted game-ending procedures and this particular situation applies, the game may end. If the state association has not adopted game-ending procedures and both opposing coaches and the umpire-in-chief agree to end the game, the game may end.

4.2.4 SITUATION B: At the beginning of the game, the opposing coaches agree to play two five-inning games. **RULING:** A regulation varsity game consists of seven innings. Predetermining a game(s) to be five innings is not legal.

4.2.4 SITUATION C: After three innings, the coach of the visiting team wants to end the game because his team is so far behind. **RULING:** If the state association allows coaches to agree, the game shall be terminated. If the opposing coaches do not agree to end the game, the game shall continue until such time the 10-run rule takes effect.

Topic 7
Record Keeping

PlayPic®

Topic:
General Information

Devices

Use of any object in the coach's box other than a stopwatch, rule book (hard copy), scorebook (3-3-1h), and use of amplifiers or bullhorns for coaching purposes during the course of the game (3-3-1k) also are forbidden.

Devices: Penalty

The umpire shall eject the offender from the game, unless the offense is judged to be of a minor nature. The umpire may warn the offender and then eject him if he repeats the offense. The warning or ejection shall be made at the end of playing action. Failure to comply shall result in the game being forfeited. For coaches who violate, the umpire may (1) restrict the offender to bench/dugout for the remainder of the game or (2) eject the offender. Any coach restricted to the bench shall be ejected for further misconduct. A coach may leave the bench/dugout to attend to a player who becomes ill or injured (3-3-1 penalty).

▨ Rationale

Technology has improved to the level that mobile devices can accurately video different aspects of the game. However, too many items in the coach's box could possibly draw the attention of the coach away from the game and the oversight of the students under his charge. Restriction of certain items while on the field creates a positive and focused environment for the players and officials.

Devices: Caseplays

3.3.1 SITUATION O: An individual occupying a coach's box has (a) stopwatch, (b) rule book (hard copy) or (c) scorebook (hard copy). **RULING:** Legal in (a), (b) and (c).

3.3.1 SITUATION P: An individual occupying a coach's box has (a) miniature radar gun or (b) any electronic device, including but not limited to a cell phone, smartphone, tablet, netbook or notebook computer. **RULING:** Illegal in (a) and (b). The umpire may either restrict the coach to the bench/dugout or eject him from the game.

3.3.1 SITUATION OO: The umpire observes the assistant coach in uniform videotaping the game from the (a) dugout or (b) stands. **RULING:** Legal in (a) and (b).

3.3.1 SITUATION PP: The third-base coach is in the coach's box using a video camera to tape the pitcher's move to first base. **RULING:** This is not legal. The third-base coach shall be restricted to the dugout bench for the remainder of the game or ejected.

Percentage Records

Percentage records are computed as follows:

- Percentage of games won and lost — divide the number of games won by total games played.

- Batting percentage — divide the total number of base hits, not the total bases on hits, by the total times at bat.

- Fielding percentage — divide the total putouts and assists by the total of putouts, assists and errors.

- Pitcher's earned run average — divide the total runs earned during his pitching by the total number of innings he pitched and multiply by seven (9-7-2).

Plays

A play is the term is also used to denote a unit of action which begins when a pitcher has the ball in his possession in pitching position and ends when ball becomes dead or pitcher again holds the ball while in pitching position (2-29-1). A double play is continuous activity which results in two putouts during a play (2-29-2).

Summary

The game summary includes the following:

- Total score and runs scored in each inning.

- Stolen bases for each runner.

- Sacrifices by each batter.

- Base hits by each batter and total against each pitcher.
- Two- or three-base hits and home runs.

- Times at bat for each player and total against each pitcher.

- Strikeouts by each pitcher.

- Bases on balls by each pitcher.

- Wild pitches by each pitcher.

- Times each pitcher hits batter with pitch and names of those hit.

- Passed balls by catcher.

- Time required to play game and name of each umpire.

- Names of winning and losing pitchers.

- Name of pitcher to receive credit for a save (9-7-1).

System

Uniformity in records of game activity is promoted by use of a standard tabulation sheet (9-2-1). The official scorer shall keep records as outlined in the following rules. He or she has the final authority when judgment is involved in determining whether a batter-runner's advance to first base is the result of an error or of a base hit. The scorebook of the home team shall be the official scorebook, unless the umpire-in-chief rules otherwise (9-2-2).

Umpires

The umpire-in-chief's duties include and correcting a scorekeeping error if brought to any umpire's attention before the umpires leave the field when the game is over (10-2-3m).

When a game is played under the auspices of an organization which permits protests to be filed, the umpire-in-chief shall inform the coach of the opposing team and the official scorer when a protest if field (10-2-3i).

Umpires: Caseplay

10.2.3 SITUATION K: What happens if a scoring error concerning the number of runs a team scores or outs a team has is detected (a) before the game has ended, or (b) after the game? **RULING:** In (a), the scoring error is corrected immediately. In (b), if by changing the scoring error the outcome will be affected, the corrected score shall be brought to an umpire's attention before the umpires leave the playing field. Otherwise, the score that both teams thought was correct stands.

COMMENT: The scorebook of the home team shall be the official scorebook, unless the umpire-in-chief rules otherwise. Individuals who keep their team's scorebook should pay particular attention to the score that is posted on the scoreboard, or that is announced over the PA system. If there is any confusion about the number of runs scored, the official scorekeeper should be consulted immediately. Umpires are not required to sign the scorebook to make it official.

Topic:
Offensive Statistics

Each player's batting record shall include his name and position, the number of times he batted, the runs he scored and the base hits he made (9-3-1a).

In addition, the summary shall include:

• The number of total base hits and the type (single, double, triple or home run), sacrifices, and number of runs he batted in (9-3-1b);

• Slugging percentage, which is total bases (i.e., double = two bases, triple = three bases, etc.) divided by official at bats (9-3-1c); and on-base percentage, which is the number of hits, walks and hit by pitch divided by the number of official at-bats, walks, hit by pitch and sacrifice flies) (9-3-1d).

Base Hit

A base hit (also called a safe hit or single) is one which enables the batter to advance to first base without being put out (2-5-2) and not because of a fielder's error (9-3-2a). It is not a base hit if any runner is out on a force play caused by the batter advancing toward first base (9-3-2a-1).

Base hits include any fair hit which cannot be fielded in time to throw out or tag out a batter-runner or any other runner when he is being forced to advance. Illustrations are: ball is stopped or checked by a fielder in motion who cannot recover in time, or ball moves too slowly; or ball is hit with such force to a fielder that neither he nor an assisting fielder can handle it (9-3-2a-2).

A base hit is also scored if the batter advances without liability of being put out because a runner is declared out for being hit by the batted ball or the umpire is hit by a batted ball (9-3-2b) or because of a fielder's choice when a fielder attempts to put out another runner but is unsuccessful and the scorer believes the batter-runner would have reached first base even with perfect fielding (9-3-2c).

An extra base hit is one which enables the batter to advance to first base and then to one or more succeeding bases. A two-base hit (double), three-base hit (triple) or home run enables him to reach second, third or home base, respectively (2-5-3, 9-3-3).

Base Hit: Caseplay

9.3.2 SITUATION C: While advancing to second, R1 is hit by a batted ball that prevents an obvious double play on him and the batter-runner. **RULING:** Both the runner and the batter-runner are declared out. The batter is not credited with a base hit (8-4-1h).

Run Batted In

A run batted in is credited to the batter when a runner scores because of a base hit, including the batter-runner's score on a home run; a sacrifice; any putout; a forced advance, such as for a base on balls or batter being hit; or an error, provided there are not two outs and that action is such that the runner on third would have scored even if there had been no error (9-3-5). It is not a run batted in if there is a double play from a force or one in which the batter is put out or should have been put out on a batted ground ball (9-3-5 exception).

Sacrifice

A sacrifice is a bunt which enables any runner to advance, or a fly ball (sacrifice fly) which enables a runner to score. In either case, the result is the batter-runner being put out before he reaches first base, or would have resulted in his being put out if the batted ball had been fielded without error, and provided two were not out when the ball was hit. A sacrifice is not listed as a time-at-bat (2-31-1, 9-3-4).

Sacrifice: Caseplay

9.3.2 SITUATION A: With R3 on third, R2 on second and R1 on first, B4's fly ball to center field is caught by F8, who then throws to second base. (a) His throw is in time to retire R1 attempting to advance, (b) R1 arrives ahead of the throw, or (c) R1 remains at first base. How are all advances recorded? **RULING:** In (a), (b) and (c), R3 scores by virtue of a sacrifice fly and R2 advances on a fielder's choice. In (b), R1 advances on a fielder's choice, even though the throw was late (2-8-4).

Stolen Base

A stolen base is an advance of a runner to the next base without the aid of a base hit, a putout or a fielding (including battery) error (2-34-1,

9-4-1). A double steal is two runners advancing on such a play (2-34-2). A triple steal is three runners advancing on such a play (2-34-3).

No runner is credited with a steal if after reaching the base, the runner overslides and is put out; or in an attempted double or triple steal, any runner is put out; or opponents are in collusion as in a deliberate attempt to help establish a record; or there is defensive indifference and no play is attempted (9-4-1 exception).

Strikeout

When a strikeout involves more than one batter, it is charged to the one who received at least two strikes. If no batter received more than one strike, it is charged to the batter who received the third strike (9-3-6).

Time at Bat

The time at bat is the period beginning when a batter first enters the batter's box and continuing until he is put out or becomes a runner (2-39-1).

A batter is not charged in the records with a time at bat when he makes a sacrifice hit, is hit by a pitched ball, is awarded a base on balls, is replaced before being charged with two strikes, is replaced after being charged with two strikes and the substitute does not strike out, or when he advances to first base because of obstruction by a fielder (2-39-1 exception).

Topic:
Defensive Statistics

Each player's fielding record shall include the times he put out a batter or runner, the times he assisted a teammate in putting out a runner, and the number of errors he committed (9-5-1).

Assist

An assist is credited to a fielder each time he handles or deflects the ball during action which is connected with the putout or he handles the ball prior to an error which prevents what would have been a putout. If several fielders handle the ball or one fielder handles it more than once during a play, such as when a runner is caught between bases, only one assist is credited to each of such fielders (9-5-3). After a pitch, if catcher tags out or throws out a runner, the pitcher is not credited with an assist (9-5-3a).

Double or Triple Play

A double play or triple play is credited to one or more fielders when two or three players are put out between the time a pitch is delivered and the time the ball next becomes dead or is next in possession of the pitcher in pitching position (9-5-4).

Error

An error is a misplay by a fielder or a team, which is recorded in the error column of the player's or team's record (2-12-1). An error is charged against a fielder or a team for each misplay that prolongs the time at bat of the batter or the time a player continues to be a runner, or permits the runner to advance one or more bases (9-5-5). Misplays that are not recorded in the error column but are included in the game summary include a balk, wild pitch, batter hit by pitched ball and passed ball (2-12-2).

Certain plays that meet the above criteria are not charged as errors:

• A pitcher is not charged with an error for a base on balls; or a batter being hit, or a balk, or a wild pitch.

• A catcher is not charged with an error for a wild throw in his attempt to prevent a stolen base unless the runner advances another base because of the wild throw.

• Neither catcher nor infielder is charged with an error for a wild throw in an attempt to complete a double play, unless the throw is so wild that it permits a runner to advance an additional base. But if a player drops a thrown ball, when by holding it he would have completed the double (or triple) play, it is an error. A passed ball is a pitch the catcher fails to stop or control when he should have been able to do so with ordinary effort and on which a runner, other than the batter, is able to advance. When a passed ball occurs on a third strike, permitting a batter to reach first base, score a strikeout and a passed ball.

• A fielder is not charged with an error for accurately throwing to a base whose baseman fails to stop or try to stop the ball, provided there was good reason for the throw. If the runner advances because of the throw, the error is charged to the team or fielder who should have covered that base.

• If a fielder drops a fair fly ball but recovers in time to force out a runner, he is not charged with an error. It is recorded as a force-out (9-5-5 exceptions).

Error: Caseplays

9.5.5 SITUATION A: F2 touches the bat of B1 as he swings at the ball. How is this entered in the records? **RULING:** F2 is charged with an error. B1 is awarded first base and is not charged with a time at bat (9-3-1a).

9.5.5 SITUATION B: B1 hits a pop-up behind second base that could easily be caught by either F4 or F6. The ball is not caught. **RULING:** Since the ball could have been caught, it is a team error and is not a hit.

9.5.5 SITUATION C: R1 on first base attempts to steal second base. F2 makes throw to second base that should have been caught, but neither F6 nor F4 was at the base to receive the throw. **RULING:** This is a stolen base and a team error if R1 advances at least to third base on the play.

Fielder's Choice

A fielder's choice is the act of a fielder with a live ball, who elects to throw for an attempted putout or to retire unassisted any runner or batter-runner, thus permitting the advance of another runner(s). Scorers use the term to indicate the advance of the batter-runner who takes one or more bases when the fielder who handles his batted ball plays on a preceding runner; to indicate the advance of a runner (other than by stolen base or error) while a fielder is trying to put out another runner; and to indicate the advance of a runner due to the defensive team's refusal to play on him (an undefended steal) (2-14-1).

Fielder's Choice: Caseplay

9.5.4 SITUATION: With R2 on second and R1 on first, B3 bunts to F3. F3 fields the batted ball, then throws to F4 who returns the throw to F3 for a double play. How shall the scorekeeper record this action? RULING: R1 and B3 are retired (3-4-3) as R2 advances by a fielder's choice.

Passed Ball

A passed ball is a pitch which the catcher fails to stop or control when he should have been able to do so with ordinary effort, and which enables a runner including the batter-runner to advance (2-26-1).

Putout

A putout is credited to a fielder who catches a batted ball in flight, or who tags out a runner, or who puts out a runner by holding the ball while touching a base to which a runner is forced to advance or return (9-5-2).

There are exceptions to the putout rule:

- The catcher is credited with the putout when batter is out for illegally batting the ball, for a third strike bunted foul, for being hit by his own batted ball, for batting out of turn or for batter's interference.

- For an infield fly that is not caught, the putout is credited to the fielder who would ordinarily have made the catch.

- For runner being out because of being hit by a batted ball, the putout is credited to the fielder who is nearest the ball at the time.

- For runner called out for missing base, credit putout to fielder at that base.

- For malicious contact by a runner, credit the putout to the involved fielder (9-5-2 exceptions).

Putout: Caseplays

9.1.1 SITUATION I: With R2 on second, B2 hits a fly ball to F8. R2 fails to tag second after the catch and goes to third. After proper appeal, the umpire declares R2 out for leaving early. Which defensive player receives the putout for R2? **RULING:** Credit the putout to the nearest designated baseman, who in this case will be F4 (9-5-2c).

9.3.2 SITUATION B: B1 hits to left field and reaches second. However, he is called out for not touching first base. How should this be entered in the scorebook? **RULING:** The putout should be credited to F3. B1 is not credited with a hit.

Topic:
Pitching Statistics

The number of bases on balls, batters being hit by a pitch, strikeouts, and base hits allowed by each pitcher shall be recorded in the summary. If batter is hit by what would have been the fourth ball, it is recorded as a hit batter (9-6-2).

Earned Run

In order for a run to be earned, it must be scored without the aid of errors, or passed balls. To determine whether runs are earned or not, reconstruct the inning without the errors and passed balls. If there is doubt as to whether or not a run is earned, the pitcher shall be given the benefit (9-6-3). A relief pitcher shall not be charged with any earned run scored by a runner who was on base when such pitcher entered, nor with any hit or advance by a batter who had more balls than strikes when such pitcher entered (9-6-5).

Save

In order for a pitcher to be credited with a save, he shall meet all three of the following criteria: he is the last pitcher in a game won by his team; he is not the winning pitcher; and he meets at least one of the following:

• He enters the game with a lead of not more than three runs and pitches at least one inning; or

• He enters the game regardless of the count on the batter with the potential tying run either on base, at bat or on deck; or

• He pitches effectively for at least three innings (9-6-7).

A starting pitcher who is replaced and then re-enters as pitcher can be credited with a win but not a save (9-6-7c-4).

Strikeout

A strikeout is credited to the pitcher when a third strike is delivered to a batter even though the batter might reach first base because the third strike is a wild pitch or is not caught. It is also a strikeout if an attempted third strike bunt is an uncaught foul (9-6-4).

Wild Pitch

A wild pitch is one which cannot be handled by the catcher with ordinary effort (2-41-1). A wild pitch shall be charged in the summary to the pitcher when a ball legally delivered to the batter is so high, or so low (including any pitch that touches the ground in front of home plate), or so far away from home plate that the catcher does not stop or control it with ordinary effort so that the batter-runner advances to first base or any runner advances a base. When the catcher enables a runner, other than the batter-runner, to advance by failing to control a pitch that he should have been able to control, it is not a wild pitch but a "passed ball" (9-6-1).

Wins and Losses

If the starting pitcher has pitched the first four innings or more and his team is ahead when he is replaced and the team holds the lead for the remainder of the game, he shall be the winning pitcher (9-6-6a).

If a game ends for whatever reason, having gone less than seven innings, then the starting pitcher shall have pitched three or more consecutive innings to be declared the winning pitcher. If the starting pitcher cannot be declared the winning pitcher, and more than one relief pitcher is used, the winning pitcher shall be determined using the following criteria:

• If the score is tied, it results in the game becoming a new contest so far as judging who is the winning and losing pitcher.

• If the starting pitcher is removed before having pitched four or more innings and his team is ahead, the official scorer shall determine the winning pitcher to be the relief pitcher who has been the most effective.

• If the opposition goes ahead, pitchers up to that time in the game cannot be credited with the win. However, if the pitcher pitching subsequently takes and maintains a lead the remainder of the game, said pitcher is credited with the win.

• Generally the relief pitcher credited with the win is the pitcher when his team takes the lead and holds it for the rest of the game. However, if the relief pitcher pitches only a short while or not effectively and a succeeding relief pitcher replaces him and does better work in keeping the lead, the latter shall be granted the win (9-6-6b).

If a pitcher is removed for a pinch-hitter or a pinch-runner, the runs scored by his team during the inning of his removal are to be credited to his benefit to decide the pitcher of record (9-6-6c).

▨ Rationale

Pro rules require a pitcher to go five innings to qualify for the win. However, pro games are nine innings long. The requirement is based upon the number of innings required for the starting pitcher go more than half the game.

The starting pitcher shall be charged with the loss when he is replaced and his team is behind or falls behind because of runs assessed to him after being replaced and his team does not subsequently tie the score or take the lead (9-6-6d).

A pitcher cannot be given credit for pitching a shutout when he does not pitch the complete game except when he enters the game with no one out before the opponents have scored in the first inning and does not permit the opposition to score during the game (9-6-6e).

Signal Chart

Do Not Pitch; Ball Is Dead

Play

Strike

Foul Tip

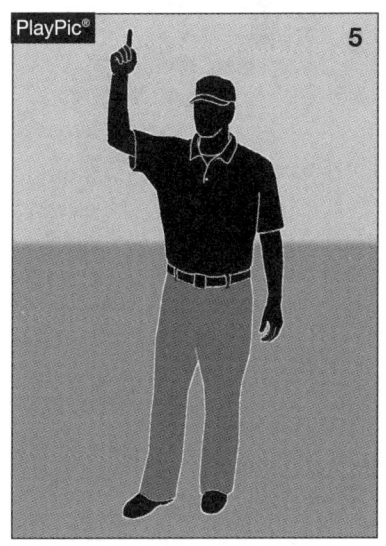

Infield Fly

Foul Ball, Time Out Or Dead Ball

Fair Ball

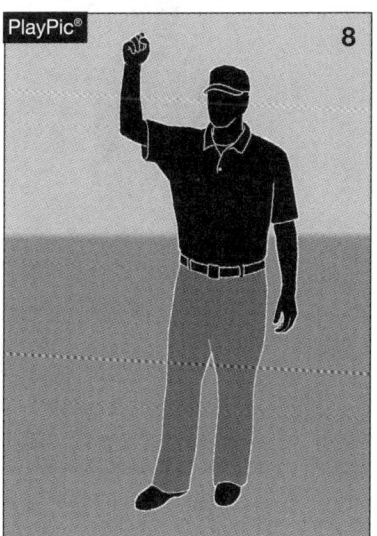

Out

Safe

Count

Time play

Double Tag Rotation

13

Correct Rotation

14

Information Available

NFHS PUBLICATIONS

Prices effective April 1, 2019 — March 31, 2020

RULES PUBLICATIONS

Baseball Rules Book.....................................$10.00
Baseball Case Book......................................$10.00
Baseball Umpires Manual (2019 & 2020) $10.00
Baseball Simplified & Illustrated Rules $10.00
Baseball Rules by Topic $10.00
Basketball Rules Book..................................$10.00
Basketball Case Book...................................$10.00
Basketball Simplified & Illustrated Rules $10.00
Basketball Officials Manual (2019-21) $10.00
Basketball Handbook (2018-20)....................$10.00
Basketball Rules by Topic $10.00
Field Hockey Rules Book...............................$10.00
Football Rules Book $10.00
Football Case Book......................................$10.00
Football Simplified & Illustrated Rules $10.00
Football Handbook (2019 & 2020)................$10.00
Football Game Officials Manual
   (2018 & 2019) $10.00
Football Rules by Topic................................$10.00
Girls Gymnastics Rules Book & Manual
   (2018-20)..$10.00

Ice Hockey Rules Book $10.00
Boys Lacrosse Rules Book............................$10.00
Girls Lacrosse Rules Book $10.00
Soccer Rules Book.......................................$10.00
Softball Rules Book......................................$10.00
Softball Case Book $10.00
Softball Umpires Manual (2020 & 2021) $10.00
Softball Simplified & Illustrated Rules $10.00
Softball Rules by Topic $10.00
Spirit Rules Book $10.00
Swimming & Diving Rules Book $10.00
Track & Field Rules Book..............................$10.00
Track & Field Case Book $10.00
Track & Field Manual (2019 & 2020) $10.00
Volleyball Rules Book...................................$10.00
Volleyball Case Book & Manual....................$10.00
Volleyball Simplified & Illustrated Rules $10.00
Water Polo Rules Book (2018-20) $10.00
Wrestling Rules Book....................................$10.00
Wrestling Case Book & Manual....................$10.00

MISCELLANEOUS ITEMS

NFHS Statisticians' Manual $8.00
Scorebooks: Baseball-Softball, Basketball, Swimming & Diving, Cross Country, Soccer,
   Track & Field, Volleyball, Wrestling and Field Hockey $12.00
Diving Scoresheets (pad of 100)...$8.00
Volleyball Team Rosters & Lineup Sheets (pads of 100) $8.00
Libero Tracking Sheet (pads of 50)..$8.00
Baseball/Softball Lineup Sheets – 3-Part NCR (sets/100)...$10.00
Wrestling Tournament Match Cards (sets/100) $7.25
Competitors Numbers (Track and Gymnastics – Waterproof, nontearable, black numbers and
   six colors of backgrounds numbers are 1-1000 sold in sets of 100 .... $15.00/set

MISCELLANEOUS SPORTS ITEMS

Court and Field Diagram Guide $25.00
NFHS Handbook (2018-19)..........................$12.00
Let's Make It Official $5.00

Sportsmanship. It's Up to You Toolkit $19.95
High School Activities – A Community
   Investment in America $39.95

ORDERING

Individuals ordering NFHS publications and other products and materials
are requested to order online at **www.nfhs.com**.

National Federation of State High School Associations

2019-20
NFHS RULES BOOKS

Published in 17 sports by the National
Federation of State High School
Associations, rules books contain the
official rules for high school athletic
competition. These books are designed
to explain all aspects of the game
or contest. They are good for
participants as well as coaches and
contest officials.

The NFHS also publishes case books,
manuals, handbooks and illustrated
books in several sports to help in
further explaining the rules.

Customer Service Department

PO Box 361246, Indianapolis, IN 46236-5324

1-800-776-3462

or order online at **www.nfhs.com**

ARE YOU READY TO JOIN?

ANY GAME. ANYTIME. ANYWHERE.

You are Covered!
- $3 million Annual General Liability Coverage
- $50,000 Game Call and Assigners' Coverage
- $10,000 Assault Protection
- Free Consultation and Information Services

EVERY GAME. EVERY SPORT. EVERY LEVEL.

The Finest Training Resources
- Referee Magazine — 12 Monthly issues
- It's Official — 16-page members-only newsletter every month
- Access to NASO members-only app
- 20% discount on all Referee training products
- Monthly NASO digital LockerRoom newsletter
- Online sport-specific quizzes

For Officials, By Officials
Your dues also support NASO's efforts to improve working conditions for all sports through such efforts as:
- Assault and independent contractor legislation
- Taking informed stances on select issues in the media
- Recruitment and retention efforts
- Celebrating officials and officiating with national awards

For more information or to join
www.naso.org/bookjoin or call 800-733-6100

NATIONAL ASSOCIATION OF SPORTS OFFICIALS

Notes

Notes

Notes

Notes

Notes